Voices of Strength

Voices of Strength
Sons and Daughters of Suicide
Speak Out

By

Judy Zionts Fox RN, LSW and Mia Roldan

New Horizon Press
Far Hills, NJ

Copyright © 2009 by Judy Zionts Fox RN, LSW and Mia Roldan

New Horizon Press
P.O. Box 669
Far Hills, NJ 07931

Judy Zionts Fox
Mia Roldan
Voices of Strength: Sons and Daughters of Suicide Speak Out

Cover design: Wendy Bass
Interior design: Susan Sanderson

Library of Congress Control Number: 2008921806

ISBN 13: 978-0-88282-333-1
ISBN 10: 0-88282-333-7
New Horizon Press

Manufactured in the U.S.A.

2012   2011   2010   2009   2008   /   5   4   3   2   1

Authors' Note

This book is based on the authors' research and personal experiences. In order to protect privacy, some names have been changed and identifying characteristics have been altered. For purposes of simplifying usage, the pronouns his/her and s/he are sometimes used interchangeably. The information contained herein is not intended to replace any necessary therapy with mental health professionals.

Dedication

Mia Roldan and Judy Fox would like to dedicate their labor of love to their respective mothers: Jeanne N. Knutson and Beatrice Steiner Zionts.

Mia and Judy would also like to dedicate this book to the parents lost to suicide by all of their participants, who so openly and generously shared with them and the readers their individual stories of survival.

Table of Contents

Foreword

The year was 1972, and I had just spent a memorable afternoon with the legendary Muhammad Ali. When I returned to my Las Vegas law office, I was given an urgent message to call my mother at our home in Searchlight, Nevada. That is when I learned my father had shot himself. Prior to this moment, I had never thought of suicide as something that would affect my life. Suicide was something that only happened in other people's families.

Suicide is like a haunting fog, having no boundaries and forever lingering in the thoughts of those who have survived it. I speak from experience when I say there is nothing more devastating than losing a loved one to suicide. Afterward, my family did not talk about it, and we bore the heavy burden of that tragedy in secret. Like many survivors, I wondered who was to blame and what I could have done to prevent it. My embarrassment and shame made a melancholy situation even worse. It was difficult to explain to others, especially when no one wanted to talk about it.

For many years, I kept my feelings to myself. That finally changed when Mike Wallace, the normally stone-faced CBS news journalist, testified before the Senate Special Committee on Aging. Mr. Wallace had tears in his eyes when he spoke about thoughts of taking his own life, and I was forced to finally confront my feelings about my father's suicide. His soul-baring experience gave me the courage to be open about my father's death. For the first time, I found myself sharing with my Senate colleagues the fact that my father killed himself.

Since 1997, I have been on a crusade to bolster suicide prevention efforts, and through it all I have come to learn many things. I now understand that my father was not alone, and neither was I as a survivor. Suicide is not just an individual's health problem; it is one of the leading causes of death in our country. Every time someone commits suicide, we all lose in many different ways. Someone once said, "The person who completes suicide dies once, but those left behind die a thousand deaths."

Voices of Strength speaks to the mourning sons and daughters on how they can survive and eventually go beyond survival to a meaningful and fulfilling life. Survivors should know that it is not shameful nor a betrayal of the deceased for the son or daughter to start thriving at some point. Rather, thriving is a way of honoring our deceased relative. The book shares accounts by suicide survivors which convey the lasting impression suicide leaves on an individual, regardless of age or sex.

This book is helpful, because it addresses the benefits of reconciliation with family members. Furthermore, it attempts to educate the survivors, friends, relatives and professionals (i.e. therapists, clergy and first responders) about how the suicide might affect sons and daughters who were at different stages and ages (birth through adulthood) at the time of the parent's suicide. *Voices of Strength* is sure to offer reassurance and comfort for the son and daughter through their journey of recovery from the suicide.

I am grateful for the opportunity to talk about losing a parent to suicide. My family and I have come a long way since the days when we didn't mention it. Together, we must lift the veil of secrecy that for too long has kept us in the dark about the dynamics of suicide and surviving the loss of a loved one. I hope that by sharing my story I have helped give hope to those considering suicide and insight to those coping with the loss of a loved one.

Harry Reid, 24th U.S. Senate Majority Leader

Acknowledgements

The journey of this book has spanned ten years; from an idea to an outline, from a rough draft to the actual publication of our manuscript. In that time, we as authors have had significant changes to our lives, as anyone would in a decade. We've had children and grandchildren born, we've changed careers, we've moved, we've watched close friends become sick and die, we've had our own serious health issues, we've lost a stepmother, a grandmother, a cousin and an aunt. This book with our stories of survival is something we fervently wanted to write. Neither one of us would have ever predicted in our careers we would one day be published authors. However, once we decided to write the book, we knew with unwavering certainty that *Voices of Strength* would be published. Our drive and determination overcame all the obstacles and odds that were stacked against us, and here we are today. The process for this book mirrors the message that our book gives: that even when you're faced with a difficult task, one that you don't think you're experienced enough or emotionally equipped to handle, you can achieve so much fulfillment from your efforts. Life will go on around you—the good and the bad—to inspire you and to throw you off track. But keeping the goal in your heart and mind, planning small steps to get there and asking for and receiving help from others will all lead you to where you eventually want to be.

I (Judy) wish to thank my dear husband Jack of forty years for his patience, devotion and unwavering support during these many years of writing *Voices of Strength*. He helped edit, gave his input, addressed envelopes and cooked dinner when I was too busy, to name just a few of his many contributions. The ways he helped go on and on. Next, I wish to acknowledge and thank our four daughters, not only for their interest in this huge endeavor but for making my life fulfilled. It has been a wonder to me that having had unfortunate fate as a daughter with mothers, that I have been blessed with four daughters whom I love dearly. Thus, I have been given a second chance to work out the mother–daughter relationship. Beginning with our oldest: Elaine Fox Concklin, Janette Fox Klocko, Linda Fox Besher and Susan Fox Metcalfe. I also thank with much love my son in-laws: Wes Concklin and Bryce Metcalfe. My appreciation extends to our grandchildren, beginning with the youngest two, Parker and Claire Metcalfe, Emery Besher, Jasmin, Savannah and Dylan Klocko, Michelle Concklin and Joshua Concklin and his wife Heather. Our great-grandchildren include Payton, Mason and Rebekah Concklin. All of these family members were instrumental in giving me a life separate from our book as well as being helpful in other ways. I appreciate the evening my brother Stanley Zionts and I sat down and discussed our different perceptions of our lives together. We shared the same history but yet, being five years apart in age, experienced different happenings and viewpoints. I want to extend a special thank you to Andrea Michael, who played a key role in my recovery and stood unfalteringly by me throughout my healing. I wish to thank my co-author, Mia Roldan, for her compatible, refreshing and youthful yet mature point-of-view in the creation of our book. We believed from the beginning that our age difference was a real plus in giving two different perspectives in our writing.

I (Mia) would like to thank first my husband and best friend, Christopher, who believed in me from the very first moment and always listened, supported and gave me whatever I needed to go on year after year. I want to thank my two sons, Desmond and Darby, who were born during this time, for making me a mother and giving me such love and happiness. I want to thank my father, David Knutson, and my siblings, Leslie Giuso, Stephen Knutson and John Knutson, who were always there for me and bravely told their own stories in this book. Lastly, I would like to thank my writing partner, Judy Fox, who gave me the motivation and encouragement whenever I needed it and without whom I never would have written this book.

We couldn't have written this book without the love and support of so many friends and family members. The number of people we want to acknowledge and thank is large. We apologize in advance for anyone who we inadvertently left out of this lengthy list. Some individuals wanted to remain anonymous, and we respected that. We thank those who wished not to be acknowledged in the book for their participation in which they so generously shared their deepest thoughts, feelings and life stories. Less than half of those below are sons and daughters of suicide. Many contributed by helping to edit, encouraging and motivating. Others were great listeners who supported us with their confidence in us as friends. Many did favors that definitely impacted the writing of the book itself, such as helping with computer and software issues. Our list is a general one and does not differentiate survivors from those who helped us in other ways. Included are our cousins, friends, acquaintances, professional contributors, support group facilitators who assisted us in finding participants and, of course, participants who contributed to our book, those voices of strength that we refer to in our title. They are in alphabetical order by their first names.

Amanda Conley
Amy Van Meter
Annie Melvin
Barbara Buie
Barbara Digby
Barbara Robin
Betty Dimmick
Billi Sue Allen
Bonnie Carter
Bonnie Cross
Bonnie Day
Boyd Smith
Caryn Steerman
Carolyn Martin
Chaplain Dora Robinson
Char and Art Roldan
Charlotte Nacozy
Charul and Doyal Alexander
Cheryl Bias
Cheryl Painter
Cheryl Swanson
Cindy Sanders
Cynthia Boom

D'Anna Sims
David Baer
David Morales
Desiree Roldan
Diane Robertson
Dick and Ele Amos
Dick Concklin, in loving memory
Donna Oakford
Dr. Gary D Kinnaman
Dr. Sydney Harriet, our agent
Elaine Ward
Elizabeth Lewis
Ellen and Ralph Loeb
Ellen Steinberg Karch
Elsie Pierce
Erin Thomas
Father Benedetto
Father David Hoster
Father Larry Mattingly
Harriet Goldman
Harriet Jett
Helen Holden
Inetha Anderson

Irene Parker
Jan and Bob Burnside
Jane Burkett
Janelle Jones
Janet Bohmann
Jaynelle Nestle
Jennifer Lyon
Jill Sharp
Jill Wallace
Joan Cline
Joan Hilgers
Julia Henninger
Joan Soffer
Julie Scales
Karen Cristobal
Kathy Morgan
Kay Kleeber
Keyna Kellogg
Kimberly Rogers
Kristine Dibert Errecart
Laura and Sam Evans
Lauren Bajwa
Leann Gouveia
Lesley Lewis
Lori Handelman
Lorraine Fleury
Lowell Goldman, in loving
    memory
Lucinda Newell
Lydia and Harold Servetnick
Lynn Knutson
Margaret Berton
Marianne and Richard
Stephens
Marilyn Christian
Marilyn Koeing
Mary Ann Johnston
Mary Lee Hopkins
Melanie Fox Vanicek

Michelle and David Rosenblatt
Minister Davidson Loehr
Minister Jack R. Harris
    Bonham
Monet and Patrick Lessner
Mort Batlan
Pastor Dan Davis
Pastor Tracey Davenport
Patricia C Bravo
Patti Hadrava
Patti Hirsh
Rabbi Alan Freedman
Rabbi Richard Zionts
Rabbi Steven Folberg
Rachel Gould
Rebekah Davis
Rosa Raskin
Roseann Woodka
Rosella Levinson, in loving
    memory
Rowdy and Ashley Stovall
Roz and Bill Poynter
Sandy Candler
Sandy Pollard
Shanna Arciniaga
Shannon Kaiser
Shelley Green
Sherwin Robin, in loving
    memory
Shirley Kaminsky
Stacey Ross
Steven Towler
Suzann Madeley
Tammie Garza
Terri Parsons Smith
Vicki Dempsey
Virginia Wedeikes
Vonny Manna

These photos tell the stories of Judy and Mia. The photograph of Judy and her mother (top left) is the only one ever taken of both of them, two days before the act of suicide. One can easily see the despair and detachment in her mother's face as Judy is not being held but is just lying on her mother's lap. Mia's mother looks down smiling at her daughter (bottom right), but there's a sense of distance as this pose was staged and not spontaneous. Both mothers met the same fate, which was when Mia and Judy became daughters of suicide.

INTRODUCTION

Silence Ceases
and Hope Emerges

The foundation for this book began in 1942 for Judy and in 1981 for Mia. These are the years that our mothers took their own lives. In 1998, we met at a local group for women who had lost their mothers. We were the only ones whose mothers had died from suicide. We had each individually felt the need to write a book about our loss of mothers through suicide and to connect with others like us whom we knew existed in the world. Meeting each other and sharing our stories was the spark that was needed to honestly and openly discuss what our mothers' illnesses and suicides had done to our families, our lives and us. We wanted to explore what other individuals who had experienced parent suicide had to share as well. We began our book by creating questionnaires for conducting interviews with participants, clergy, therapists and a first responder. We surveyed sixty-three survivors throughout the United States and Canada. Of these sixty-three, fifty-seven participants chose to be interviewed. What is amazing to us both is the realization that without that single, life-changing event, we might not be the professionals, women, wives and mothers we are today.

Our book's message is strongly based on the surveys and interviews of our participants, as well as our own testimonies. We also have interviewed a number of therapists, clergy of different faiths and a retired criminal investigator who have all had experience dealing with survivors

1

of parent suicide. In talking personally with almost each and every person, we have been inspired and encouraged to produce a book that will reach a diverse audience; not only survivors of parent suicide, but also their families (including the surviving parent), their friends, community members who might come into contact with them (therapists/counselors, mental health professionals, clergy and first responders) and, hopefully, anyone who might be contemplating taking his or her own life.

We feel that all of our participants have been heroically honest with us about the personal details of their lives and feelings. When we played and replayed lengthy tapes to transcribe each individually recorded interview, Judy's husband, Jack, commented one day that these are voices that finally are being heard. As we discussed the stories that we heard, we were awed by the courage we heard in each and every participant's voice. That is why we chose to name our book *Voices of Strength: Sons & Daughters of Suicide Speak Out.*

Our stories, research and experiences, we believe, shed light on the ways survivors of suicidal parents cope and on our strong feelings as to why the information in this book is needed.

Judy's Story

I was nine or ten years old at the time that the following incident took place. In our McKees Rocks, Pennsylvania, public housing development, which was built during World War II, I was washing dinner dishes when my stepmother came into the kitchen and announced: "I have something to tell you. I am not really your mother. You had another mother who gave birth to you." I reflected for a moment surprised, because on a conscious level, I thought that she was my mother. But then on another level, I thought maybe I already knew that there was another mother. She went on to say that my mother killed herself and that she drank poison after I was born. I was told this was a secret and not to talk to anyone about my birth mother, not even that there was another mother. I knew my stepmother meant this, that I best not tell a soul, because I would be in serious trouble and would never hear the end of it. To me, this also meant I should not talk to her either. Neither she nor my dad brought this topic up again, never asked what I felt. It was a clear statement that I should not bring this up with my dad or stepmother and I didn't, at least not until my later adolescent years. This conversation with my stepmother in the kitchen was very brief, having only taken a couple of minutes. I had no one to discuss my shock with, a huge load for anyone at any age to carry. I already was a silent child and I became more withdrawn. I had a new option to consider: suicide. Fortunately I never did exercise this option nor did I even have a plan, but I did think about it. After that, I was repeatedly reminded by my stepmother that she was not my "real mother." She looked pretty real to me, and that hurt, because I wanted a real mother. I thought if I tried hard enough, I could become the person I thought she wanted me to be and then she would like me. One day, I figured out that wasn't going to happen. Up until right before she died at age ninety-two, she would tell me, "I wish I had my own kids."

My mother's suicide was not discussed in our family. The only explanation I ever heard from my father was one short sentence: "She was very ill." Then, he would follow this up by saying, "This happened in the past, keep it there." (End of discussion) Other typical responses were, "You have another mother now. Forget everything else," or, "You were too young to feel anything and it didn't affect you." Information was something I never did get from him. Well, I did get one other piece of his thinking concerning my mother, or perhaps it said more about my father. He questioned my paternity. Maybe, just maybe, I was not his child. Eventually, that issue was discarded. There was no denying that I definitely resembled him. Was this question based on fact or was he creating this scenario to deal with guilt that he felt, real or imagined?

My aunt, my mother's sister, was a little more informative but really not by much. She asked why I wanted to know and then did not listen to my response. Once in a while, my persistence in bringing up the topic won. But not often. My uncle, my mother's brother, didn't want to talk about my mother at all. So, this was the way it was. But I needed to know. I needed to know who my mother was; what she looked like, about her personality and interests and why she took her own life. I needed to know about my own life history.

The fact was that my mother died from suicide when I was a newborn. Finally, my persistence in learning more about my mother won out fifty-seven years after her suicide. One month before her own death, my very ill, disabled, elderly and dying aunt talked to me about my mother's suicide. On the day I visited, I knew her remaining days on this earth were to be brief. Fortunately, I tried one last time to speak with her of my mother. To my surprise, she wanted to talk to me about my mother's death, as upsetting as the topic was to her. Perhaps she just needed to die at peace. Even though our talk took place more than five and one half decades after my mother's suicide, the start of our conversation centered on whether or not I would use my aunt's name. I told my aunt I would only use her name in the book I planned if she wanted me to.

She emphatically replied that she did not want her name cited, even with her awareness that her days were numbered and that her death would come soon. "You won't mention my name, will you? I don't want anyone to know who I am." Her feelings of shame at the way my mother died remained with her. However, she did agree that I could identify her as my aunt. As she spoke of her sister's suicide, sobs emerged from her throat. Her grief sounded as fresh as if my aunt's tragic loss had been recent, not fifty-seven years earlier.

As her condition worsened, we spoke of what her belief was as to the cause of my mother's suicide. She replied, "Well, because I told her that I was getting married, and she didn't like the man I was marrying. She didn't want me to marry your uncle." I injected some dark humor when I said, "If that were a reason for killing yourself, then a lot of people would be killing themselves, because many people are getting married to people who others would not choose for them." She seemed to breathe a sigh of relief and responded saying, "I know you're right." Then I asked my aunt, "Had you ever thought about that?" My aunt replied, "No, I never thought about that."

She was not sobbing or even crying during this dialogue. In fact, she laughed with each realization that her plans to marry did not kill her sister. She did go on to say during this, our last conversation together, "She could still be living, you know. It's been tough. I miss her a lot, because she and I were close." Then she added some other factors that really might have been the reasons for her sister's suicide, including mental illness. As our talk came to an end, she proudly responded, "That's the story. Are you going to put all that in your book?" When I said I would, she nodded and for the first time ever, my aunt spoke more comfortably of her sister and her sister's death. The next day she died.

When secrets about a close loved one's suicide are kept and our inner thoughts are not verbalized, what we once believed as common sense cannot be accessed so easily. Feelings do not lose their intensity. Fears emerge of even mentioning the person's name, much less talking of what happened. The end result is that family and friends suffer in silence. It is a myth that if such an event is not talked about, we will spare others and ourselves pain and sadness. Contrary to what many believe, it does not help survivors to pretend that the suicide of a family member never happened. The truth is that the pain never leaves and does not even lessen when one remains silent about the shock, grief and feelings of guilt. The survivor cannot move forward with his or her life.

Of course, mental health care in the 1940s when my mother died was still rather primitive compared to what it is today. The hardships from the Great Depression and the personal demands resulting from World War II caused extreme overcrowding and deterioration in the state mental institutions. Because many military personnel suffered from combat-related mental illnesses, civilians were mostly treated outside the usual mental hospitals. Insulin shock therapy was a widespread treatment for mental illness, and during this period of time, electroconvulsive therapy was introduced in the United States, which eventually replaced insulin therapy. Still, two decades later when I was a student nurse, insulin therapy was still used on occasion. The Mental Health Act (which provided funding for research into causes, prevention and treatment of mental illness) was not enacted until 1946, four years after my mother's suicide. Drugs such as Thorazine and other tranquilizers that treated mental illnesses weren't available until the mid 1950s. These drugs reduced the need for hospitalization. Until then, shock treatment, restraints and seclusion rooms were of widespread use to manage mental illness. It wasn't until the late 1960s that psychologists and social workers started treating mental illness (The New York State Archives, a program of the State Education Department, with its main facility located in the Cultural Education Center on Madison Avenue in Albany). In addition, the stigma of suicide was even more prevalent back then and survivors were all too frequently punished and scorned rather than supported and understood. Generally, our society was intolerant toward survivors of suicide. It was extremely common that other people wanted nothing to do with the survivors and added immensely to the survivor's pain with punishment and scorn. I have no doubt that my aunt survived the very best way she knew and did her best with the scanty information that was available to her at that time. In those years, silence was the only coping device she knew and perhaps the solution that most individuals chose. Today, we know that the silence past generations utilized is understandable, considering the stigma that was imposed upon the survivors. Nonetheless, there was and is a terrible price to pay for silence.

Mia's Story

I remember the moment perfectly. My father sat my sister, my two brothers and me down to tell us the news. We had just come back from Paris, where we'd spent the holidays with our sister. We were exhausted, ready to go to bed and, most of all, curious. I also remember telling my sister that Mom would be angry if she knew that Dad was keeping us at his apartment so long before bringing us back to her house (They had divorced three years earlier). He said it just with the facts, the main idea of what had happened, "Your mother killed herself on Christmas day. She was alone in the house." We all reacted in our own individual ways and emotionally broke away from each other. My father was relieved when our pastor arrived and took over the role of consoler. My dad then emotionally checked out, out of necessity and out of habit, and the period of silence began.

I don't know how many days passed before my mother's funeral. All those days seem like one very long afternoon in my memory. When we got back from the cemetery, there were family and friends, a variety of foods and a claustrophobic atmosphere of guilt. Everyone did his or her part to help us children "cope." But the mix of people was so segregated that I never felt a message from anyone that it was okay to have any and all of the feelings I had. Being twelve at the time, it was almost like I needed to be told what I was feeling and what to feel next. One of my sister's friends sensed how angry I was and gave me a dozen eggs to throw off the balcony onto the street. It was a wonderful gesture that brought me a brief moment of sanity and relief. But in these feelings too, I was alone. Surprisingly enough, I was already seeing a psychologist at the time to deal with my parents' recent divorce. She, like all the others, just felt sorry for me and offered no answers and no comfort.

My most prevalent feeling was anger. I was angry with everyone: my mother for a lot of reasons besides her suicide, my father, his wife of eight months, my siblings, my friends and all my other relatives and acquaintances for a general feeling of abandonment. In fact, I was angry with strangers and anyone who looked at me with pity in their eyes. When I returned to school after a few absences, I was penalized for being officially "unexcused" without a note explaining what had happened. So, I was sent to the attendance clerk, a bitter grandmother-type woman, who seemed like she had been there since the school opened in the early 1900s. I was angry with her through my fear and silence towards her. And when my sister came to the school to explain it all, she expressed her anger with them for their mistreatment of me. After that day, all the teachers and administrators felt so sad for me, and they expressed that with every passing glance in the halls. But no one (like the counselor or the principal!) ever called me into his or her office to talk. And I remained angry and resentful for a long time in a world of silence.

I was raised as an Episcopalian, baptized and confirmed. I viewed my church like a familiar and understanding relative that you look forward to seeing at the holidays. I don't think I really believed all the concepts and teachings of the Bible that I had learned. But, nonetheless, it had been a constant in my life amidst all the changes. So, being very adult and employing my survival strategies, I called my pastor and made an appointment with him. I questioned him about the suicide, the divorce, all the recent changes, my general unhappiness and the terrible fights that occurred between my father and my mother and now between my father and my stepmother. I had a lot of needs that had been building for a while, and I looked to him to answer it all and make sense out of what had happened. I tried to link it all to God, believing that He had made it all happen, but why? Why was I being tested so? Again, I felt angry and let down, and I returned to my existence of silence.

My six years of middle and high school were spent being very quiet about the suicide. After two years, my brothers and stepbrother had all gone to college, and I was truly alone. I felt like I rented a room in a boarding house. I got my driver's license the day I turned sixteen and drove off in my used Honda. I bought my own groceries that I stored in the refrigerator in the garage and made all my own meals. I got a job and worked every day after school and full-time in the summer. My stepmother told me six months after my mother's suicide to stop mourning. I rarely saw my dad or stepmother. I stayed with the same therapist for five of those years. My dad came to my sessions occasionally, but only when he and my stepmother were fighting about me. I was so lonely in those years. I knew I needed someone to take care of me, to be there for me. But I was so angry with all the people who should have done it (my mom, dad and stepmother) but didn't. The self-imposed exile into my private world of silence was only reinforced by everyone's behavior around me. I did turn to self-destructive behaviors and I am lucky that I didn't do any permanent damage. I have spent many years working at the emotional damage that I caused myself. I can truly say now that I'm the happiest I've ever been.

Our Lives Today

Judy is married, a mother of four grown daughters, a grandmother and a retired registered nurse and social worker. Mia is married with two boys, an elementary special education teacher and currently working on her master's degree in social work from the University of Texas at Austin. We feel there is a serious void in information available to those like us who have struggled with the legacy of suicidal parents and sought help. Though there are other books, counseling and support services, what we believe is truly needed is compassionate means to obtain and utilize coping skills. As we searched for and read books on survivors of suicide, we did not find one book that specifically addresses the needs of survivors of parent suicide. We looked for one that provided an outlet for sharing individual experiences. Through our own experience and research, we feel that sons and daughters need a book that shows where and how to find help. We believe others will be helped by learning how survivors have coped at various stages of recovery and what different avenues they have used to create fulfilling and meaningful lives after their tragic event. Ultimately, we wanted to share with our readers that it is possible to thrive as well as survive. We also know that misinformed family, friends and various community members who may or may not be trying to help actually complicate the pain of parent suicide. We wanted to hear, record and then share the positive and negative experiences of our participants.

Benefits for Other Readers
You may be the surviving spouse of suicide and want some ideas to help your child/ren cope with the other parent's suicide. If you are a friend, co-worker or an acquaintance of someone who has had to endure a parent suicide, here are many narratives on what our survivors found helpful and not so helpful in the aftermath of the suicide. If you are a therapist or counselor, a representative of a religious faith or a first responder, we also hope this book will be helpful about what approaches our participants found useful and compassionate and which were not. Sometimes an approach that one participant found beneficial, another found annoying or useless. Should you be a student studying for a vocation or a profession that may bring you in contact with those who have lost a parent to suicide, we hope our book will increase your knowledge and result in your listening first to the survivor and then thoughtfully pondering your responses. If you have contemplated suicide or if you have attempted it in the past, in this book you will learn of the ripple effect that occurs with such an event and how that effect really never stops its motion for the survivors. It is our hope you will conclude that suicide never is an option.

Our Hopes for Children of Suicidal Parents
It is our wish that you will read and find this book helpful. If you have lost a parent to suicide, we hope that you will not only find comfort in the knowledge that you are not alone and that your experiences and feelings are similar to others who have been through a parent suicide, but also that you will become more informed about the issues sons and daughters who experience parent suicide face and the steps towards healing. We hope you will also be inspired to begin or continue working towards integrating the past and building a fulfilling life.

Prologue

One day, Judy's grandson, Joshua Concklin, came forward and shared with us his frightening but telling story of his perspective on the long-term effects of suicide on generations. This young married man stated, "I was never a child of suicide, but I did become quite serious about making my baby one."

Here is his story:

As for my childhood, I was forced to grow up at an early age in order to make a home life for myself, my sister and mother as Mom worked very hard to overcome an abusive marriage and to provide for the two of us. While Mom struggled and worked to climb the corporate ladder, family time became rarer. It was difficult for me to make friends as we moved often until I was a teenager, and I had obligations in the house as well.

Fortunately, I did have an extended family consisting of my grandma and grandpa. I spent a couple of weeks with them every summer and saw them frequently. I greatly enjoyed the time we spent around the holidays when the family got together; those were happy times.

I met the love of my life and my best friend a few weeks before my twentieth birthday. By the time we had been together for two weeks we both knew that this was it and had started a list of things that we wanted for our wedding and had even discussed how many kids we wanted. My life started becoming what I always wanted it to be. After we were married, our lives became better but more complicated, as I was in the military and had to deploy out to sea fairly regularly. I was deployed for our first anniversary, which got me down, but soon after I came home we learned we were expecting our first child, and I couldn't have been more overjoyed. Then something changed. As I struggled to spend as much time at home with my expecting wife, work also had a higher demand on my time. My supervisor didn't seem to like me very much and tried to get me in trouble on numerous occasions, which weighed very heavily on my mind. Then one afternoon, I overdosed on prescription medication; I tried to commit suicide. I was trying to make the voices go away when I overdosed; I just needed to get away...and so I took more and more medication until...

I had a revelation:

I remembered what it was like to grow up without a father.

I remembered what it was like to feel lonely.

I remembered seeing how my mom struggled to raise two kids on her own.

I remembered how the man I now call Dad came into our lives during my adolescence and really tried to make a difference.

I remembered the personal sacrifice he made for me.

I thought about everything that I would miss if I left. I would never get to see my child, much less see what he would become.

I remembered what my grandmother said she felt like when her mother died when she was a child, and I knew that I never wanted to put my child through that.

People who have parents who have committed suicide have a very difficult road ahead of them. Questions (such as "Was it my fault or was it your fault?") often plague these individuals as they may be either looking for someone to blame or blaming themselves.

The thought of what effects my actions might have on my family is what saved my life. My unborn saved my life. Not a day goes by now, no matter what happens or doesn't happen, that I don't look back and remember where I've been, what I've done and know that there isn't anything that I can't overcome.

I did not survive a parent committing suicide nor can I completely comprehend it, but I almost made my firstborn a survivor of parent suicide, and I will never forgive myself for that. I now have three children...number four? Maybe, maybe not, we'll just have to see what the future brings. As for those who have had the unfortunate experience of losing a parent to suicide, I hope this story may give you some solace that it was not your fault, could never be a child's fault, because a parent's love for a child runs so deep and strong. My heart goes out to you who have survived. I hope you can remember the good as well. I hope you find comfort and that your own lives will be happy and fulfilling.

Joshua's story gives us a first person perspective on the questions that go through the mind of a parent contemplating suicide. Although no one can know the true last thoughts of a parent who succeeds in suicide (even when there is a note), Joshua's account of the revelations that led him to choose to live are what the authors believe to be a fair representation of the inner struggle that most suicidal parents face. Some parents are able to rationalize the act nonetheless; other parents realize the devastation they will leave in their absence.

Joshua's description also touches on a significant issue brought up in our book by many survivors—the guilt a survivor feels that the parent's suicide was their fault. The authors would like to reiterate along with Joshua that no survivor is responsible for their parent's suicide. This act is contemplated and completed solely by the parent.

Parents are role models, and when they attempt or succeed at suicide, they unwittingly set an example for their offspring by their attempt or final act of suicide. This act can potentially provide their children with just one more choice for solving problems. Statistics show that the offspring of parent suicide are at higher risk for taking their own lives. It is up to the sons and daughters to stop this tragic cycle in their families.

PART I

A Parent's Suicide

■ ■ ■

From *The Loss That is Forever: The Lifelong Impact of the Early Death of a Mother or Father* by Maxine Harris (New York: Penguin Group, 1996):

> *The suicide of a parent shatters a child's belief that he or she is lovable and worthy of being loved...When death happens suddenly or violently or after a long illness, a child must contend with the uncertainty of the world and with a parent's inability to prevent disaster. Yet that child knows that his or her parent did not want to die. Given a choice, he or she would prefer...to be there forever.*

> *When a parent commits suicide, a child must contend with the fact that the parent died willingly, that he or she sought death and knowingly...left the child behind. The refrain of "If my mother or father loved me, how could they have left me?" haunts the lives of the survivors of suicide. Children may come to doubt their own worthiness and inherent goodness. Perhaps it was because they were not good enough that the parent chose to leave them. (p. 29)*

CHAPTER 1

Small Children: Birth to Ten

■ ■ ■

I am somewhere; I just have no idea where. It is an unfamiliar, poverty stricken place full of strange people. While wandering about this place, I see this small child about two or three years of age who is looking for her mommy. I walk around with her trying to sight her mother, who I am unable to locate. At first I am carrying this tiny child, and later I think we are holding hands while walking and searching. We keep encountering women on our mission and stop to inquire about the identity of each and every one. We find no answers for the child as each woman we run into manages to not admit nor deny that she is her mother. The child tightens her grip and clings. Her bewilderment intensifies, as each of these strange, poorly clad, vagabond women move by in an unrecognizable blur. It is a dreary day; the air is dingy, blurring the details of each face.

I am no longer with the child. Instead I am an observer. I see another female plodding along with the little girl as the exploration continues for her mommy, whoever she is. I don't think this person is the mother, but I am confused as to how she entered into the picture. She is holding the child's hand and is dragging her along, not walking with her. I am very uneasy having allowed the girl to go with this other woman. I do not even know when I released the child over to her or even if I had.

I reflect back thoughtfully over my revealing dream of many years back: this sweet little girl and the adult assisting the little one to find her mommy.

Who were they? While this part of my dream was immediately clear because unquestionably they were both me, I wonder about the identity of the female who plodded along dragging the tiny me behind her as the pursuit continued to locate my mother. Who was she? With thought, it occurs to me that she is me as well, the vulnerable and weary part of me who was on this unavailing quest looking for my mother. Who is my mother, the one who loved and thought the world of me? Is she my birth mother? Is she Marguerite, my gravely ill grandmother's private duty nurse who mothered, loved and cared for my brother, Stan, and me until I was two years, ten months? Could she be my grandmother? Is she the cruel housekeeper who was supposed to be caring for us after Marguerite left until I turned five and one half years? I don't think so. Certainly the woman who married my father when I was three and one half and adopted me when I was a preteen couldn't be my "real" mother. At age ninety-one, she continues to claim not to be my mother, maintaining that I am "someone else's child."

"Will my 'real' mother please stand up?"

Judy was only seven weeks at the time of her mother's suicide.

Absence, Loss or Both?

Judy always felt that there was an empty space inside her. This is an emotional response commonly felt by children who have experienced a parent's death during their infancy or young childhood.

I never knew my mother and didn't feel a sense of loss for her, just this empty space inside me, because I had never really known her or learned to love her. I felt this sense of nothingness regarding my absent mother. However, this does not mean that loss did not co-exist in me along with the absence. I felt a terrible loss inside me, which I did not understand until adulthood.

After the death of a parent of a newborn or infant, it is likely that there may be a substitute parent with whom the baby or child has bonded. However, this person is frequently not a permanent figure in the child's life, causing the young survivor to experience an additional loss or multiple losses thereafter at an age when he or she is not equipped to deal with another loss in his or her life. This was Judy's experience:

My family (my father, brother and I) moved in with our paternal grandparents after our mother's suicide. A nurse was already caring for our grandmother, who was seriously ill with uncontrolled diabetes and a leg amputation. This nurse, Marguerite, took over the care of my brother, Stan, and me, bonding and becoming in essence a real mother to us. I called this nurse "Mommy" and truly believed that she, Marguerite, was our mother. Two months before turning three years of age, Marguerite left her job and an abusive housekeeper took charge of us. Profound loss and waiting became very much a part of my identity into most of my adult years until my late forties and early fifties. At that time, I found a therapist who knew how to deal with my huge loss. During therapy, I wrote this piece:

I don't want to move. I can't move. I cry for Mommy. Penny smothers my cries with her hand burying my mouth. I can't breath. She releases her hand and I make no more sounds. Inside I keep crying for Mommy. I want to roll up in a ball and I do. I listen. I watch. The phone! It's ringing! Is it Mommy? I'll wait. I'll wait till I find her. I can't find her. She's not coming. I won't give up until I find her. I'll become a nurse just like Mommy and I'll work in the hospital. I'll find her there. I become a nurse and I work in the hospital. I keep waiting, looking and listening for someone. I just can't remember who.

When a Parent's Suicide Enters a Child's Life

When the death of a parent sneaks into a child's life, the child is not equipped to deal with this loss. Survival is the immediate concern, because a child cannot survive without an adult's intervention. He or she needs either the remaining parent to be the responsible party or some other adult to provide the necessities for survival. Insecurity becomes the main issue as the child is well aware of his or her own inability to stay alive without an adult figure. Children are dependent on adults and are keenly aware of this. Generally, the remaining parent takes over total care of the child, but new fears begin to surface for the child. What if the other parent should die, leave or commit suicide?

As if this particular issue isn't, in and of itself, enough to cope with, children do not have the resources that are available to adults. Unless they have an insightful surviving parent who is able to provide needed emotional support, love and therapeutic help when the time is right, they are helpless to fend for themselves. Very young children do not have the vocabulary to express their feelings, grief and fears, which are generally intensely overwhelming. They do not comprehend what has happened to them. They have no words to sort out and comprehend this event, and yet it deeply affects the rest of their lives. They may never have been able to achieve closure with their mothers or fathers. They probably haven't been able to say good-bye or, if by chance they did, can't recall doing so later in life. They no doubt have not gone through the normal stages of grief and thus become chronic grievers until they find a therapist who knows how to deal with chronic grief. What has happened to them is calamitous and tragic. Without therapeutic intervention, this can disrupt and halt emotional growth and cause lifelong fears and suffering.

The strong, long-term effects of an early death of a parent apply to not only young children but also adolescents as well. (We'll discuss this further in Chapter 2, "Adolescent Transitions.") As you read on, please keep in mind that not only are these young people dealing with an early loss of a parent through death but also they have the added burden of coping with the stigmas of suicide as well. It is not unusual that these children have a long string of memories of this parent's repeated attempts at suicide. These children not only face the catastrophe of this loss but also very frequently face the abuse and rebuke of family members and society. Just trying to absorb what children go through when a parent takes his or her own life is no doubt incomprehensible in the minds of most adults.

Judy's brother, Stan, who was five years old at the time of his mother's suicide, accurately fits the young child's inability to recall and understand the magnitude of the death even over sixty years after the suicide. As Judy and he talked, he repeatedly answered questions with, "Can't say, too young" or "I can't remember." When asked about his story, he replied, "There is no story." Judy responds: "Our family refused to discuss our mother, her death and suicide; it was a taboo subject to even talk about with one another. My brother thinks he might have been the one to find our mother after the suicide."

Finding Adult Survivors of Parent Suicide as Infants and Young Children

Eleven people with whom we spoke, including Judy, were nine years or younger at the time of their parents' suicides. Eight are in the helping professions today: four psychotherapists, one registered nurse, one registered nurse/social worker and two teachers. All our participants are older than eighteen years of age. When we make reference to a baby or child, we speak of the person's age at the time of the parent's suicide or event. Three individuals were infants (five months and younger) at the time of the event. We had difficulty finding these participants. We spoke with four participants who were two to five years of age at the time of a parent's suicide who sought us through a mental health organization, and two others we already knew. Four people with whom we spoke ranged from six to nine years of age, two from a mental health professional organization and two from suicide survivors support groups. As mentioned earlier, we confined our study and interviews to people with resources in their lives. We wanted to be sure that our participants had friends, family, therapists or support groups to talk with if any issues were raised during our research. They assured us they had resources should they need them. Many participants reported to us that they found the survey and interviews therapeutic. We were not surprised by this reaction. They reported that the questions we asked were thought provoking and inspired them to speak on issues not discussed previously with siblings, parents and extended family members either for the first time or on a new level. In addition, many expressed that it was exciting that their words could help other survivors worldwide. Their voices were finally heard and, in our book, could make a difference to an infinite number of people who suffer similar tragedies.

Numbers of Childhood Survivor Participants

1. Secrecy of parental suicide is so very strong, perhaps to the extent that there may be those from this group of survivors who might actually not know that the cause of their parent's death was suicide. The cause of death may have been ruled an accident and/or the children and others may never have been told the truth, even when the child grew into adulthood. However, in the case of a baby or very young child, there are specific issues related to this age group, such as a family's inability to bond with the baby and the child's fears of attachment. It will mask their understanding of why the survivor suffers from these problems. The life struggles may still be there but without the knowledge of what caused such difficulties. Judy tells of her family situation:

My pregnant grandmother died from the flu during the 1918 flu epidemic at the age of twenty-nine. Her oldest of four children was five years of age. My mother took her own life when she was twenty-nine years of age and attempted suicide many times while pregnant with me, her second baby. My brother was also five. At this same age I was pregnant with my second baby and had a most difficult year filled with intensive fears that I was going to die before my next birthday. I did not comprehend why I had these exaggerated fears. I knew my mother died at age twenty-nine, but I was not suicidal. I had no knowledge that my maternal grandmother also died at this age. On the eve of my thirtieth birthday, I was unable to sleep until after midnight at which time I felt total relief and these fears ceased. On my thirtieth birthday, my father said to me, "You are still alive and you are thirty. Family members believed you would die at age twenty-nine." I had no conscious memory of such conversation among my extended family but obviously such discussion took place in my presence during my young childhood. My husband, Jack, heard my father saying this and exclaimed, "Whoa, this has been Judy's worst year!"

Many years later, my psychotherapist had me do a timeline, a map showing the events taking place at certain ages of my grandparents, parents and myself. This timeline was very revealing to me in many ways, one being the disclosure of my pregnant grandmother and her death during the epidemic, my mother's pregnancy with me and multiple suicide attempts with eventual success after my birth and my pregnancy with exaggerated fears of dying. All of this took place when all three of us were age twenty-nine.

2. Sons and daughters who were infants and small children at the time of the suicide did not come forth to volunteer in our study. They may have thought they were just too young at the time of the event, believing they could not contribute much to our research and that their situation simply did not apply to our study. We found this not to be true; the effects on babies and children are clearly pronounced and damaging.

We did not find these sons and daughters in support groups. They may not have considered joining such groups for suicide survivors, believing they were too young at the time of the event and would be an outsider. They might also mistakenly believe that they were too young to recall anything significant and would thus feel out of place.

We found these young survivors by advertising in support group periodicals throughout the United States. Also, we personally knew some adults who had lost parents to suicide at very young ages. These were our primary sources for finding participants who were very young at the time of the suicide.

3. The chaotic beginning in life for these babies and young children definitely may result in the youngster being emotionally unhealthy and lacking stability. If the caretaker does not seek therapy, s/he may not be

emotionally strong enough to actually participate.

At one time it was confidently believed that a young child soon forgets his mother and so gets over his misery. Grief in childhood, it was thought, is short-lived. Now, however, more searching observation has shown that this is not so. Yearning for mother's return lingers on.

John Bowlby, *Attachment and Loss, Volume III: Loss: Sadness and Depression* (New York: Basic Books, Inc., 1980).

4. Suicide as an option for solving problems is only one consequence that a son or daughter of parent suicide may adopt. Because of their disordered beginning in life, the infant or young child might become more predisposed to self-destructive behavior when bonding does not take place with the remaining parent or a parent substitute. Some survivors at such a young age may become suicidal or actually complete suicide successfully.

Fears of Mental Illness after a Parent Suicide

Eleven participants reported that they worried "frequently" or "occasionally" versus "rarely" or "never" about the following:

- Six participants fear becoming mentally ill and four are fearful of also taking their own lives.
- Three participants fear family members becoming mentally ill. There was a fourth participant who said that "this has already happened." All four worry about family members becoming suicidal.

Abuse and Psychological Trauma of Children of Suicides

- Seven participants admitted to physical and/or sexual abuse during their childhood from the deceased parent, remaining parent and/or parent substitute.
- Another participant did not report abuse, but the fact that she was the one to find her dead parent after the suicide is, in reality, severe psychological abuse.
- One other participant often took on the role of a parent to her mother, who felt enormous stress over fears of losing her home and being separated from her daughter. Extended family members tried to have the child adopted and also felt entitlement to the property

this mother and child lived on. They imposed an extended legal fight of many years on this already small, traumatized family.

- The surviving parent's words can stab the heart of the child more deeply than even physical abuse. When the surviving father loses his spouse after the birth of his child, a blend of feelings (guilt and anger, to name a couple) might result in projecting his own feelings toward his child to explain the behavior of others.

Judy relates:

When I, as an adult, commented how my stepmother always complained of illness when they visited us, my father's explanation to me of his interpretation of her behavior was, "Maybe just the sight of you makes her ill." Actually, to this day I consider this statement a half truth. I believe the sight of me made both of them ill. I looked enough like my mother that, unknowingly, in essence, I haunted both of them.

- Especially if the mother is the parent who has died, family members of these children frequently believe that they now have free rein to discipline the children in any manner of their choosing. The woman who cared for Judy and her brother told Judy of this incident:

Marguerite, who cared for my brother Stan and me, took a weekend off. That Sunday relatives were visiting and my brother, age six at that time, had a tiff with our cousin. Our aunt, the cousin's mother, went to spank Stan and chased him all over the house trying to do so. My brother hid under the bed and stayed in his hiding place for a good bit of time until they left. My brother evidently was so scared that he felt physically ill and could not attend school the next day. Marguerite spoke with our aunt after her return that evening and advised her that just because we were motherless did not entitle relatives to spank us.

Before and After the Suicide of a Parent

One day, our whole world changes and we are no longer the same. Some children recall the day their world changed and how it was before. In many situations, those around us change and suddenly seem to view us differently. Behaviors and attitudes from society may include avoiding and ignoring the survivor. Others might see our parent who completed suicide as having been a lesser person because of their act of suicide. They might also view the survivor as an inferior being. For infants and newborns, there is no *before* and *after*, there is only an *after*. Fortunately, not all people are insensitive to families and children of suicide, but almost all of our participants who lost a parent to suicide related to us unkind experiences and rejection. Of our eleven participants ages nine and younger, three reported their parent's suicide as "a defining event," six said it was "one of the most defining events" and the other three called it "the most defining event of their life."

In the Beginning: Issues of Infants who Lose a Parent to Suicide
1. A disastrous beginning in life

Judy saw this news clipping concerning her mother's suicide:

> April 4, 1942: "As a result of swallowing poison in her home yesterday, Mrs. Beatrice Zionts, twenty-nine, of Stowe Township, died in Ohio Valley Hospital last night. The mother of two children, one less than two months old, was found unconscious in the bathroom of her home by her husband. According to a report of the coroner, it was the third time that Mrs. Zionts tried to end her life. About seven weeks ago, it was reported by police, Mrs. Zionts attempted to leap from a window of the Ohio Valley Hospital a few days before her child was born."

Revealing how she found the clipping, Judy comments:

When I found this newspaper clipping in my uncle's Bible (much to his consternation), I realized how close I had come to not surviving until birth and being here today. I always thought my mother's suicide was caused by postpartum depression, but clearly her psychoses occurred before delivery. Much later, I learned from my aunt that my mother overdosed more than once while pregnant with me. For most of my life, I would experience from time to time a dread of pending disaster. I now know why!

Close family members of a suicide find their lives unmanageable and chaotic at the time of the tragic event. No doubt they probably were severely dysfunctional before then. Infants are raised in this chaos. Their lives begin in an out-of-control environment. Their lifelong task may be making their lives manageable by bringing order to their lives. This is done one day at a time and might be the only way of life that the child knows. Even though this is a huge task, it is possible to do. Judy tells here of her beginning of life being a time of total disruption:

Life was disrupted and changed dramatically for my family after my mother's suicide. My father had to find someone to care for us and moved us all in with his parents since the nurse caring for his mother agreed to care for my brother and myself. My grandfather was stubborn and difficult, putting extra burdens on my father by insisting he take over medical expenses for my grandmother. My dad had to work a second job to meet the added financial load. Family members were making comments on the shame of my birth and blamed my father for getting her pregnant. In addition to this, two months before I turned three years of age, this nurse whom I loved and called Mommy was no longer our caretaker. A catastrophe occurred and I could not heal from it, at least not until I found my psychotherapist in my later forties who knew what to do with my very early grief. I lost my mother again, and never again would my family speak of her with me, just as they would not talk of my birth mother. Both mothers disappeared from my life as if they never existed. Instead, I woke up to a stranger, a cruel housekeeper.

The mother of David M., two months of age at the time of his father's suicide, was in a terrible emotional state when he needed her the most:

My mother went through a horribly regressive emotional experience after the suicide. My father's parents blamed her for his death, as well as his siblings. She still has a difficult time reliving these memories.

Ashley, four years old at the time of her father's suicide, shares her feelings about the chaos in her life.

I had a very chaotic childhood. The suicide was only one of many family secrets. There is a history of substance abuse and mental illness, especially depression.

2. Blaming the newborn or infant and/or the remaining parent
It is not infrequent that children are blamed for the suicide of a parent.

Even if this is not the case, children tend to blame themselves. They might believe that they could have done something to prevent or stop their parent from taking his or her own life. Children have magical thinking. They might believe that the parent will return to life and continue to parent them. They might remember getting angry or misbehaving and then believe that is why the parent killed him or herself. So the child may keep trying to be extra good and even start fearing that the other parent might also leave if the child is disobedient. Newborns also may be blamed as the cause of suicide, particularly if the parent happens to be the mother. If this is the case, the child is invariably likely to overhear some comment made that their birth "killed" their mother.

Mary Higgins Clark, the "Queen of Suspense," says this so aptly in her novel, *Daddy's Little Girl*. (New York: Simon & Schuster, 2002):

Over the years I came to understand that when grief is not shared, blame is passed around like a hot potato instead, thrust from one to the other, eventually sticking to the hands of the one least able to throw it away.

In this case, that person was me. (p. 41)

Judy relates:

We had some relatives over for dinner and I (twelve years old at the time) was seated on the front porch when one family member casually commented to another: "Too bad Beatrice (my mother) ever became pregnant; if she hadn't had a baby, she would be alive today." Interestingly enough, this individual not only blamed my birth (the newborn at the time of the suicide) but she also spoke in front of me as if I did not know the English language. This was twelve years after my mother's suicide and such conversation was still taking place in my presence.

Before I even understood that my mother was dead, I believed as a child that I had killed someone. That thought kept running through my mind. No doubt I overheard some comment when I was quite young and not old enough to make sense of it. I recall my first day at Sunday school at the age of six. We discussed the Ten Commandments, and by the time we made it to the sixth commandment, "Thou shalt not kill," I ceased to hear any more of what was said. Instead I became absorbed in my own thoughts that when I was too young to recall, I broke the worst commandment of all. Yes, I thought I had killed someone; I just had no idea who.

Blame heaps additional pain on the baby's family and the baby, making it more difficult (perhaps sometimes impossible) for bonding to take place between family members and the baby. In addition, the infant has no cognitive skills to recognize what is happening, to verbally express feelings or to consciously understand or remember what is taking place. All the infant can do is cry. Caretakers may not be sensitive to the cries when life is already so chaotic. Because this baby will grow up to have no conscious memory nor be able to make sense of his or her frenzied world does not mean the suicide is not real for this son or daughter or that there was no impact on the baby's present or future life.

The dilemma of feeling a lack of belonging in one's family and community tends to be quite strong in our infant survivor participants of parent suicide. Children are totally helpless and vulnerable to psychological, spiritual and physical harm by grieving, shocked and/or angry family members and friends. Our data and personal experiences indicate that the child who is handled in a warm, loving, accepting and supportive environment after the suicide is, unfortunately, the exception rather than the rule.

Ben, age three at the time of his father's suicide, states his relationship with his mother was always very good. He reports being able to discuss his father and the suicide freely with his mother, and his greatest support after his father's suicide came from his mother, sister and maternal grandmother. Only the information that he wanted and needed to know was shared with him. His family was approachable but cautious with the topic of suicide. Ben said his father's suicide was one of the most defining events in his life. He found his stepfather to be a very good man and parent, and his relationship with him ranged at times from very good to good. However, Ben never really wanted to talk about his birth father's suicide with his stepfather:

I can remember my stepfather and me discussing what my birth father was like. However, I can never remember talking to him about the suicide. My stepfather also has never used my real father's suicide to make himself look better in my eyes. He never compared himself to my real father, which I really appreciate. I think our relationship would not be good if he had. In my mind, my stepfather is the only person in my family who knows the least about the suicide and the reason for it. The reality, however, is that my stepfather and mother probably know the most about that due to my mother sharing everything with him. My mother has told us before, that my step-dad is the only person who knows what all has happened to her with regards to my real father.

3. How could life have been different?

For those of us who have lost a parent as an infant, it is totally speculative as to what our lives would have been had the suicide not happened. We certainly have beliefs as to what might have been different. The one and only thing we know for sure is that our parents' suicides have shaped our lives from the beginning. How our lives would have been is only a guess.

Stewart, a three month old twin at the time of his father's suicide, states the suicide as being the most defining event of his life:

I definitely believe that had our father not committed suicide, my life would have been different. I would have had a childhood and would not have married at such a young age. Instead I took care of our mother so she could take care of us.

David M., two months of age at the time of his father's suicide, reveals his thoughts on this topic:

I would say yes, it has changed my life. To put that into words—you know that it's changed your life, but you don't know how because coming from a reference of, say, like my brother, who has kind of the "typical caring home" with his dad (my stepfather) and our mother, who has been in a better state of mind during his upbringing for obvious reasons. I've wondered how my life would have been different had my father survived and this is what I think. I'm maybe not as friendly and as comfortable with feelings, touch and signs of affection—fatherly things. I think maybe if I had both parents it would have been different. Maybe I would be more affectionate with others. I'm not very affectionate with my mother, not in terms of hugs, kisses and phone calls. You see what the media shows you on TV as a family, how you should be. Then you see others, and you make your own perceptions or make your own judgments and then you see how yours doesn't fit into either of those.

With my stepfather, he's a good guy. I was, however, not open to his parental input or fatherly advice. He never really stepped in and acted in that role, possibly because I wasn't receptive. He's more of a good listener. We have mutual respect for each other. I love and admire him, but it's never "warm and fuzzy" like what you see on TV.

These points bring up how infant survivors think in terms of personal losses. Our point of reference of how ideal families should be is often modeled for us on old television sitcoms such as *The Brady Bunch*, *Leave it to Beaver* or *The Cosby Show*. Of course, these were not generally realistic or typical of the average family with a father and mother. Certainly, while being an infant and losing a parent to death (and then suicide as the cause of death) has its own unique issues, it doesn't mean that children brought up with both parents intact necessarily have the "warm and fuzzy" life that we dream they do. Nonetheless, the infant survivors of suicide start life out with a major disadvantage, a significant handicap that is not visible to the outside world. Trauma can be minimized with an outstandingly attentive and nurturing family, but we have found among most all of our participants that families generally show serious dysfunction when there has been a suicide. The infant clearly has no control over influencing the family.

4. Lack of bonding with the newborn

Due to the many serious issues that specifically occur when an infant is born and a suicide occurs, lack of bonding with the newborn on the family's part is sadly a common consequence. Grieving over a serious loss and then bonding at the same time with a newborn are antagonistic to one another. For most, it is extremely difficult to bond when grieving and in post-suicide shock. Infancy is the most critical time in a person's life to experience bonding and to receive love, nurturing and a sense of belonging. If it is not provided one way or another, there is a strong possibility of a lack of good mental health and stability among this group of survivors.

David M., two months of age at the time of his father's suicide, feels:

Most of my time was spent with my grandmother. I realized when I got closer to graduation from college that I didn't really spend that much time with my mother when I was a baby or a child. I recall that when I was with her, she would be in her room just crying while I was watching TV. As an adult, I've talked with her about it and basically she tells me that she was an emotional wreck, very depressed and shocked. The doctor had prescribed her valium, and she was pretty much doped up; she wasn't in a place to take care of me at that time, and I believe that really kept our bond from developing. Because my early years really weren't spent with her, I was closer to my grandmother up until I was about five or six.

Judy offers a similar theory:

My father, not to be blamed, was never able to really bond with me, and when I asked him how I was during this time, his reply was, "You were too young and couldn't feel anything. It didn't affect you." He was totally wrong! I always felt this empty space inside of me, yearning and longing for someone I didn't know: my mother, whoever she is. I also believe my father did the best he could at that time with the limitations that existed within him and his environment.

The Child's First History Lesson

Judy's hypothesis is that people who lose a parent (particularly the mother) as infants or young children around age five or younger may lose a certain point of reference as to who they are, where they belong and frequently about their connection to the family. In essence, a person's first lesson in history and geography happens to be their own personal lineage. Judy relates her situation to this hypothesis:

Generally, mothers are the ones to provide a baby and child with their own personal history. It was a thought that I had when I was struggling throughout my adulthood to figure out who I was and where I came from. I started out adulthood knowing very little about me, from where I came. My father, most of the time, had his usual reply when I asked about my natural mother, her suicide or any questions about my childhood at all: "Don't worry about it; it's in the past; let it go; start living in the present; all you need to know about is now." I wondered how I could let go if I wasn't sure what it was I needed to let go of.

This was my own personal history, and I was entitled to know what it was. Gradually, I began to relate this to my disinterest and struggle to learn in history classes. I was told not to be interested in my own past, and yet at home and in school I was told that I was supposed to be interested about the past of our state, our nation, our world and from where we come as humans. In Sunday school, we were taught about the history of my heritage and my people. Yet, I never learned my earliest lessons in history: my own past, my own history! How could I branch out and go from there and learn the more advanced concepts of this subject? It is like learning algebra if you haven't first learned your numbers.

For me, geography was just as bad. I had no concept of knowledge from where I came. I wasn't even sure who my mother was, no less where she was. How was I to know which direction that I needed to go to fall into her arms?

Tammie, two years old at the time of her mother's suicide, tells of her experience with these school subjects:

Geography and history were so unbelievably tough for me. It was like a fog. Everything was all jumbled up in my head: dates, places and people. I couldn't keep anything straight. I couldn't remember what happened when, who bombed who and who was the king of where. I couldn't put them in order in my head, let alone remember them. Geography was just as bad. There are no roots, there's no anchor, there's no background. You can't put yourself together, can't put your own pieces together, no sense of identity as to who you are. You had to memorize and it was impossible because everything was jumbled up to me when it came to geography or history. My sense of direction is miserable.

In looking at the seven participants who were age six or younger at the time of their parents' suicides, we see that five reported dislike and/or difficulty in one or both of these two subjects. One participant had a mother who managed to give her child a stable upbringing in spite of the tragedy, and interestingly enough, he had no difficulty with these subjects. Our seventh participant did not choose to have an interview. Another participant, Margaret, who lost her father to suicide when she was twenty-nine, states that history was a real puzzle to her. We learned that Margaret's mother died from a cause other than suicide when Margaret was about three and one-half years of age.

When we asked her about history classes in school, Margaret replied:

I recall history as tedious and (more interestingly) remember virtually NOTHING I ever learned. My husband and I even share humor about my extreme lack of knowledge of the world in terms of history.

My mother died when I was three years, ten months. Obviously I don't remember "conversations" with my mother. My memories of her are like movie scenes, and I have only a couple. They are more visual than they are recalling verbal content. After her death, we were rather estranged from her family, particularly after my father remarried about two years later. I saw my grandparents twice that I recall during my formative years, once because they came to visit (which I recall as an awkward event because of my stepmother) and once when my sister married. My grandfather attended the wedding, as my maternal grandmother had completed suicide when I was in the fourth grade. I learned more of my history at a family reunion at age twenty-one. I attended it with my eighteen-year-old brother who had never met these people. We had a life-altering weekend, staying up until all hours as I shared our family history with him. I was hurt for him and appalled to learn that he was unsure whether his biological sister was his sister or not. (In our family, we also had a half-sister and two step-siblings.)   My brother was two or three when my father remarried so he really didn't remember not having all these siblings. When I was having my own family is when I became more interested in medical history, etc. However, I never really became interested in history (world or American history) beyond my own narrow knowledge of my personal past. It has only been in the last two years that I have developed any interest at all in learning more about world events such as the Middle East conflict, probably because of trying to understand more about 9/11 and our future risks. Also, geography is something I know nothing about other than an image of the globe. I am okay if I have been somewhere and have to locate it on a map. Beyond my local travels, I am really ignorant. I believe I was so self-absorbed as a child that my concerns did not at all expand beyond my small world, my own experience.

Dick Concklin, who lost a grandparent to suicide, expresses so articulately his support of this hypothesis connecting early loss of a mother and the comprehension of history and geography:

Aside from some primal sensations in the womb, we all arrive in this world unaware of space and time. Space, the geography of the environment, is first learned at the mother's breast or at the nipple of a bottle and continues to develop throughout life. The mystery of time is explored first in the history of days that begin with the dawn of self-awareness. Therefore, it is not surprising that these personal focal points of reference are vital to putting all that is learned into perspective and establishing one's identity. From the simple relationship of one's house to a neighbor's down the street, the relative distance and direction of Houston to New York can eventually, over years of development, be understood.

It is not surprising, therefore, that the deprivation of early access to the basic starting points can make geographic and historical capabilities difficult to develop. Trauma and frightening experiences during one's early childhood can make later return to those excruciating times very painful. Yet those times are precisely where the baselines and focal points of reference lie. An analogy might be the experience of astronauts operating in a zero gravity vehicle. Without the orientation of gravity, they can't tell up from down or east from west. In a similar way, those affected with impaired recall might find a wall that separates them from their critical early history and all that has gone on before.

Should Children be Told that a Parent Committed Suicide?

There is controversy among our participants, as well as between the authors, on this topic because of the pros and cons in sharing information about a parent's suicide with children. Judy believes that, if possible, small children should not be told that the cause of death is suicide, particularly if this information is not going to be passed on by other family or friends. In certain cases, it could be wise to wait until young adulthood. Frequently the child's finding out may be inevitable, in which case a parent must explain it with the help of a professional therapist who knows how to do this. Parents often are the child's role model, and when one takes his or her own life, the child often considers this an additional option for solving problems: "After all, if Mom or Dad can do it, so can I." What and when to tell a child of a parent's suicide is strictly a judgment call.

Psychotherapist Andrea Michael states her opinion on telling small children that Mom or Dad died from suicide:

I wouldn't tell small children. I would talk to them as Mom, Dad, Grandma or Granddad having died and gone to Heaven. I think this is too difficult a subject and too hard to comprehend, even for adults. I don't think children can emotionally or cognitively understand this. Children don't even begin to understand that death is forever until they are five, six or seven, and we don't begin to comprehend the impact that forever means until much later in life. If they are going to find out from other children or others, I would work with the child a long time and deal with it as Mommy (or Daddy) was terribly ill and couldn't survive that. That is why they left their suffering, but most of us don't suffer like that. I think they would need a lot, a lot of help in coming to grips with suicide, working within play therapy so they could express their anger, confusion and sadness. I think it would take a long time for a child to sort it out.

It takes a long time for a child to sort out the death of any parent, but if it is suicide and they know about it, I believe that would be incredibly traumatic. I would hope they could be protected from that information until they are much older and able to cope with it. I would certainly see that the child was in therapy with a qualified child therapist.

More than once in our survey, it was demonstrated how young children cannot come to terms with the concept of mortality. This fact shows how important it is to talk to the child about his or her parent and be aware of what the child thinks and believes. They may have been told that their parent has died, but they tend to pretend otherwise and even believe it by making excuses to themselves and others for their parent not being around, such as their parent is gone on business or even divorced and living elsewhere. They see that other children have two parents, and they don't want others to realize that they are different in this way. Sometimes it may take until preadolescence or longer for the child to acknowledge that their parent is not coming home and is dead.

Sometimes, there is no choice or chance to use discretion as to when the child learns that there was a suicide. The child may have been present. Unfortunately, adults frequently talk recklessly in front of children and say things that young survivors do not need to hear. Neighborhood children or younger members of the family might repeat what they have heard from their own parents to the son or daughter of suicide.

Typically, our participants complained that they were told too much, more than they wanted or needed to know or that they were not told the truth. This is truly a dilemma for the remaining parent or guardian. If the son or daughter is not told, he or she may feel lied to. If he or she is told, the son or daughter may feel it is more than they want to know or are capable of handling. It can be considered a no-win situation for the parent, no matter what explanation is given. The child may grow up to express dissatisfaction in how this was handled by the remaining parent. The parent will just have to weigh the pros and cons of each approach and say what he or she believes is in the best interest of the child. Additionally, after being told about the parent's suicide, the living parent frequently becomes unapproachable in discussing the child's or their own feelings. When they were told, participants mostly reported they were either told not to tell or talk about this, or the environment was such that the child simply knew this was a taboo topic in their household. Then the child must either disregard the parent's orders not to tell or carry the burden of keeping such a secret.

Barbara felt she had two losses at age six when her mother took her own life. Barbara and her father moved in with her paternal grandparents, but her father avoided her: "My father didn't tell me how she died until I was a few years older. It was at the same time he told me the facts of life." She did go on to say that although her father was unapproachable prior to telling of her mother's suicide, her father became approachable once she was told, which she appreciated.

Judy relates her burden of keeping the suicide a secret:

I was instructed not to tell that we even had another mother, no less talk about the suicide. I was supposed to pretend that our stepmother was our birth mother. My parents were unapproachable when I wanted to ask questions about my mother. I kept the secret. My brother, however, said he told whoever he wanted about our mother and her suicide.

Here are some suggestions for questions for the surviving parent, stepparent or guardian to consider as to when and what to tell their children about the suicide in their families:

- Is anyone else likely to tell the child?
- Do neighbors or any others who might tell your child know of the suicide?
- Is it going to be helpful and useful to your child to know this yet? If yes, how?
- Has your child asked questions, and what specifically are his/her questions?
- Does your child understand death at this time?
- Have you discussed this with professionals, primarily a good child therapist? Have you read books on the topic?
- Can you trust and get cooperation from family, friends and school teachers to respect your approach and not interfere with it?

This will be a very individualized and personal decision as to when it is appropriate to tell your child. Our advice is to be cautious, know exactly what you are going to say before even approaching him or her on the topic of suicide and have resources available for the child.

Memories and Longing for the Child Survivor

Memories may be absent, few or many. Basically it depends on the age the child is when the suicide occurs but not necessarily.

Joan narrated the following about her young incident with suicide:

I was nine when my mother ended her life. My father was very difficult and refused to talk with us about her. Once he listened as I talked with him about how the whole episode had affected us and the fact that we couldn't talk about it. He just looked at me and said, "That was the only way we could survive at the time, just not talk about it and go on and figure out the problems and do what we could." I didn't have a mother and I yearned for her. The whole business of being without a mother became my entire career. I didn't know who she was; I didn't even know what kind of food she liked or what color she liked. The biggest problem with me is I remember nothing before that day. I have total amnesia.

Ben, who was three years old when his father took his own life, said at the time we spoke that he still thought about his dad three to six times a week. He recalled two interactions with his father before the suicide:

The first was while my father and my mother were still married. Sometimes, after he came home from work, he would take his keychain that had a yellow bird on it and hide it in his hand. He would then begin whistling like a bird and tell us he had a bird in his hand. Then he would show us the keychain with the bird. I thought it was so neat that he could whistle like a bird.

The other incident was after the divorce. My father came to get my sister and me to go to his mother's house for the weekend. I recall him turning his head away from the table to cough or sneeze several times. I also remember that at some point during the meal that I was crying (I am not sure why). He told me that if I didn't stop crying, he'd give me something to cry about. I was not punished, so I assume I quit crying.

Judy told of this nightmare:

During my childhood and adolescence, I experienced a repetitive nightmare in which I heard discordant banging coming from our piano. I became immobilized in bed with terror wondering who might be downstairs making this disquieting cacophony. I could not move and I could not wake up. One day, I mentioned this to my brother who replied that our mother pounded on the piano during her moments of emotional torment.

Feelings about Parents
Judy reports:

It is my experience of as far back as I can recall that I felt that God told my mother to return to protect me, that I needed her. I thought she stayed with me but was invisible. When I was so alone or at times in danger, I would cry out inside me to my mother to please protect or save me. Inevitably, I would get help. It was almost as if a person would drop from the sky to rescue me.

David M., two months of age at the time of his father's suicide, felt his father was with him:

There have been several unexplained events over the course of my life. I've kind of attributed that to my father in some sense watching over me. When I've turned to my father for help or for guidance (kind of like my father is God), but more specifically when I've turned to my dad, something will happen and my life will fall into place or there'll be some turn of events. I've always felt like I've been taken from danger as I've had some really close calls.

Katherine, who was seven and one-half at the time of her father's suicide and almost eight years at the time of her mother's murder, says she feels her mother is still around:

My last dream of my mom happened about one and one-half years ago when she came to me and told me that she knew that all of this was very, very difficult for me. She assured me that it was okay and that she was okay.

The Problem of Isolation
Sometimes others offer to adopt the child after a parent suicide, particularly when s/he happens to be a newborn or infant. In Judy's family, a paternal uncle and aunt came forward wanting to adopt her, as they had only boys. The obstetrician of Judy's mother also made an offer to Judy's

father to allow him and his wife to adopt the seven-week-old baby. This would have been taboo for Judy's father to separate family members.

Family members are often callous and escalate the pain and worries of the surviving family instead of helping to keep the family and home intact after the suicide. A family of one of our participants pressured the surviving parent to put the baby up for adoption. This pressure continued to the point that this young child understood what was happening. They even had someone in mind to adopt the child. More than once in our surveys, it was illustrated that extended families felt they were entitled to some or all of the surviving family's money or even the property that the family lived on. This was not only true for families of baby and child survivors but also adult survivors. The legal fees just add an extra burden. This not only causes insecurity and angst among the surviving parent but the young child as well, who is fearful of losing his or her remaining parent or becoming homeless. The remaining parent's mental health may become compromised and, in order not to lose their surviving parent and/or home, the child may attempt to take on adult responsibilities, such as caring for the parent in an effort to make sure that this adult is okay. They cease to be a child and believe they have power and control when they are clearly out of control of the family situation. If and when things go wrong, the child frequently feels that s/he is to blame.

Isolation often occurs for the pain-stricken family because of the stigma of the suicide. People and other family members may avoid them. Either the baby (particularly if the mother takes her own life shortly after giving birth) or the remaining spouse is often blamed and this can be used as an excuse to avoid them. Self blame and feelings of horror over the suicide often result.

Others may avoid the newborn in order not to be reminded of the suicide. Stewart speaks of his own and his twin brother's situation:

We only were able to play with our cousins on my mother's side of the family. My father's family stayed away from us after his suicide.

Making the Decision to be Childless
Four of the people we interviewed do not have children. Two of these want children in the future but worry about being unable to nurture and commit as a parent. One participant remains undecided, and the other states that the decision has been made not to have any children.

Seven participants have children, and most of these say their parenting has been definitely affected by the suicide. A participant who had decided against having children because "mothers die" married a man who was thought to be infertile but wasn't; she ended up having children. Three say they are much more open, honest and emotionally available because of their own negative experiences, but one of these spoke of both positive and negative effects in parenting. Two participants reported that the suicide has impacted their parenting in a negative way. Two deny that suicide has impacted their parenting at all but went on to reveal ways during their interviews that they did parent differently because of the suicide.

Making the Decision to have Children
Judy tells:

When I married Jack, he already had custody of two children from his previous marriage. For me, this was instant marriage and motherhood. I knew I wanted to be a great mother to them, but they weren't cute little babies; they were very cute kids who did things that weren't so cute! They were excited when their dad got married, but angry as well. Certainly they wanted their birth mother, who already was remarried. In any case, I had clear-cut examples in my own life of what I shouldn't do, but that still posed a problem; how would I find the answers that exemplify what I should do? I thought about this quite seriously before I married and, of course, experienced panic over and over.

I started on my own quest for an education on child rearing, and I needed to develop a line of attack to get the education necessary to parent my new family, and my first approach just happened upon me. Since I was getting married, the nurse I shared an apartment with found a new person to split the rent with. I needed a place to live prior to marriage and another nurse friend with five sons offered me a room in her home for a couple of months. For almost two months, I became part of another family and had the opportunity to observe some new parenting skills of both my friend and her husband. I did learn some ideas of what I wanted to do and, of course, some of what I thought I didn't want to do. But I did live in a family home different from my childhood family. Meanwhile Elaine and Janette (my two daughters to-be) knew that their dad and I were getting married. The girls were excited but that did not last forever. Eight-year-old Elaine said they needed to call me Mom before we married, and five-year-old Janette liked to copy her older sister. So, very prematurely I became Mom. I had them at the park playing one day, and they were trying to get my attention with one of their voices repeating over and over "Mommy, Mommy, Mommy." I was sitting on the bench, not in any way responding back. Finally a woman nearby poked my arm and pointed at the girls, "Aren't they your children?" I looked at the young gals and said, "Oh yes, you're right, they are." That was my initial introduction into motherhood.

The bookstore and library became frequented places for me as I began my extensive quest for knowledge from the experts on how to become a mother. More and more books on child rearing accumulated in my library, and I acquired and read book after book. Our oldest daughter, Elaine, who read quite well, would look through the books that I was reading and would pronounce, "That won't teach you what to do with us." From the mouth of babes, but she wasn't exactly correct. Of course, I quickly discovered that one book wasn't enough. Different authors had different suggestions, and while one approach worked for one child, maybe next time, it didn't. The next child may need still another approach. Many books were read and reread. However, despite my studies, I felt I knew less and less.

I conversed with mothers every chance I could find and found myself unofficially interviewing them. They related something their child did, and I asked, "How did you handle that one?" Of course, mothers generally love to talk about their kids, and I learned.

Still, one more method for me to learn parenting was to do volunteer work called "Lay Therapy" for Travis County Child Welfare. We were taught skills to re-parent parents who had come into the Child Welfare system. The training to do this volunteer work was extensive, and we had continuing education as we did our work with clients. One such opportunity consisted of parenting classes. I took advantage of all that was offered to satisfy my thirst for parenting skills both for teaching our clients as well as, of course, for my own parenting role.

Eventually, I decided that I needed a professional to help me with those situations where I just couldn't find solutions. I started out aiming for perfection but a therapist taught me a whole new concept called "good-enough."

Becoming a mother was the most challenging job I ever undertook. As for starting out with a ready-made family, it was undoubtedly a good thing that I had not a clue of what was in store for me. We had fun and loving times. However, as relationships were now changed and more complex, there was anger to work through for not just the girls and my husband (their father), but for me as well.

I started out with a marriage and two daughters, and then a year and a half later I gave birth to Linda and three years after Linda came Susan. During these years I also "gave birth" to Elaine and Janette. The labor to be a family was extraordinarily long. Then one day I actually had four daughters, not just in language but in my heart. We stuck together. One of our two oldest daughters as adults said to me on one occasion that it amazed them that with all I put up with, I stuck by them through everything. I was thinking the same thing, except a reverse version. I thought about the mistakes I made and how it turned out that we ended up loving each other as much as we do. I believe Elaine and Janette had a good point; maybe what we have to do is stick by each other and just "keep on truckin'".

Fears of Parenting

It is not unusual to be fearful of whether or not you are capable of being a loving parent and to worry that you might not be able to bond, particularly if you did not bond with your parent. This was David M.'s fear. He was only two months old when his father took his own life. His mother found bonding extremely difficult during the time that she was in mourning and shock. At the same time, having family members blame her for the suicide undermined her spirit even more, and she struggled to show her love towards her infant. Although currently David M. has no children, he hesitantly told us he would like to: "In raising children, I fear that children require a lot of attention and guidance. I fear that I will not be able to provide enough love and care."

The Issue of Giving Birth

Judy reports:

When your mother did not live even long enough to get you through your second month of life, this adds fears about having children. In addition, I did have fears of dying when my children were young. Nonetheless, I wanted children. I was stubborn. Fear did not stop me from doing what I knew was right for me. But I do recall the terror and aloneness that I felt before giving birth. Just shortly before I delivered Linda at the hospital in which I worked as a nurse, my supervisor came into the labor room to see me. I don't recall much of anything of what she said, but I do know that I lost my fear of giving birth and becoming a mother. For that short time, she became a mother to me.

Concerns of Ability to Commit

Ben, three years of age at the time of his father's suicide, speaks of this issue:

I've always questioned the level of commitment my father had to us as his children and am somewhat fearful that some of his personality/commitment level may also be in me. I've backed out of relationships with girlfriends when the relationship was requiring more commitment. I now regret that. One of those relationships would likely have resulted in marriage had I been more committed. Sometimes I wonder if I got that trait from my father (I suspect he did have that trait).

Joan, nine years old at the time of her mother's suicide, tells her story:

Earlier on, I thought I did not want children and married a man who had been told he could probably not bear children. Years later, after we were parents, I discovered the reason why I did not want children at first: Mothers die. I always felt uncertain about raising my children, especially during their adolescence. I felt I had no role model since my family was estranged from each other and even my aunts (my mother's two sisters) were uninvolved. Not a good time for me as a child.

The Impact of Parent Suicide on Present Relationships

We asked all our participants if they believe their parents' suicides affected their present relationships. All participants who were in the age bracket from zero through nine years at the time of their parents' suicides responded "yes," but this did not mean that their relationships were affected necessarily in a negative way.

Joan feared her relationship would not last with her husband:

I lack trust that a relationship will last. It's probably fortunate or God's will that I became a military wife because of the nature of how we lived. You know, you make friends and then you leave and then they show up again someplace else or they don't. You keep in touch or you don't. It's very transient. I think the biggest problem was my relationship with my husband, and I did not really trust that this relationship would last, but it did.

David M., two months of age at the time of his father's suicide, fears relationships:

I don't get warm, caring and affectionate feelings, especially when I've been in a relationship. It feels uncomfortable to me. I struggle with myself to know why

I don't feel "warm and fuzzy" inside. I feel like I have mutual respect for people, but I don't like hugs and kisses. In some respects, I'm resentful that I got dealt these cards and that my brother has my stepfather and my mother and has the picturesque kind of family. It's really messed up a lot of things in my life to some degree that I have to process and take care of.

Janelle, ten years old at the time of her father's suicide, shares her thoughts:

I think my dad's suicide has changed my life, but I can't describe how it is different, because I was so young (still developing) when it happened. I never know if I am the way I am because I was exposed to suicide so early or if this is just my personality. I consider myself more pessimistic and untrusting than the average person. From what I've learned in school, I would likely qualify for a depression diagnosis with anxiety features. I know suicide is a risk for me. My husband gets subjected to some of my irritability/pessimism, and he has put up with this for years. I tend to take on too much, function under pretty high levels of stress and rarely take time to relax. Why do I try so hard? What am I trying to prove? Am I just a type-A personality or is part of me still a little ten-year-old girl trying to be good enough or gain approval that I will never get? Maybe my dad's suicide impacted my path in life, but I guess I'll never know; it happened before I knew what path I was on.

Children's Grief After a Parent Suicide

Chronic grief is a major issue for many childhood survivors of suicidal parents. Eight of our participants (including those who were infants at the time of loss) admitted they were still mourning. Judy shares her experience:

Until I had extensive therapy with a social worker who knew what to do with me, I was still grieving. I would say that my grief was truly over in my early fifties. I experienced emptiness and longing intensely, and these feelings would immobilize me. I believe my most painful loss came from the mother figure who really loved me and was out of my life two months before I turned three. She was the nurse for my very ill, diabetic grandmother, as well as the caretaker for my brother and me. I thought she was my mother. Determining how much was grief as an infant and what I started to experience almost three years later would probably be impossible and not necessary to know anyway for my recovery. Probably the grief was very mixed. It simply was clear to me that I also had leftover grief from birth on. I am feeling emptiness and longing minimally if at all from my childhood, and for me, that is a very dramatic change.

Tammie, two years old at the time of her mother's suicide, expresses her long-term reaction:

Grieve my mother, I thought that was funny. What are you talking about, grieve my mother? She's been gone forever, fifteen years. What is there to grieve? I learned about grieving my mother later when digging up photos and every time I found myself without a mother at the time of a significant event in my life. I was jealous of every female who had a mother, and I still am. I attach to older women. I always feel safer around older women, you know. I hate it when they leave. I am really missing my mom. This was true even when I dated guys and their mothers were really good to me. That's when I realized I had to grieve my mom. With the help of more therapy, I started to work on forgiving my mother so I could love her for the part of her that loved me. I always had clean clothes on in the pictures and stuff. She cared about me on some level and on some level she didn't. I didn't know what to do with my own kid now, so I began to understand maybe what my mother had gone through. I relate to her. That's when the forgiveness started to come in.

Sons and Daughters Tell What Was Not Helpful

1. When a parent of a young child dies, no less to suicide, it is a most unnatural condition. Frequently, the child develops a vulnerable appearance that tends to elicit mistreatment from people who feed on those who are easily hurt. Children are already easy prey to maltreatment, and sometimes this maltreatment centers around the suicide. It is up to teachers, adults and other parents to put a stop to this and teach their children to show empathy to the survivor's situation.

Stewart, a twin who was three months of age at the time of his father's suicide, explains:

You can't tell people or children not to pick on you. Teachers did not help. The teasing and scorn about my own past of being fatherless stuck with me all through school from the first to the eighth grade. I would beg my mother to not send us to school, but she did anyway.

2. Callous, judgmental comments generally originate from the adults, filtering down to the children. Some of our participants were told by the

other kids that their mother or father was going to hell.

3. Some participants reported that although they were old enough and wanted to, they were not allowed to attend their parents' funerals. These survivors report that this still bothers them and that closure with that parent becomes even more complicated. On the other hand, it is necessary to be aware of harsh statements that could be made at any time during the funeral from clergy or others in front of the children.

4. Some say they lost two parents, because the living parent either became emotionally detached from the children or they ceased to be with the children most of the time, leaving others to attend to them.

5. Although sons and daughters of parent suicide have a higher incidence of attempted suicide, we spoke with many participants who said that this act is not an option for them. No one has the right to suggest to anyone that the son or daughter will follow suit.

Barbara, age six at the time of her mother's suicide, says:

I was in my early twenties and attending the University. I had a social work professor to whom I revealed my mother's suicide. I had never been to counseling at that point in my life, and she said, "Well you need to go to counseling because you have a ninety-eight percent chance of committing suicide." That was real abrasive to me. It was like, wait a minute! I'm not depressed! My intent was not to end my life.

6. Trying to keep the suicide a secret is a nightmare. More often than not, our participants were not allowed to talk about the deceased parent and all too often told to deny the fact that the parent ever existed.

Angela, nine at the time of her father's suicide, reveals:

We never went to the funeral and we were just supposed to forget that he ever lived. It was not a good situation... A month after my father's suicide, my mother changed our name and a year later we moved and were supposed to pretend like our stepfather was our only father. We were not supposed to acknowledge that we had that past life. I split off from that part of my life.

Today things are totally different with my mom, and if I need to talk with her, I call her and we talk. I ask her questions and she's very helpful. But in those days, she didn't have a clue that I needed to process anything.

Katherine, seven and one-half years old at the time of her father's suicide and almost eight at the time of her mother's murder, shares:

The deal is nobody ever told me anything. The way the whole thing was all set up for my even finding out that my father was dead was unbelievable. I had a favorite uncle who would come and visit, and when he did, it would mean fun time for me. I was at school and my uncle walked into the classroom, and of course, I immediately thought fun time, and that we would go to the zoo or play. I saw him talking to my teacher and my teacher looked very sad and they were looking at me and of course, I'm still not getting it. I get into the car and several of my brothers were in the car and they're sad and I can't figure it out because no one still said anything to me. My brothers are upset with me because I'm not sad. But you know, I thought we were going somewhere fun so why would I be sad? Then I walked into our house and people were crying everywhere and I still didn't know what was going on. I walked into the kitchen and my aunt turned around to hand me some juice and then said how brave I was for not crying. And I'm thinking, crying about what? At that point I turned around and I saw my mom across the room talking to someone on the phone and I heard her tell them that my father was dead. There was a period of sitting back and listening. No one ever told me.

7. Having age-inappropriate expectations of and conversations with the child after the loss of a parent.

Janelle, ten years at the time of her father's suicide, tells what was not helpful:

Others said I had to help take care of my mother now. My thoughts were, *I am ten years old, don't make me responsible for adults.* I didn't want to hear about everyone else who had committed suicide. That wasn't comforting.

Unhelpful Explanations that Our Participants were Given After the Suicide

Judy's brother Stan was told: *Your mother stopped breathing.*

Tammie heard: *Your mother died from natural causes.* Young people do not die of natural causes.

Your mother died of headaches was conveyed to Barbara, who then worried about dying when she had headaches.

Judy's father's response was: *The past is the past. Let it go; let us not talk about it.*

Joan says: *One of the things my father said to me once was when I said something about missing my mother, "You have a roof over your head, three meals a day, what more do you need?"*

Tammie overheard a neighbor saying: *"Oh those are the kids of the woman who killed herself."*

Sons and Daughters Describe what was Helpful

Stewart, the twin who was three months of age at the time of his father's suicide, said:

I can still remember there was one boy, I still remember him. He and I are still good friends today. He didn't avoid us like the other kids and was just kind. He would play basketball and baseball with us.

Stan, five years at the time of his mother's suicide, shared:

Some other families helped to take care of us and let me play with their kids.

Overview

Losses and separations are a fact of life. As we go through life, we experience sadness by losing and being separated. Normally, as babies and small children, our losses are temporary. Babies and very young people are totally dependent on Mom and/or Dad. A parent puts them to bed for the night and then leaves the room. Or they have a baby-sitter when Mom and Dad go out for a while to refresh and have adult time. For an infant or a young child, just a few hours feels like an eternity when the parents leave, but this is a learning experience, because within a short time, parents return and the grief is quickly over and the effect of this temporary loss is not lasting. When separated from a parent for what adults consider a short time, the very young child grieves as an adult may mourn when an actual death occurs. But the young person comes to understand when parents go out and come home that the parent or parents haven't abandoned them. The children learn this when the parents return to show their love and caring once again. Such experiences are painful for the little ones, but they are necessary occurrences for them to understand temporary loss and to grow and mature into human beings who are better prepared for future temporary losses and, later, permanent ones.

As an adult, when a good friend or close relative such as a parent is lost through death, grief overcomes us and we feel as if a piece of us has died. We cry, we sob and the pain of loss may feel excruciating, and yet we as adults understand that this happens in life. We have resources, maturity, community, friends and family to be there to hold us and comfort us at this time of bereavement. If we are involved in a religious community, loving arms come forth not only with comfort, visits, meals and flowers, but spiritual guidance through this harsh period in our lives.

However, when the death of a close family member is not a death from illness or old age but is a violent death such as suicide, when one chooses to take his or her own life, this loss becomes, for many adults, beyond comprehension. There are so many unanswered questions that will never be satisfactorily solved. Almost always we experience feelings such as remorse and anger as well as total grief.

If we are helpless babies or small children who have lost a parent to death, the loss is more inexplicable and comfortless. Adults around us are weeping and quite distressed. They may have trouble caring for us. This is not simply a learning experience that other very young people experience of a parent leaving for a short period of time and then returning. This is forever and the child feels totally helpless. Not only that, but children do not have the words to make sense of it all. They become inconsolable. They think the parent may come back, and they wait and wait and wait until they finally despair because it does not happen. The parent does not return. Eventually the child forgets how it all started, but they continue to wait for and long for someone whom the child may not even remember well. Children don't understand what happened.

Lastly, in the child's parent's death as a suicide, adults usually are blaming themselves and each other for this individual's end of life. Often some are a bit out of control, not only wailing but also fighting amongst themselves. And the child hears and sees it all. The adults, feeling resentful because of their own suffering, might even be blaming the child. They might be angry that the child was ever born or resent the child because he needs so much. After all, blaming the child might seem to take the focus off themselves. It might serve as avoidance of feeling one's own feelings and remorse. The child does not have any resources to in any way protect, defend or nurture themselves. The child needs the protection and nurturing but many times they are not getting it. Now this does not happen in most situations, but it happens more often than not.

When the child is past early childhood at the time of the suicide, s/he may have the vocabulary to express his or herself but still the finality of death is difficult to comprehend. Even if others are not blaming the child, the child is old enough to understand blame and place it on him or herself. Maybe the child was mad at this parent before the suicide or perhaps this young person misbehaved. Certainly to a child, those are very real reasons to feel blame, or so the child believes.

However, as gloomy as these circumstances look and, in fact it is a dismal situation, adult survivors tell us that surviving and at some point thriving is definitely achievable. Be aware that it takes a lot of work to achieve this goal. While some very painful and negative outcomes result for children who experience the suicide of a parent, many of our participants also report that as they matured, they have learned to strongly value their present family and friends, particularly after receiving helpful psychotherapy and support. Many say they are more loving and caring of humanity and have learned openness and honesty. Nine of our participants who were children at the time of parent loss have chosen for themselves helping professions. If one works and achieves a life beyond survival after such a loss, compassion for mankind becomes a natural outcome. This does not mean that this individual comes out of such a horrific experience unscathed. It does mean that one still can survive and eventually thrive with help from loving friends, family, caretakers, teachers and qualified psychotherapists when needed.

To effectively get through a suicide in one's family, the person surviving must at some point admit his or her pain, feel it and be open about the emotion. In our experience, this, of course, does not happen immediately for most children of any age. It is important for the child to know about his or her past in a language that the child can comprehend. Caretakers need to be open and answer questions in ways that are age-appropriate for the child. When a child's questions are countered with comments such as, "This is something we don't talk about," this reply is harmful to the child. Denial of our experiences of suffering and recollections is the negation of our existence, our very own being. Without memories, no matter how tragic they may be, we are individuals without pasts who cannot give credence to our present and build a rewarding future. It is through the piecing together, admission and validations of our life experiences as we learn to understand what we encounter, even when it is the tragic death of a parent, that joy can eventually reclaim its way into our hearts.

■ ■ ■

CHAPTER 2

Adolescent Transitions

■ ■ ■

Mia reveals her own understanding of the pain of experiencing a parental suicide in the tumultuous adolescent years:

Growing up under the shadow of my mother's suicide was almost as difficult, if not in some ways more, than experiencing her death. We were never as close as I wanted and never had the opportunity to be best friends. I always recall that sense of regret and loss that I felt. Moreover, looking back, our relationship was not solid or even an enjoyable one. I feared her when she was alive due to her frequent and unpredictable violent rages induced by alcohol and prescription drugs.

Despite her addiction, she was a busy woman, a true female role model with two Ph.D.'s who traveled extensively and was multilingual, authored several books, started her own international society of political psychologists and was the mother of four. Most of my time with her was spent accompanying her to the beauty salon, the gym and other miscellaneous errands only to wait for her while I looked at some outdated magazines. She was a stern disciplinarian, a trait she inherited from my grandfather. My mother made sure that I had trendy new outfits to wear to school each fall and made a big deal out of my birthdays. On the positive side, she encouraged and fostered my intellectual as well as cultural growth and awareness. She wasn't the mother I had wished for but she was my mother. Losing her to suicide when I was twelve years old was a traumatic ending to my unhappy lifetime with her.

The anguish of losing my mom to suicide brought with it so much pain, but also a lot of questions and curiosities. How could she have done that to me? What does her suicide say about me? What does it say about my father and his choice of a spouse? Why didn't she get the help she needed? Why was it taboo to talk about her death and suicide with my family? Why did so many people stop talking to me?

When I first met my husband and would describe my mother and childhood to him, he was confused by the conflicting stories I told him. One story I told him was of the time she was drunk and on Valium while driving back from dinner with only me in the car. She was pulled over for drunk driving, refused to get out of her car and dragged (while screaming profanities) to a police car. She threatened me to get into the police car with her "or else." I was eventually driven to a neighbor's house where my mother called my older brothers and me all night to come get her out of jail or she would never forgive us. Then there were the stories I told my husband of the Christmases full of gingerbread houses, dozens of cookies and huge parties; or how every school year she would take me shopping for new clothes and a special first-day-of-school outfit. Even through all the horror stories that have scarred me for life, I continued to idealize my mother because she was my mother. I didn't want to feel like I came from this scary, abusive and tragic person.

Losing her has been difficult at various times in my life. There have been the milestone experiences like getting married, moving out of state, buying my first home and having my first child. I expected to miss a maternal role model and friend to guide me through those times. But my other, less emphasized moments in life without her have been much more painful to accept and live through. For instance, having her to just drop by my house with some dinner when my son was sick or sharing stories of work experiences that I would have liked her advice on. But here again, I'm fantasizing the person I would want her to be in these situations, not the person she probably would have been.

Still, I can't help but long for what I don't have. I envy people who have good relationships with their mothers. Her suicide has changed the direction my life took. I feel awkward at times for saying this, but I really feel as though my life has been more successful because she isn't in it anymore. She held me in fear and taught me traits that lowered my self-esteem, such as yo-yo dieting and trying to control everything around me. At this point in my life, I think of my mother and I feel respectful of all her professional accomplishments and her generous nature. I have worked very hard since her death to appreciate these qualities in her so that I can feel like that is what she really taught me, and I remember those qualities so that I can tell her grandchildren.

The evolution of Mia's feelings and the insight they have brought her will, we hope, resonate with other survivors.

Suicide and the Preadolescent and Adolescent Survivors

Preadolescents and adolescents who experience a parent's suicide are often expected to carry a heavy load. The multiple tasks that they frequently find themselves burdened with are generally not acknowledged, never explained and are usually unappreciated by those around them. Such chores may include housecleaning, cooking, laundry, parenting themselves (and for many their siblings as well) and keeping up with their studies. Sometimes they reverse roles and feel responsible for their remaining parent. As if that is not enough, they are dealing with society's imposed shame and stigmas while having to explain to their friends and others what happened to their parent.

In our adolescent years, we work to define ourselves as we face the approaching road of adulthood before us. Naturally, the first place we look to understand who we are is within our family. Where do we belong? Our community, school environment and the people we live with all help us to comprehend who we are. Adolescence is quite a journey itself, trying to navigate through a world that expects more responsibility and maturity from teenagers. What happens when one parent suddenly leaves one's life between the ages of ten and twenty? How does that event further complicate an already confusing process? How does one become a functioning adult while being raised by only one parent?

Shelley was sixteen when her father committed suicide. He left home when she was seven years old after almost six years of molesting her. She told us not only about her difficulties in relationships with men, but also of establishing one with her son:

I have really missed male guidance and male role modeling, the experience of growing up with and being around an adult male and witnessing a good marriage and relationship. Having borne a son, a male child, I am now having some difficulty in relating to him as an intimate grown-up male. My comfort level with adult men who are healthy, strong and mature is extremely hampered.

Stephen, Mia's brother, who was fifteen when his mother took her own life, discussed the effects of being so young when it happened to him:

It's hard when it happens as an adolescent because you don't know who you are at that time that it happens. You're still developing and working on what you're going to be and how you're going to carry yourself. As I'm finding out, it hindered a lot of my development. So I have a lot of issues with accepting and with being accepted.

Kimberley lost her father to suicide when she was twenty years old. She says:

Who I am as a person was shaped by my father's suicide. Hopefully, it has made me a more mature and compassionate person. I do not take life—anyone's life—for granted.

Adolescence is a vital time in human development when young people are preparing themselves for the future and what role they'll play in society. The decision is made to get involved in plans for a livelihood, whether it is a job right out of high school or one which requires further skills or schooling at a trade school, university or any other such continuing education. It's a time when preparation towards marriage versus single life or just living together as partners and becoming a parent versus not having children may be pondered. It can also be a time that this is not thought about, just recklessly acted upon. Adolescents go through major biological changes during the ages between ten and twenty. It is a time of going through maturation into adulthood and working towards becoming a more independent adult. It also can be a time when one goes astray and begins to lead a life of destruction to one's self and/or others, perhaps a life of antisocial behavior, a life that may lead to prison at some point and time.

Professor Robert Sylwester, in his article "In Search of the Roots of Adolescent Aggression," states:

From ten to twenty, we (adolescents) focus on learning how to be productive, reproductive human beings—planning for a vocation and exploring emotional commitment and sexuality. We go through seven profound biological changes during our life, and three of these generally occur from ten to fourteen: the onset of our reproductive capabilities, the maturation of intelligence, and the maturation of our personal and social identities." (Association for Supervision and

Curriculum Development) It's a constant push and pull between parents and adolescents to assert their independence and define themselves during these important changes. Sometimes they need their parents for guidance, then they act embarrassed by them and avoid them. Complicating this matter further is the fact that adolescent brains are not fully developed and matured in most people until their early twenties.

Robert Sylwester, "In Search of the Roots of Adolescent Aggression," *Educational Leadership* vol. 57, no. 4 (September 1999).

Ambur, fourteen at the time of her mother's suicide, speaks of her feelings of instability in the absence of her mother's influence:

When I was in high school and college, my goal was to go to medical school. It was in college that I really experienced the impact of not having my mother because she is the one who really understood me emotionally. I always had that support-based security with my mother and I didn't feel that with my father. When I was in college, I became afraid of taking the huge risk of going on to medical school. I became desperate for stability and security and made some really bad choices, like being desperate to find a man who I thought would understand me and give me some security and stability. I almost know that if my mom had lived that she wouldn't have let me veer in that path. She was the one who kept us on track and guided us in the direction of what was important for our future.

Lesley, thirteen years of age at the time of her father's suicide, speaks at age twenty-two of wanting to explore her issues before having children:

I hope to have kids but I have some issues to truly deal with beforehand. I am just now realizing that my dad's suicide directly affects most areas of my life. It is very frustrating! I don't want to pass on any residual baggage to my children.

Lesley also wants to share her experience with other survivors:

Move one minute at a time. Allow yourself to feel if possible, and grieve the way that works for you. Never feel ashamed of your loss. People can be so uneducated and ignorant so talk to those you feel comfortable with. And remember, "Death ends a life, not a relationship." Don't fool yourself in thinking that you are superhuman and are unaffected by your parent's suicide. It happened and it has consequences on your life, your future. If you are holding any sort of grudges, you must forgive.

It is difficult for an adolescent to comprehend both the concepts of death and suicide—two of those "abstract ideas." A parent's suicide magnifies fears that adolescents already had previously about their own world. Mia, twelve at the time of her mother's suicide, tells of her fears that escalated:

I know that I felt extremely afraid after my mom took her own life. I would sleep at night with the light on and be afraid that she was under my bed waiting to "get me" when I fell asleep. I had said goodbye to her before I went away for Christmas vacation with my siblings and two weeks later when we returned, she was gone. It seemed unreal that she was gone forever, let alone that she was dead. I convinced myself that her coffin was empty at the funeral.

Carla, eleven at the time of her father's suicide, describes her fears of getting close to others:

Because of my father's death, I have a fear of intimacy in two forms:
   1) I have this fear that anyone I let in too close is going to die unexpectedly (morbid, I know, and I have been working on this—I know it's irrational.)
   2) I also have issues depending on other people—I felt like my mother was trapped after my father's death and I didn't ever want to be in that situation, so I have made an effort to be as self-reliant as possible.
   The best analogy that comes to mind at the moment would be comparing my father to a security blanket, once it has been taken away from me. I was terrified of not being able to survive without it and resolved to never have that feeling again. I more or less turned into a control freak (in the sense that I try to control everything in my life—not control other people). Basically I want to do everything myself with no help from anyone. Luckily, I am a "work in progress" and am learning to let go a little more each day.

Dr. Alan Wolfelt is a clinical thanatologist and the director of the Center for Loss and Life Transition in Ft. Collins, Colorado. In his book, *Healing a Teen's Grieving Heart: 100 Practical Ideas for Families, Friends and Caregivers*, he emphasizes the importance of acceptance, honesty and compassion toward a teen who has experienced a traumatic loss:

If teens are to reconcile the loss, they must have a safe, accepting atmosphere in which they can mourn. Often teenagers don't want to mourn because mourning makes them feel vulnerable and dependant. Feeling this runs counter to their natural need to separate from parents and other authority figures. Grieving teens need permission to mourn. Sometimes what they need most from adults is an awareness that it is okay to feel the many emotions they feel and to talk or not to talk about them.

Alan Wolfelt, *Healing a Teen's Grieving Heart: 100 Practical Ideas for Families, Friends and Caregivers* (Colorado: Companion Press, 2001).

Adolescent Loss and Fears of Becoming a Parent

One of the worries that sons and daughters who lost a parent when they were adolescents expressed was their fear of the parent's depression or illness being passed on to their children. Two concerns they spoke of were their apprehensions about whether their children would grow up to be suicidal and how to tell them about their grandmother or grandfather. The fact is that these are common issues among all age groups with children. Mia, age twelve at the time of her mother's suicide, speaks of her fears:

I know that having my son a little over two years ago has been one of the most truly wonderful events I will ever know in this lifetime. At times, it seems unreal that I'm a mother! I still feel like a child needing to be mothered myself, because that process came to a halt at age twelve. I always wanted to have children. I do feel my spirit is more complete, and I'm much more self-assured that I'm doing what I was meant to do. But my fears now center on if I will subconsciously be the "bad" mother to my son that my mother was to me. Will I abandon him in any way? Do I love him too much (hear me out...) to try and make up for the love that I didn't have? Will he feel smothered by my love? Am I being a healthy role model for him physically, emotionally and spiritually? And are these all just "normal" new mom fears or really the fears of an emotionally neglected child who prematurely lost her mother?

I believe that there is no greater bond in human existence than that between a mother and her child. It has been idealized and immortalized for centuries in the image of the Madonna and child. Over and over, it is revealed that if one does not grow up with a healthy image of his or her mother and is not given a mother's unconditional love, this reality becomes a lifelong desire and a need to be fulfilled.

There are numerous stories of mothers who abuse and/or neglect their children and yet those children still grow up to say they love their mothers. What one perceives as love for a mother in the case of emotional abandonment is really that person's inner child still crying out to be nurtured and protected by a mother's love. Frequently, people who are abandoned by their mother feel a fervent and unexplainable love for their mother. This feeling grows in their subconscious in proportion to their unfulfilled basic needs that a mother's love provides for a child.

I have spent two-thirds of my life without my mother. I have been living without her twice as long as I knew her. Yet I still daze off and think about her absence and wish that she were here for me. Often I ask myself, do I just miss the idea of her and what a stereotypical mother represents, or do I actually miss the person she was and yearn for the qualities of her I can still recall? This question continues to confuse me, and I still end up with the same result: I feel alone in my heart without that foundational love that is given by a mother.

Given this, I am raising my son with all the consistent and unconditional love that I can. I dread the day when I will explain what happened to his grandmother. I hope he doesn't have to face life's cruel realities anytime soon and lose his innocent belief that his world is a place of trust, beauty and wonder. But at least he will grow up knowing truly in his heart that my love is something he can always count on.

Hannah was eighteen at the time of her father's suicide. She reveals:

I often feel empty and sad inside and wonder if this will affect my relationship with my children. I am not sure I am emotionally strong enough.

Kate was sixteen at the time of her father's suicide. She tells:

I'm also afraid that suicide might be in my blood and in the genes that will be passed down to my children.

Erin was nineteen at the time of her mother's suicide. She states:

I worry that I might be crazy, because some people think that she was...I guess. I worry that because I am a part of her, I might be just like her by not being a good mom and leaving my children as she left me. At times, I stress on these issues.

Helpful Advice for Preadolescents and Adolescents

Those who were older children at the time of their parents' suicides commonly felt that the best thing others did for them was "to just be there for them." So how did this group define "being there"? They felt those friends who simply listened when the survivor needed to be heard who validated their feelings expressed at that time were there for them. They wanted to be called when friends made plans to go out. They wanted to have their wishes respected when choosing not to talk about the suicide. They wished for their friends to remain friends just as they were before the suicide. Mia speaks of this issue in her life:

I appreciated those friends who let me feel and do whatever I needed to do. They didn't try to shield me from what had happened, because I "was a child" and "couldn't handle it." They didn't pity me and make me then feel like I needed to make them feel better because they were so sad for me! I'll never forget standing on the balcony of my dad's condo after my mom's funeral. My sister's friend encouraged me to throw all the flower bouquets and then a dozen eggs down on the street. It was so therapeutic to be encouraged to do something physical and something I normally wouldn't ever think of doing, a respite from all the pity and sympathetic looks.

Donna, fourteen at the time of her father's suicide, states:

I liked it when someone specifically took me out. I went even when I didn't want to because it felt good to have a friend to take me out, not just write it or say it but to do it. That's the difference.

Lorraine, twenty at the time of her mother's suicide, tells:

Mainly I remember the few people who would ask me about the suicide and how I was doing, then just listen patiently and empathetically allowing me to cry on their shoulder a bit when I needed that. I needed to talk a lot and for people to just be with me, close to me.

Another common theme of being in this age group at the time of a parent's death was the desire to be allowed to feel "normal," to be an adolescent with adolescent worries and issues. To some extent, it is good to maintain whatever normalcy that can possibly be preserved. The facts are, however, that for the most part life won't be "normal" for a very long time. "Normalcy" frequently can be somewhat sustained by keeping the preadolescent and/or adolescent in the same home and same school and for the remaining parent to refrain from dating or getting married too soon. It is best if the remaining parent concentrates and focuses on the children instead of any other person. However, in many cases, such "ideals" may not be reasonable. For example, if the suicide took place in the home, one may find it feasible for the family to move. If parents are already divorced and the remaining parent lives in another town or state, the young person may need to move to live with him or her. It would be better for the adult to move to where the son or daughter lives to allow for some stability and continuity in his or her life. However, most adults who have jobs and responsibilities in other areas cannot do this, so it is an individual matter that needs talking over between parent and child. Parents should include the young person in such discussions to empower them as much as possible at this time. It would be best for life to change as little as possible for at least a year or longer. However, we realize each situation is unique and many times extenuating circumstances make this impossible.

When talking to an adolescent who has lost a parent, it is important to stress that life will not be the same, and the sons and/or daughters frequently have little to no control over their situations. Pretending to be "normal" in terms of not talking about the suicide, pretending the deceased never existed and covering up the pain that family members are feeling is devastating in the long run for adolescents.

Rachel, fifteen years at the time of her father's suicide, reveals:

It was helpful when people and friends just kind of kept things normal, but not completely. I was still the same person, but something bad had happened.

Ambur, fourteen years at the time of her mother's suicide, found it helpful to have female family figures around after the event:

All of my family's members knew about it and my aunt came to stay with me and my dad because I was the youngest kid. I was the only one at home at that time. I was fourteen. One of my aunts came to stay with us for several months, and then she left and another aunt came to stay with us for several months. This was helpful to have a female figure around. I was a sophomore in high school at that time, and I had close friends and although we didn't really talk about what happened, they knew that my mom had passed away and they sort of opened up to me about things in their life. It was very helpful actually to comprehend some of the serious things that they were going through and to know that I had friends who had some understanding of trauma at a young age.

Having helpful family members close is essential for comforting and encouraging the child or adolescent to express their feelings, but unfortunately this doesn't happen often. It means that the extended family members cannot be self-absorbed at this time, must be willing and able to participate and help, able to acknowledge the suicide and then able to openly discuss it without the shame and secrecy that all too frequently accompanies the subject.

Dr. Wolfelt gives sound advice in his book, *Healing a Teen's Grieving Heart,* concerning the acknowledgement of the death. He says, "As you talk with and listen to the teen, be honest about the nature and cause of the death—even if the death was violent or self-inflicted. Teens can cope with what they know; they cannot cope with what they don't know."

Unhelpful Advice for the Preadolescents and Adolescents

Mia, twelve at the time of her mother's suicide, confides:

Adolescent peers frequently do not have the maturity to be empathetic to what the survivor is going through. The adolescent survivor can't make sense of it either, understandably so. This is where I found myself. Not only did I not know which of my friends even knew, I didn't know how we would ever talk about it. Our topics of conversation then revolved around the latest designer jeans, pop music, makeup and boys. This situation might have been made easier if my father had called my friend's parents and explained what had happened. On the other hand, when people did learn of my situation, they treated me as if I had a terminal disease. They felt so sorry for me. This simply infuriated me because the last thing I needed were more spotlights on my situation or me.

Kimberley, twenty at the time of her father's suicide, says:

I broke up with my boyfriend when he said I was the cause of my father buying straight-edged razor blades. Twenty-five years later I still think that was a cruel thing to say.

Ambur, fourteen at the time of her mother's suicide, reveals:

The neighbors stopped treating me like a person and I became more of a curiosity. I started feeling this strange feeling between myself and others.

Carla, eleven years at the time of her father's suicide, states:

To say I felt different would be the understatement of the year. For one thing, I was extremely embarrassed—the stigma of suicide is so awful and I feared that everyone must think that my father was crazy, and I knew he was not. At that time, I was the only one of my friends who had lost a parent (with the exception of one girl who had lost her mother to cancer when we were in fourth grade). I didn't want anyone to feel sorry for me and I definitely didn't want to be treated differently.

Some people deal with a parent suicide by using "catch-phrases." Whether such phrases come from an acquaintance or a family member and whether they are well-intentioned or knee-jerk reactions, these are not helpful. "Time heals all wounds" is one of those clichés that is not comforting to children or adolescents. In addition, it gives the appearance of making light of a terrible situation.

Others to whom we spoke who were teenagers at the time of their parents' suicides added to our knowledge of what remarks they found meaningless.

Josephine, nineteen at the time of her father's suicide, says:

I hated hearing, "It's God's will," or "Only the strong can handle hard things." Never say that.

John, sixteen at the time of his mother's suicide, tells:

I hated it when people constantly said, "If there's anything I can do, let me know." I found that insincere.

Issues Arising when the Preadolescent or Adolescent Returns to School

In regards to holiday grief, Mia has experienced this problem as a child and as a school teacher. She had a second chance to reenact her own distressing experience as a school teacher when the father of three children at the school where she taught took his own life:

Since my mother died on Christmas day, I was out on winter break from school. I didn't go back when classes resumed in January because of her funeral. When I returned, no one at my school knew what had happened because my father hadn't called my school. My first period science teacher gave me a hard time about my "unexcused absences" and she maintained that I couldn't come back to class without a note from home. So, I went to the office and eventually broke down in front of the school secretary talking about my mother's suicide. The secretary felt terrible and called my older sister, who proceeded to come down to school and yell at everyone in the office for their insensitivity and cruelty.

I think it is absolutely responsible and necessary for a family member to call a child's school and let them know what has happened. Furthermore, I think a family member should meet with the principal and the school counselor to make a plan for that child to smoothly transition back into school. What happened in my situation was that my story became the weekly school gossip and was passed from teacher to teacher in the lounge. There were one or two teachers who I believe would have reached out to me, but since there was no guidance from the administration and so much time had passed before they knew, they felt unsure at that point what to do.

When there was a suicide of a father of three children at the school where I taught, the school's principal used our "emergency tree" telephone contact system to let the entire faculty know that day what happened. Then, the mother met with the principal, the assistant principal and the school counselor to plan for her children's return to school. The school counselor visited the classrooms before the children came back to answer any student questions. In addition, I was asked to write and distribute a one-page letter of advice to the entire faculty. Here is my letter.

Dear Friends,

At this time of great sadness for the _____ family, I want to share some of my experience on this subject and advice for us all. For the past four years, I've been working on and writing a book for survivors of parent suicide. (My mother committed suicide when I was twelve years old.) A large part of this book is written for those people around the survivor—family, friends, therapists, community, etc. It offers suggestions on how to help the survivor. It is of course a very different situation when the survivor is a child and he/she must go back to their school life. So, the following are my personal suggestions for these children.

Try not to react and look at the children wearing the sadness and sorrow that you feel. They are seeing a lot of this from their siblings, mother and family, and they don't need to feel like they have to take care of our feelings. They need us to be strong for them right now. They need to have something they can depend on. It's difficult to come back to a school where everyone knows what has just happened, and you feel like everyone is staring at you and expecting you to talk about it. Give these children what you would normally give them: a smile, a hug, a friendly hello.

It's important for their classmates and other kids to treat them like they always have, i.e. play games at recess, eat lunch together, work in class, talk about interests, etc. These children are going to need normalcy as much as possible. They will need stability in the midst of this crisis.

We need to be sensitive around the upcoming holidays. Think carefully about Thanksgiving and Christmas activities that involve what you're grateful for, family trees, etc.

Be aware that these children will be feeling several different emotions that may be brief or may last awhile. They could be: grief, anger, guilt, sadness, fear of the unknown, a sense of responsibility to take care of their siblings and/or mom and a need to be strong for their siblings and/or mom.

If anyone would like to talk with me about this, I am available to you. The important thing to remember is that these children CAN go on to have happy and fulfilling lives. What is going to help them get there is the consistency of our love and support, counseling, their family and friends and their faith.

Sincerely,
Mia Roldan

Adolescents, like other survivors, differ in what they want or think they want when they experience the death of a parent. When the tragic experience occurs at various stages in preadolescence and adolescence, there is definitely a tendency to not want all eyes centered on them. On the other hand, those who are ignored or are not offered support or assistance feel so alone, and this approach just exaggerates the pain.

Carla, eleven years at the time of her father's suicide, reveals:

Teachers wanted me to talk about my trauma, and I really didn't want to at the time. It was one of my favorite teachers whom I think the world of to this day. We never did talk about it. I also did not like getting special treatment. While I appreciated my teachers' concerns, I did not want to be "different" from the other kids; the situation to which I am referring regards a family tree project. I had one in seventh grade and the teacher pulled me aside and asked if I wanted to do something different because of my father. I said "no," of course. The exact same situation happened once again in the ninth grade.

Dr. Wolfelt advises to move toward the pain of an adolescent's loss differently than you would the emotion felt by an adult: "The teen's naturally strong resistance to mourning does not mean the teen isn't hurting inside or isn't capable of mourning with support or understanding. Remember that because teens don't articulate their feelings well, they often do as much if not more of their mourning through behaviors rather than words." He suggests engaging in a physical sport or activity that the teen enjoys as a way to establish a comfort place to discuss their feelings about the death.

Solid Support Systems and Recovery

The most crucial aspect of helping adolescents cope with their parents' suicides is to assist them with getting a strong support network of family, friends and community members such as school or a religious congregation. Adolescents need to know who they can depend on, night or day, for anything related (or not) to the suicide. This goes hand-in-hand with supportive adults being ready and willing to give honest and age-appropriate answers to any questions older children voice. When preadolescents or adolescents are in an environment that's conducive to admitting, accepting, being open about and discussing their parents' suicides, there is a stronger chance for solid emotional health to develop.

Lorraine, twenty at the time of her mother's suicide, states:

I felt a lot of avoidance by people at the time of my mother's suicide. That felt hurtful to me. It seemed they were hardened about it, or that her death didn't matter somehow because it was a suicide, almost like she didn't matter or her life didn't have any value. I had a weak support system at the time it happened and was alone most of the time. I needed to go through the process of recovery, which meant to feel my feelings and accept them and release them, but that was a painful process. Very few people seemed to want to hang around me when I needed them the most. Finally, I became so lonely that I stuffed my feelings down so that I could try to act happier, so I could have some people in my life. That was good for the short-term, because I had more people around me. It was bad for the long-term because all of those stuffed emotions were just sitting there waiting for me to deal with them someday.

How Suicide Affects Sibling Relationships

Four of our participants stated that they were closer to their siblings after their parents' suicides. Four with siblings said they pulled away from one another after the suicide. One likeness among the adolescents in this second group was that they were prohibited by the remaining parent to talk about what happened. Mia speaks:

I include myself in the latter group of four. I am the youngest of four siblings: my brothers are four and five years older and my sister is eight years older. There are "pockets" of closeness among the four of us, but I think because we were told directly and indirectly by my father and stepmother not to discuss the suicide, our sibling relationships suffered. Before my mother's suicide, the four of us were extremely close. Part of that was a result of the bond created by my parents' separation and subsequent divorce. But after our mother's suicide, we weren't able to really be there for each other as we were before and sadly to this day we are all not as close as we once were.

Andrew, thirteen at the time when his mother murdered his two youngest siblings prior to taking her own life, confides:

No one talked about it. I think my siblings were all feeling really guilty about the whole situation and I think they just wanted to forget and deny more than anything else.

Ambur, fourteen at the time of her mother's suicide, says:

There is a feeling of closeness between us because we have this shared experience, but I don't know what he has done to deal with and reflect on her suicide. I feel like we have this unspoken bond between us. I'm glad that I have a brother. I don't feel like it was just me that this happened to.

Josephine, nineteen at the time of her father's suicide, states:

My sister and I are closer than we might have been due to our father's suicide and the resulting need to collaborate in reference to our mom's care.

Mental Health Professionals and Preadolescents or Adolescents

Many of our preadolescent and adolescent participants did not receive therapy. For some, it may not have been available. However, we the authors believe that preadolescents and adolescents need to receive some age-appropriate counseling or therapy as soon as possible after the suicide. There are many local community professionals and organizations that provide this with payment on a sliding scale. It is important for children that the remaining parent have an appointment first with the therapist to make sure that the parent feels the counselor is qualified and has values acceptable to them. The remaining parent and therapist need to discuss the approach that will be used to maintain communication with each other. And most important, the therapist and young survivor must be able to express themselves and feel comfortable. Two of our participants spoke about their positive experiences with mental health professionals.

Lorraine, twenty at the time of her mother's suicide, reveals:

They kept encouraging me to keep going through my recovery process and presented a confident vision for me that things would get better. They kept reminding me of my strong points. They kept validating my experiences, through my own eyes. And the most important thing was they encouraged me to feel my feelings and stay with them, and they were patient with that process; however long it took was just fine with them.

Ambur, fourteen at the time of her mother's suicide, states:

My counselor validated that I had been through something that was very, very difficult and had come out of it in a positive way and tried to do things for myself that were positive. That was something that I always remembered because no one in my family, none of my friends, no one I knew had ever said that to me or given me any credit. I was the youngest child in the family and I was the one who sort of took care of my dad. All of a sudden I had added burdens to my life and no one ever gave me credit for all the things I had done. Just hearing that from her made all the difference to me.

How Suicide Changes Preadolescent or Adolescent's Lives

Since preadolescents and adolescents are just embarking on their development into adulthood, suicide is almost certain to skew their development toward another direction. Some feel like their parent's suicide changed them to be less trusting and therefore more withdrawn. In many cases, the suicide acts like a filter as to how they view themselves and their relationships. Most, but not all of our participants of this age, classified the suicide as the most or one of the most defining events of their lives and say that their mourning period is not over. Their grief still comes and goes. We have some participants who think about their parent every day, with the time of the event ranging from five years to forty years prior to their interviews.

Andrew, thirteen at the time of his mother's murder/suicide when she shot the youngest two siblings prior to taking her own life, reveals:

I'm more withdrawn and shy with people in my life, and it has been difficult to make friends since the event. I returned to school after that and backed off a bit. I don't really want to get too close.

Rachel, fifteen at the time of her father's suicide, confides:

I am really skeptical of people when I first meet them and they seem nice. I wonder what they are hiding. It is not easy for me to trust people. Also, when people still love me after I tell them, I know they are quality people and then my trust in them becomes super strong.

Leslie (Mia's sister), twenty at the time of her mother's suicide, states:

I am definitely a different person because of her suicide. What I always think in my head is that it keeps on giving—the suicide continues to impact so much that it keeps on impacting, even right up to the morning of this interview. My father's second marriage was difficult, but we (Leslie and her three siblings) shared the added burden of our stepmother who came as part and parcel in that horrible period right after the suicide. Our stepmother was not a good, loving and caring person to us. So it's kind of like splitting hairs. This part belongs to Mom's suicide and this part belongs to the miserable relationship that Dad shared with us and that our stepmother influenced.

Some participants who were adolescents at the time of the event felt their parents' suicides changed them to become more empathetic and compassionate towards other people and towards life in general. An adolescent feels the weight of losing a parent during these formative and identifying years differently. When fixed aspects of our lives that we've come to depend on are suddenly taken away from us (such as a parent's death or suicide, having both parents present in our lives and losing the house we grew up in), it thoroughly uproots the normalcy we've grown accustomed to. Mia speaks on this issue:

I will never forget when my parents told me at age nine they were getting a divorce and again when my father told us three years later that my mother had taken her own life. I felt as if I had awakened from a dream, that everything up until then hadn't been real life and that this horrible fact was now my inescapable reality.

Ambur, fourteen at the time of her mother's suicide, says:

I think it has made me an empathetic person. In a way, I sometimes think I feel and sense a lot of things that other people don't sense who haven't been through something like this. Sometimes I feel, this sounds strange, that I can see a bigger picture than many others see. In a way, it is sometimes good but in another way, I feel I can't relate as well to people who have never experienced something that is life-changing, especially when they are younger.

Mia responds to Ambur:

Like this participant, I too feel like many times I can't relate to other people because I appreciate what others take for granted—the normalcy of home and growing up with both parents. Living through my adolescent years with an emotionally void father and a resentful and angry stepmother, my only motivation to surviving was to know that one day my life would be under my control. It took most of my twenties to learn how to be an adult and not seek others to take care of me. I can definitely say that the suicide has forced me to prioritize my life and focus on what is most important: my well-being, my husband and son and my relationships.

Donna, fourteen at the time of her father's suicide, says:

I have become more compassionate to people who have had anything happen that is not good, a car accident or anything. I am able to say, "I'll be here if you need something." Then I do it, realizing that life is too short. I want to make the most out of everything.

Erin, nineteen at the time of her mother's suicide, adds:

I am more grown up than my peers when it comes to responsibilities because of this event. I appreciate lots of little things more now. I take much better care of my life.

Overview

Adolescence is an in-between stage of a person from childhood to adulthood. The adolescent is transforming into a young adult, both physically and emotionally, and has the huge task of making lifetime decisions for one's self. In addition to this, the adolescent's brain is still not developed into an adult brain. The teen's judgment may frequently appear to an adult as being impaired. Couple these facts with another reality: adolescents are beginning to explore their sexuality. It is not unusual that some parents express that their children who seemed so mature suddenly act like aliens from another planet during this phase of their lives. Though they may gradually or rapidly take on the appearance of becoming mature adults, in fact they are far from it. Without a doubt, the teenager is not to be mistaken for an adult.

It is a time when teens might lead you to believe they think that you are not needed as parents anymore, and yet without a doubt they need the guidance of their mothers and fathers. Frequently, parent and child are at odds with each other during this stage of life. The child may not act like the sweet child one thought s/he was.

The adolescent may be deciding whether to graduate from high school and get a job or go onto college. Some adolescents may want to prematurely drop out of high school and get a job only to find they are not prepared for adult life. They may have definite ideas as to whether to get married or remain single and whether or not having children is in the equation. Too often, the order in which they do things is skewed. There is no question that they are not mini-adults.

With all this in mind, envision the disruption in a teen's life when a parent dies during these years. There may be additional chores to do now. S/he might need to be looking after the younger children if there are younger ones. If s/he was planning to go to college, will this stay in the equation or will it need to be postponed? Will the adolescent have to think about going to work first for financial reasons, or will the teen just feel so distraught that college is something that s/he quits thinking about? Will a job for the teen be in the equation while attending school to help with finances?

The death of a parent by his or her own hand causes more disruption than a death from natural causes because it is, in fact, a suicide. How easy it is for the adolescent to blame him or herself and feel total guilt for the death of the parent. No doubt s/he has probably become more difficult to deal with, clashing with the surviving parent and likely arguing and disagreeing more. The deceased parent may have been angry with or hurt by the teen (as teens often do) prior to the act and now amends cannot be made because the parent is dead and by his or her own hands, no less. Does this suicide sound like a rational solution now for the adolescent's pain? After all, his or her parent did it. Is the family open about talking with the sons and daughters about the deceased parent, or does all conversation cease? Is the suicide being kept a total secret from even close friends and other family members? Is the suicide now public knowledge? Is the teen experiencing warmth and caring from the community, or are they being stared at, ignored and rejected by others? Are their peers kind, or are they saying hurtful things to the son or daughter because it was a suicide? What if it is clergy speaking cruelly about the parent who took his or her own life? Will the adolescent be the one to decide to reject these peers now and just quit socializing? One could go on and on with the possibilities after such an event.

Reality can be jarring, but avoidance of it can cause underlying everlasting grief that will tarnish each day that we live. Because to avoid grief is only to prolong it for an indefinite time period until such time that you gain the courage to confront it face to face. Grief won't go away until we face it head-on.

A teen who experiences the suicide of a parent needs someone who is available to listen and hear, to encourage, to show unconditional love, to validate and accept all the feelings that the adolescent might have been hiding and is willing to share. Some days may need to be silent days when the adolescent just needs a person to be there. Many teenagers feel guilty about past arguments with their dead parents. It is necessary to talk with the adolescent so that he or she will understand that teens all get angry at their parents from time to time and say things that might later be regretted. This is not the cause of parent suicide. Teen survivors must come to understand that they are not responsible for the suicide. There is only one individual responsible and that is the deceased parent.

The most important thing needed by the teenaged survivor is for someone to be there for this person (who is not a child and yet not an adult). It is the surviving parent's responsibility to inform the adults (teachers, doctors or parents of their friends) directly involved with their child as to what has happened. It would be appropriate for teachers to guide the teenager's peers on how to respond positively, not to avoid the teen but to do the opposite, be available for visits, movies and sharing feelings. Kindness is of utmost importance. The teen who lost his or her parent needs to learn openness and to respond in turn with kindness when others come forward with attempts to console and to help, which frequently might be a bit awkward. Remember, the awkward part does not matter; it is always the caring that counts.

Survivors of parent suicide during adolescence have shared in this chapter how going beyond survival is definitely a choice, a choice that all survivors have the option to make. If you have lost a parent in your teen years, we know this is a very difficult burden to bear. But we hope that learning from others who have borne similar tragedies and gone on to find love and create satisfying lives will inspire you to continue your journey with hope and optimism.

CHAPTER 3

Adult Loss

My father could have had two broken arms and a broken leg. If he promised to take us on a hike in the foggy Marin Hills, he would. So, he was the one who taught me trust and reliability. And look what he did to me! I was turning thirty-nine, but I was still my father's daughter. And he was my daddy.

Mary Ann, thirty-eight at the time of her father's suicide.

You are only completely an adult when your mind tells you that you are grown up. It could be when you become a parent, own your first house or successfully gain your first "real" job. Being an adult on the outside because of age does not preclude many of us from feeling like our inner spirit is childlike. This feeling is enhanced by the fact that for many people, their parents accompany them through a majority of their adult years, roughly from the twenties to possibly the sixties or even longer. There are many aspects of parent/child roles. For instance, we are continually reminded that we are someone's "child" when our parents question our personal, professional and/or parental decisions. However, we expect to rely on our parents for their unconditional support and love, for only in a parent-child relationship is this potentially possible. This is lost forever when one of our parents takes his or her own life and leaves us feeling like lost adult children.

For many of our participants who were over the age of twenty at the time of their parents' suicides, they found themselves in the role of taking care of the ill parent prior to the event. Several spoke of their duties of giving constant care, reassurance and emotional support to a mentally ill mother or father, often alone and lonely after a divorce, and frequently an alcoholic or recreational drug abuser. Others spoke of their parents' despair and frustration at suffering a physical ailment that interrupted the parents' control and freedom to enjoy their lives. These parents were simply "tired of fighting it." Some parents were facing extreme financial hardships and didn't know how they were going to support themselves or their families anymore. Sometimes survivors spoke of relief after their parents' suicides, because the parents suffered so much or because the parents had abused them (physically, verbally and/or sexually) at one point in the survivors' lives. Some believe that their parents "saw suicide as a coping technique" for their pain and thus repeatedly tried to end their lives with the hope of potentially being saved at each attempt. In the case of some parent suicides, there were no obvious signs prior to the event that would explain the act. The common thread, however, among almost all our participants is that after all the speculating and questioning, there are very few answers as to why the suicides occurred.

Lori, twenty-three years at the time of her father's suicide, says:

There is one thing that my sister-in-law said to me that really took the weight of the world off my shoulders, and I have remembered it all these years and offer the words to people when they need support. She said, "When someone commits suicide, they take all the answers and leave you with all the questions." That may not sound necessarily helpful except that it released me from trying to find answers, because it framed the event in a way that I could search all day long and I could get a best guess, but I wouldn't get any answer. That was really helpful.

Feelings of Adult Survivors

We spoke with twenty-four women and two men who ranged in ages from twenty-one to fifty-three at the time of their parents' suicides. The following pattern was repeated many times. First, over half said that the suicides of their parents were one of the most defining events of their lives. Second, sad feelings were felt by almost everyone immediately following the suicide, with abandonment as the second most common emotion and anger and guilt equally felt as the third. Lastly, three-fourths of our participants felt that their mourning periods still were not over—that their feelings of grief still came and went.

We heard over and over how abandonment, second to sadness, was so strongly felt by most of the sons and daughters with whom we spoke. The feelings of abandonment, however, appeared to be more complex, and many felt that the choice to commit suicide revealed something of their parents' characters. This is a common theme across all age groups and is spurred by the notion that we are literally left most of the time (or we think we are) with the knowledge that the deceased parents felt that their children would be "better off" without them. Caryn, thirty years old at the time of her father's suicide, comments:

To lose somebody to suicide, it just shatters your whole world and anything you thought or knew about that person before… My father and I had a complicated relationship anyway. But after he did that, it just shattered my whole ideal and my whole perspective of who he was personally and who he was as my father, it totally rearranges what you know. It leaves you for a while, thinking like, "I worked my life and I thought I knew how things were and now I don't think I know how anything is."

After an exercise in "traumatic writing" that Lori (twenty-three years old at the time) participated in, she was able to put a new and healing perspective on her father's suicide:

I saw abandonment as the overall theme of my life. At the end of that writing, I realized that my father abandoned himself and that was almost an after-thought, his own abandonment.

For some, this sense of abandonment led to fear of losing other loved ones. Some participants talked about intrusive fears and worries that they themselves might die and abandon their children or that their children would die of horrible accidents. Margaret, twenty-nine years at the time of her father's suicide, addresses this issue:

It is routine for me to go into my "death fantasy" when my husband is late or he is late bringing the kids home….I imagine the police coming to the door and telling me they all died in a car wreck. I certainly don't take anyone for granted. I do not have the belief that we will have all of our loved ones forever...never have. I tell people that I live by the "we could all get hit by a bus on the way home" philosophy of life.

Another common feeling participants experienced after their parents' suicides was relief. However, frequently present along with their relief were other emotions, such as sadness and self-imposed feelings of guilt for experiencing the relief that most anyone in their situations would feel. They were relieved that their parents, who in many cases were severely suffering from some form of mental or physical illness and despair, were no longer in great pain. Some felt that their parents' illnesses or depression had taken a heavy emotional, physical and mental toll on them. Many talked about phone calls at all hours of the night, driving for miles every weekend for visits and always being "on call" for any emergency. Kris, thirty-one years at the time of her mother's suicide and the oldest in her family, was left to deal with all of her mother's affairs and estate. When she first learned of her mom's suicide, she had many conflicting thoughts and emotions:

"Gosh, Mom, I just had a baby. How could you have done this to me?" I was nursing my one-week-old baby in the middle of the night when I received the call from my sister that my mom was gone. I was pretty angry and then I also started to feel relieved. My mom had been so depressed for so long and she depended on me for so many things. I remember on the drive to my mom's house feeling frustrated that I had been doing this—worrying, driving to check on her, helping her with her affairs for so long. She had attempted suicide many times over a twenty year period, so it wasn't a complete surprise to hear that she was gone. I remember thinking, well if she really is gone, maybe this will be a blessing because I won't have to do this anymore. I won't have to drop everything to see if she's okay and try to find a way that I can help her back to feeling better. I just felt a tremendous responsibility for her health and then I was feeling a bit relieved that maybe I wouldn't have to deal with it any longer. Of course, next came the guilt for feeling all of those things.

Many participants did not have good relationships with their parents because of alcoholism (perhaps other drugs as well) and all the related problems that accompany that disease. Most survivors who lived with one or both parents who abused chemicals for much of the survivors' lives reported that most (not all) parents acted out with physical and verbal abuse as well. However if it wasn't abuse, then neglect was an issue. This seemingly endless lifetime of pain ended with the suicide and relief is very understandable to experience at the time that this cycle is broken. Shanna, twenty-seven years at the time of her father's suicide, shares her experience with us:

I think we're better off; I think he's better off. There's less stress in my life now. I was caught up in the world of taking care of my mother, taking care of my father and running back and forth. I got to the point with my father when, after my engagement party where he was so inebriated and verbally abusive to my mother, I told him he wasn't allowed to come to my wedding shower if he couldn't come sober. It was the first time in all my life that I had ever seen him really nasty, and I stood up to him so I wasn't in the middle of the two of them. I think if he were still alive that the relationship would be hard with my kids.

Not all suicides are viewed as tragedies. Relief might be experienced because the parent was not a good parent, as in the case of Brenda, twenty-nine years of age when her father suicided, she reveals:

It probably has helped my life. My father just was not a very rational man. I think he would have put constraints and been more verbally abusive. I think it was almost a relief that it did happen. My particular situation wasn't a tragic loss; I've had more tragic losses than this one.

He left a note. It was not a long, lengthy, "I love you" type note. He and my mother had gotten divorced. His whole thinking was, "I am going to show you. I'm going to kill myself." It wasn't about being sorry about anything. It wasn't a rational type of suicide. It was revengeful. I was glad it was over with.

A reaction many participants elaborated on was denial, which appeared in different forms. One such defense was to deny that the parent had any negative or objectionable traits and shortcomings that were difficult for others to cope with. After suicides, some people speak of parents as saints, whether or not the sons or daughters liked them in life. Shanna, twenty-seven at the time of her parent's suicide says:

The house was full of people who hadn't seen my father in I don't know how long. These visitors were saying that my father was this wonderful, incredible man—which there was a side of him that was—but they did not know who we knew, and they didn't know the things he had said and done to my mother. So, it angered me to see hundreds of people sit and talk about what a wonderful man he was. He was, but nobody talked about his disease; nobody talked about what brought him to this place.

Some families refuse to acknowledge that a parent actually committed suicide. This, we feel, has two purposes; one is to avoid the stigma of suicide and the other is to try to convince themselves that the death has another cause and to try to forget the actual suicide. They explain that the deceased died from a condition such as a heart attack or stroke. We learned of some situations where there was a legitimate question as to whether the death was suicide or murder. A few of our participants spoke of situations where there was no doubt that the parent died from suicide, but other family members insisted that it had to be murder, because "our loved one would never have done something like take his or her own life." Again and again, the shame and stigma of suicide paralyzes a family from admitting the truth. Patricia, twenty-two years at the time of her father's suicide, experienced this labeling:

I think when I started to see the reactions of those close to me, I probably subconsciously at that point thought if those people who are close to me can't even talk to me about it or get comfortable with this, how can I tell your average person on the street or somebody that I meet at work what happened to my dad?

Most Helpful Acts of Acquaintances, Friends and Family

For friends, acquaintances, co-workers and family members who very understandably may not have had the words to express what they were feeling, our survivor participants tell what was most helpful to them after the suicides. What meant so much to the survivors were people who were not afraid to call, to follow up on them and to be around them. Caryn, age thirty at the time of her father's suicide, tells what she found helpful. Not all survivors are as comfortable as was Caryn being this straightforward with others. Therefore it is important to know the survivor very well before being so direct:

The most important thing for me was for others to ask me questions that they had or had expressed their curiosity about. For me, this was more helpful. I would rather someone ask me and if I don't want to talk about it, then I will say so. But if they asked me, then I could see where they are coming from and I could explain it to them.

Billi Sue, fifty years old at the time of her mother's suicide, has a suggestion for the survivors. She found her own candid attitude brought everything out in the open and was helpful in finding people who would be supportive:

My mom killed herself. She did not "just die." When someone has lost a loved one to suicide, they have to say what it is. Don't hide it away like it's a big dark secret, like people are going to point a finger at you. When I started talking to my colleagues and being very straight with them about what happened, I found out that one of my very closest friends had lost her dad, almost in the same way.

We heard from some participants who actually found seeing what their parents looked like in death helped to provide closure through a last image of the parents at rest. Many times after a suicide, this is not allowed by law enforcement. Some participants needed to read the police reports or view their parents' bodies to digest what happened. Shanna, twenty-seven at the time of the suicide, speaks of what she found comforting:

I told my mother I wanted to view the body, and she said no. I told her that she couldn't tell me that I could not see my father. I was the only one who was going to view the body, but I insisted that I wanted to see him. Other family members then decided to do the same. I swear as I sit here, he was smiling and at peace. It was the most calm I had ever seen him in my life. I was glad that I did get to see him and to view him, because being at peace was the last picture I had of him.

James, twenty-five at the time of his father's suicide, also needed closure:

Images of my father's last moment nagged me. I couldn't get them out of my head partly because there was nothing concrete to visualize. I can imagine forever. Through a friend of my father's, I was allowed access to the photos of the scene taken by the police. Strangely enough, the photos provided a sense of calm for me, no more wondering what he was wearing and how he looked. It was all there in brutal color. I imagine some people thinking, "Why would you ever want to see something like that?" All I can say is that it helped and I don't regret it for a second.

Co-Workers' Interaction

An adult survivor may be established in either a career or a steady job. Many identify who they are through their work. (A third of those we interviewed were either psychologists or teachers.) A job frequently is a place where the majority of time and mental energy is spent. Friends are made frequently at work, sometimes two people interact only on the job, but sometimes these friendships cross over to establish relationships outside of work. Co-workers often know about each other's lives and personalities. Many feel awkward about how to handle with others at work something as intimately personal as the suicide of a parent. Certain people are easier to talk with about one's pain than others. Many of our participants who were in emotional turmoil after the suicides put themselves in the difficult position of trying to be distracted by maintaining a busy life through work while simultaneously hoping for life to return to a "normal state." Lori, twenty-three years old at the time of her father's suicide, shares what it was like for her at work after the suicide:

Everyone that I worked with just kind of ignored my tragedy and didn't want to talk about it. I don't remember a single person comforting me because my father died, not a one. There were lots of people around and we were really close too, I thought. We worked around the clock a lot, and it was not a huge office. We hung out together. We went canoeing on the weekends together, and they would have just liked it if I hadn't said anything about it. My boss said, "Take as long as you like and need, three days before you come back." He was calling me after two days for me to come back. No idea whatsoever. It was cold and not very sensitive.

Sharon, forty-two at the time of her mother's suicide, reveals what her life at work was like after the suicide:

I took a leave of absence from work because there were so many complications with my mother's estate. Therefore I didn't have much contact with co-workers. When I returned, they really seemed uncomfortable talking to me and so I just didn't really deal with the issue at work; I just dealt with it in my personal life.

Control is an issue for survivors that comes up throughout *Voices of Strength*. When a parent's suicide occurs, frequently close family members often feel their own lives are out of control. It is not uncommon to focus at such times on whatever part of one's life that a person feels he or she has some control over. This frequently is the person's job. At work, some people want to be portrayed as self-reliant, competent individuals who can't be shaken by anything, not even a parent's death. Suicide presents even more of a challenge to maintain this steady façade so the survivor is not seen (or does not feel) as out of control as their deceased parent and the surrounding situation. Aside from work, the individual might also feel that s/he has to be "strong" for other family members and/or for his or her children. Under this pressure, a survivor may not know how to ask for help. Often this depends on the environment and the people one works with. This points to an important question: "What is the best approach for a work place to use when an employee has lost a close family member to suicide?" Ultimately, this decision falls mostly to the person in charge, whether it is an employer, supervisor or manager. He or she should immediately talk privately with the survivor, and if the survivor is not able to work or needs private time, the supervisor should make arrangements for the survivor to take off as much time as is allowable. He or she should also ask the survivor's permission to disclose the suicide to co-workers. This will alleviate the awkwardness of the survivor having to retell the story, and it also prevents them from wondering who knows and who doesn't. If possible, it would be helpful if the employer/supervisor and at least one co-worker attended the memorial service if one is scheduled. For many individuals, work comrades are like a second family. And co-workers should be guided by the employer/supervisor to show the survivor compassion and empathy after a parent's suicide, just as they would with the loss of any loved one.

Vicki, thirty-five at the time of her mother's suicide, reveals the difficult emotional state of some survivors:

When I got the news of the suicide, we were having a busy week at work. I felt an obligation to take care of the only thing I could control—my work. I didn't ask for help or time off or sympathy at the time, and I got none. Later, I realized I had always worked hard to portray myself as self-reliant, competent and able to handle everything by myself, so people let me. Now I know there are events where your family, friends and co-workers should insist a person take the time and space needed to get through certain traumas. But I also know how hard we can make it for anyone to help or even approach us to offer an understanding.

Raising Children and Their Issues

One third of our adult participants do not have any children and most of them made a conscious decision not to. Some didn't believe that their parents' suicides had any effect on their decisions. They had different reasons and fears that they stated:

- Not wanting to continue what they thought of as their legacy of abusive and dysfunctional families
- Being unable to give enough attention and love to children
- Always knew since childhood that they never wanted children
- Fear of loss, maybe something catastrophic happening with their children
- Apprehension about dying before their children are raised
- Concerns of the changing and complicated world we live in
- Unease concerning the enormous responsibility of the task

At least some of these reasons appear to us to be interconnected with each other and with the dysfunctional family behavior that may have led the parent to take his or her own life. Two participants definitely claimed that they did not want to have children because of their parents' suicides.

Lori, twenty-three at the time of her father's suicide, says:

I didn't plan to have children because:

1) I was afraid I would perpetuate the cycles of abuse in my family despite my best intentions and

2) I wanted my genes NOT to be continued in the world. The generations of suicides were definitely a factor, alongside generations of alcoholic, drug-abusing rapists. I was always told that "I was just like my father," and I believed I was the inheritor of his miserable legacy of suicide in his family: his father, his grandfather and his great-grandfather.

Cynthia, age twenty-five at the time of her mother's suicide, was also afraid:

I fear that depression may be inherited and I do not want to pass depression onto my child. I also am afraid of more painful experiences or losses—i.e. loss of a child or constant worry about my child getting hurt or in an accident.

Other than fearing that their children might turn out to be like their depressed and suicidal parents, survivors frequently have dread that because, through the suicides, they have intimate knowledge that horrible and unpredictable losses can happen, how can they trust that they won't experience something tragic happening to either their children or to themselves? Kris, thirty-one at the time of her mother's suicide, tells of her fears:

I am constantly in fear of dying tragically (not by suicide) and leaving my children abandoned and alone to be raised by people who won't care for them as I would.

After my mom passed away, my fears turned to a chemical imbalance. I started receiving a newsletter for suicide survivors and the more I read, the more aware I became that depression can be handed down from generation to generation. I started worrying about the effect on my children. And this was after I had them. I never ever thought about it beforehand. My only concern before I had children was if I could raise this child on my own. But now my fears are whether my children are going to be mentally healthy. I don't know if I could deal with it this time. How could I possibly live through losing one of my children? I lost my mom, I lost my husband, and how could I possibly live through the same with one of my children? I am extremely cautious and have my eyes wide open when it comes to how my children are behaving.

When Should Children be Told of a Grandparent's Suicide?

We asked our participants who already had kids when their parents committed suicide, if and how they told their children, and if they did, what age they thought was appropriate. We believe if the children are going to find out from others, then it is better they hear it from their own parents first. If there is not a chance that they will hear from others, it very well might be worthwhile postponing giving them this information. By giving young children this information prematurely, problems can be created that are preventable. It is best, however, to be cautious as to deciding at what age the child is told, and it is advisable to have a therapist available to work with. It is wise to think out first what the pros and cons are and to think carefully before saying anything. This is an individual decision and needs to be well thought-out. Knowing what happened to a grandparent at a younger age may unfortunately be unavoidable. If people around them are discussing the suicide, there certainly is a good chance that the grandchild may find out and then be too afraid to ask the adults any questions. Children overhear conversations. Sharon, forty-two at the time of her mother's suicide, tells how she handled this:

I just told him that his grandmother had taken her life, and I was just straight forward about what happened. I described that she had shot herself. He cried and asked questions about that, and I tried to be as open with him as I could be. I told him that Grandma wasn't in a rational state of mind. We had family dinners together, and we always talked about what was going on. He knew that Grandma was having a hard time and that she was not thinking clearly. I explained to him when he was twelve that she was not thinking clearly and that she was in a lot of pain and that was the nature of our talk.

He was always a great little happy child and until he was fourteen or fifteen, he was really open with us. Closer to age sixteen, I started to notice changes in him, becoming more secretive and other such indicators that things were not right. He was smoking marijuana at a friend's house. We were so scared for him. I remember that night that I could not sleep. I told my husband to get all of the guns out of the house; I told him I don't care what you do with them, just get them out of here. I felt like we had to be so vigilant. We sent our son to several psychologists. He was such a charming child that he would just buffalo them. We just dealt with him very directly all the time. I would talk with him about suicide and about how he was feeling. In some respect, I probably drove my son crazy because I felt like I had to be so vigilant. I had to have a ticker tape every day to know if my son was okay.

Children pick up on their remaining parents' anxieties and fears about the suicides and it being passed on. It is helpful for the survivor to see a qualified therapist in dealing with this topic so his or her own anxieties and fears can be monitored and not subconsciously passed onto the children. However, this is easier said than done and usually requires skilled help. Shanna, twenty-seven years old at the time of her father's suicide, shares her plans for handling this problem:

I will be very honest and tell them clinical depression, alcoholism and addiction run in our family. All the professionals that we talked to say that you don't want to make it happen by overstressing it, but you need to watch for it. You only answer children's questions; you don't give them more information than they ask for. As they ask, I will tell them.

How Judy Handled her Mother's Suicide with her Four Daughters

It was a relatively uncomplicated, clear-cut decision for me to make about telling my four daughters about their grandmother's suicide. I personally believe I was too young myself at age nine years to know that my mother took her own life and how she did it. Even more so, it should have been done quite differently. Since I was not going to hear about the suicide from other sources, it may have been wiser to let me know the cause of her death when I was a bit older. Certainly it would have been better to wait until I was asking questions about why she died. Of course, there are other factors here. My brother and I were adopted by our stepmother when I was in the sixth grade. At the young age of nine, I learned that my stepmother was not my birth mother, then was told in a very brief conversation, lasting just a few minutes that my natural mother was dead and how she took her own life. Afterward, I was told not to talk about it. I certainly needed to learn long before I was told of the suicide that my birth mother had died and went to Heaven when I was a baby. It would have alleviated my vague memories and confusion tremendously if I had known this at a younger age. Instead, I recall a vocabulary lesson in school when the word "kidnap" was defined, and I thought that explained my bafflement. I thought that I had been kidnapped. But knowing the morbid details of her suicide haunted me.

I made a decision not to tell our children about their grandmother's suicide until their later teenage years or young adulthood. I did not see any reason why they needed to know sooner. After all, they never knew their grandmother. At some point, when they were children, I told them she had died when I was a baby; I felt no hurry in even sharing that with them. I did not want them to feel insecure that I would die and leave them. I had the added security that no one was going to be telling my children about my mother's suicide, so I had the freedom to tell them when I thought it was age-appropriate.

One of my four children became depressed when she was a preadolescent, and I took her to a doctor who, in my opinion, was very much out-of-bounds in handling my daughter. She spoke to me privately and I was honest with her about my mother's suicide, assuming she was a professional and wouldn't use such appalling judgment by sharing this with my depressed twelve-year-old without discussing it first with me and receiving my permission. When she called my daughter back in, she started discussing her grandmother's mental illness and suicide. I was very angry that the therapist did this.

I feel this occurrence should be a warning that survivors must be vigilantly aware not to assume anything even with mental health professionals or doctors. Clarify first where they stand in their attitudes and beliefs. Definitely do not leave any child with any mental health worker who will not respect parents' wishes on such an issue or whose values do not meet with your approval. There is a huge difference between secrets and confidentiality. Being appropriate with your child in sharing information is not being secretive. It is a very individualized issue as to what to tell children and when to tell them. Once a child is informed, it is extremely important for the parent or guardian to be approachable and knowledgeable on what is said and how. If a child asks a question that you are not prepared to answer, I suggest that you tell your child that s/he asked a very good question, one that needs some thinking about. Then assure your child that you will get back to them. Be sure to follow through and get back to your child; however, first consult with a knowledgeable, qualified professional, support organization or a reliable book to learn what to say and how. Suicide is a difficult issue to discuss with children and must be handled appropriately.

I asked for feedback from all four of my daughters as to whether the knowledge of their grandmother's suicide affected them and if so, how.

Judy's thirty-two-year-old daughter, Susan, tells how she learned of and handled Judy's mother's suicide:

I would say I was affected by your mother's death and probably was more aware of how lucky I was to have had such a good childhood when at later times I saw how it was for you. It made me appreciate family more and the bond we all have and the different ways you learned to cope with it. I don't recall at what age my mother told me of her mother's death or suicide, but I think I didn't really understand it until later on. I was not sure why anyone would take their own life. I recollect my mom showing me a newspaper clipping telling of her death. I think my reaction was more to the effect of how could anyone leave a little bitty baby and her five-year-old child, that thought to be amplified later when I had my own babies.

Judy's daughter Linda, age thirty-five, speaks of her grandmother's death and suicide:

I do not remember finding out about your mother's death, or suicide. It seems like at one point in life I knew only that she had died and that the grandma that I knew was not my biological grandmother. Then, as a late teen, I remember knowing she had committed suicide, but didn't know why, when or how. I don't remember the actual "finding out" point.

I always thought it was peculiar to have an immediate family member that had actually committed suicide. I can only imagine what someone would be thinking at that moment when they actually take the plunge, so to speak. I know I've been affected by depression at varying points in my life, sometimes for a reason, sometimes without a reason, but I've never seen suicide as a personal option. I don't think that knowing a family member committed suicide has affected my choices or thoughts on that topic. Actually, that's not true. In seeing (or really just hearing about it) the aftermath of that action, it has impacted me, and caused me to be more conscious of my moods and temperament as well as my child's and to be watchful for depression. It reminds me to keep a check on this and take medical action if necessary.

The suicide issue is a tough topic but if such disorders can be hereditary, one must keep up with the smaller pieces and problems that precede such a drastic measure as suicide. I never knew my grandmother and therefore I've never really taken it "personally" or felt too close to that issue. I guess I've always felt detached from that.

Judy's daughter Janette, forty-two years old, tells of her reaction:

I was an adult before I found out that my mom's (Judy, my dad's second wife) mother had committed suicide. I think I was truly shocked for two reasons. One, I had never bothered to press for details. I assumed when she said that she lost her mother, that her mom had abandoned her as mine had when my parents got divorced. Two, I felt bad for her and wished I had been nicer, particularly during those hellish teenage years.

After my parents divorced, I had my own issues to deal with and would not have been able to shoulder any guilt associated with that knowledge. I am grateful that I did not know. I actually think it was a selfless act to keep that information from me. She never used that as an excuse for any shortcomings as a mother. I just thought (as a child) that she had no idea what it was like to lose your mother. She was taking my father and I could not see past that. The sad thing was, mine was still alive and yet I had NO contact with her for over eight years.

Mom married my dad when she was twenty-five years old. He was ten years her senior. He already had two children, ages five and nine. I was the five-year-old. Suddenly, she had a family. She gave birth to two girls and she never treated us any differently than her own flesh and blood, and I am grateful for that.

It was not until I was an adult with three children of my own that I could truly understand. I don't think I would share that information with them if this was my situation. Children do not need to carry the pain of their parents, and it is not their responsibility to help them deal with that kind of tragic loss. I think she did the right thing and for the right reasons. I will always be grateful for that.

Elaine, Judy's forty-five-year-old daughter, tells about her experience of learning about Judy's mother's suicide:

I was a pubescent pre-teen when my mom told me about her mother's death when she was a baby... I was shocked to hear this, but as the oldest of four sisters, I also felt privileged and honored that I was the first and only daughter to know about this very significant event. As a very young teenager, Mom and I were most often at odds and I did not understand a great deal about why she did things the way she did. I often thought of her as the wicked stepmother (even though she adopted my sister Janette and I shortly after she and my dad were married). My sisters were too young at the time, and each of them were told when Mom felt it was their right time. More than any of these feelings, though, I slowly began to develop more of an appreciation about where my mom was coming from. The more I learned as an adult about her childhood and the enormous losses she suffered as a result of her mother's suicide and the chain of events that started at that time and continued through her adulthood, my understanding of Mom grew deeper and deeper. As I got older (and past the terrible teens), I developed a very close and special relationship with Mom that has only continued to strengthen throughout the years.

Losing a parent by any means at any age is traumatic, but losing one through suicide has so many more traumatic implications. My mom has worked very hard for many years to deal with her issues related to this and she has a tremendous amount of insight that can help others cope and get on with a great life.

Judy responds to her daughters:
I was glad that I did ask our daughters to write their thoughts for me and for the book. I did tell Elaine after I married her dad that my mother had died, wanting her to know that I did empathize with and experience the quandary of maternal abandonment.

Positive Support Groups for Adult Survivors of Parent Suicide
Over half our adult participants attended support groups after the suicides. Some received counseling as well. We want to make a distinction between grief groups and support groups, specifically for survivors of suicide. Grief groups deal with the death of loved ones or friends. Suicide survivor support groups specifically deal with the loss of a loved one or friend through suicide. One participant recalled feeling like an "outsider" at a grief group and found a suicide survivor group online more helpful.

The majority of our participants felt they benefited from meeting with other survivors to share what had happened and to hear that they weren't alone on the road to recovery. Participants who found support groups less beneficial to them felt affected by all the sadness and pain expressed by those who shared their experiences at the meetings. Support groups are hopefully carefully planned meetings led by trained professionals but need skilled monitoring, because the feelings and events shared can be very raw and shocking. People who attend are at various stages of their recovery process and emotions can be intense. Patricia, twenty-two years old at the time of her father's suicide, discusses her negative experience:

It was a little overwhelming for me, so I'm not sure I'm prepared to do that again. Certainly going forward, I'd like to be able to become more comfortable and be able to speak out as an advocate for suicide prevention. So, I feel like I'm taking steps towards that. But I don't think I was quite ready to attend a group of these survivors. I know that most of them had just recently lost someone so they were in a pretty significant amount of pain, the individuals that were there. I would like to continue that at some point, but I don't think that I'm ready yet.

Mia tells what she experienced:

I share a similar experience to some of these participants when I attended a suicide survivor group. A twelve-year-old girl had just committed suicide, and her story was front-page news. Her parents were there discussing what emotions they could identify at the time. Other people who spoke were angry and that feeling intimidated me so that I did not share much of my story. I tried it three more times but stopped going and instead continued to see my therapist. Looking back on the experience, it would have been good to talk privately with the group leader before the meeting to know more about what to expect. We had talked on the phone, but that was more about my own situation. Also, I could have brought my husband with me for support. You can bring anyone along to these meetings, and in retrospect, it would have helped me not to feel so alone.

Participants who regarded their support group experiences as helpful felt that they were in safe places and could express anything they needed to say. They also felt comforted to know that they weren't alone in the emotions they were dealing with. They felt the need to talk with other survivors. Caryn, thirty years old at the time of her father's suicide, found:

I went to a support group for the first two years after my father died. I did find it helpful because when that happened. No one was around me other than obviously my mother and my sister. None of my friends experienced anything like that, I would feel very alone. My friends might have experienced a death; however with suicide, when your family member chose to take his or her own life, it is just extra baggage to have to deal with. It is easy to feel really alone even though you know in your head that there are other people out there who have experienced a suicide close to them. It was reaffirming to go there and hear people talk and know that even though people and their experiences are really not alike, that there were others who had similar thinking to me. It was helpful to know that it is something that impacted me so greatly that I was never going to get over it, but that is okay as I would learn to live with it. It was really so good to have a place where I felt like I could say anything I wanted or I could just sit there and take it all in if that is what I needed to do. Wherever I was at that time was okay.

Leann, thirty years old at the time of her mother's suicide, tells:

I had just lost my mother when I attended a survivor group for the first time. The first time I went to a support group meeting, I felt that these people were in so much pain I thought, "Oh my God, I am never going to get well," because there were some survivors that had been there for years and here I was in the first month. I had gone the month after she died. I thought, "I am never going to get well." I had no hope! As it turns out, for me, the SOS (Survivors of Suicide) group was extremely helpful. Going to support group meetings is good for some people but it is not right for all.

How Does Suicide Change Survivors?
Those people to whom we spoke who were adults at the time of their

parents' suicides felt that they were stronger individuals in various aspects of their lives and personalities as a result of the lessons they learned from their life-altering events. We saw a common theme within this group: They had a solid support base and attended either support groups or therapy or both.

Louise, thirty-nine years old at the time of her mother's suicide, shares:

I feel my whole life was cut down, just like a rose bush pruned to the bare root. It was the only incident, no matter how hard other things have been that I could not ignore or "barrel through." My heart was closed and filled with anger and pain. The person I am now is different in many ways. I feel I have to learn to live all over again. Reluctantly, I'm shut down and shut in. I don't have any friends or family I talk to except my kids and the people I talk to at work. No one is close to me. My relationship with my father is indifferent. I have not told anyone. I have had several medical problems since my mother's death.

Sharon, forty-two years old at the time of her mother's suicide, speaks of her self-image changing:

I think it has changed my life immeasurably and I miss my mother every day. I have become a better person. There is no question in my mind that I like myself better now than I did before. I've become more introspective and it has changed the way I view my life and I view my role here on Earth and my purpose. It has changed my life, I think, for the better. If I had to do this over again, I wouldn't choose this particular way to learn these lessons but I guess I've been able to turn it around in a way that I think has helped me.

Billi Sue, fifty years old at the time of her mother's suicide, tells how the suicide affected her:

It has made me go after things with such gusto as if there's not a moment to spare. I was always a go-getter. I just pursue things, set deadlines for myself and I follow through with things. There is no procrastination at all. I realize that, whatever it was at that split moment or whatever it was weeks in advance of when this occurred, it was very well planned. This was not a split second decision. Something had to have snapped in my mom, and so I'm guarding myself against the same thing happening to me. I just don't feel I have any time to waste. I pretty much have my life all planned out.

Vonny, thirty-three years old at the time of her mother's suicide, shares how she has matured:

Mom's suicide taught me that another person's decisions and actions are not a reflection of my worth as a person. A person's actions are all about that person, and it isn't my responsibility to "fix" anyone who makes hurtful decisions, no matter how much I may care about them or how adamantly I may disagree with what they say or do. It was a huge lesson in personal accountability—that everyone is responsible for themselves and their own actions. My own accountability rests in how I choose to react. Since I've now survived the worst possible thing a human being could ever live through, I've discovered—after a period of healing—that I have more control over how I choose to deal with people. I no longer tolerate abusive behaviors from anyone. Life is much too short. I treat myself and others with more respect and compassion now.

Candice, twenty-two years old at the time of her father's suicide, talks of her spiritual evolution:

Sharing this experience has allowed me to get in touch with my own depression and the acceptance of the fact that I have a strong family history of depression and bipolar disorder. For many years, spirituality was not even on my radar screen in spite of a strong religious background with my father, grandfather and several uncles being ministers. Eventually the experience of my father's suicide strengthened my relationship with God, with others and even with myself.

Cynthia, twenty-five years old at the time of her mother's suicide, learned about who she really is:

It was extremely devastating to me. I lost a lot of self-confidence and a lot of self-esteem because my mother built me up all the time. She used to say, "You can do anything in your life, Cynthia. You're so beautiful. You're so wonderful…" She was just like that. We talked every day on the phone. A lot of my self-confidence went away. A lot of my self-esteem went away. That was in the beginning now, but I've been gaining a lot. And at this point in my life, it'll be almost ten years, I feel like I'm a stronger person because of it. I feel like I can handle almost whatever comes my way in life because I've been through so much. I appreciate the people in my life so much more. I let them know that with words and cards and by saying "I love you." I feel like I have a lot more empathy for my friends and my family when they have problems. I try to help them however I can. I just enjoy the little things in life I didn't really pay attention to before, not take life for granted so much. That's at this point. If you had asked me that question five years ago, it would have probably been a very different answer. It changed when I went to therapy.

Vicki, thirty-five years old at the time of her mother's suicide, tells of how the event has changed her life:

I've tried to view her suicide as her legacy to me, but in a more functional way. It made me eventually willing to admit I need help at times and am driven to seek the resources she rejected and to do what it takes to keep from becoming her (an ongoing, unspoken fear). It shattered my willingness to postpone life and happiness.

Caryn, thirty years old at the time of her father's suicide, speaks of how her values developed:

I think one of the biggest ways it impacted me is that I realized that one of the most important things you can give to someone is your time, because you don't know how long you are going to have that person around. I realized that relationships are more valuable than anything else that I have in my life. Even though that person may not be around any more, the time you took with them in cultivating that relationship and memories you shared with that person are always going to last. It leaves me a lot more aware of making myself more available for people even if they want to do something real simple like go out for a cup of coffee or something. I really try to keep my schedule as free as possible to be able to just take time with people, enjoy them and talk with them. I really didn't realize how valuable that is until after this.

Overview

Adults, as a general rule, have many more resources available to them than children or adolescents. However, it must not be underestimated that the death of a parent is most always an unsettling event at any age. Parents are thought to be the most constant people in our lives. So the physical death of our mother or father can be a loss in more than one way. It can be the actual loss of the individual we knew from birth and who has always been there for us, loving us and accepting our love in return. The physical death of a parent at other times may mean something different for those without rapport with the parent, either because of the rising divorce rate and its effect on parent/child relationships or because of other estrangement. Physical death can mean another type of death, the death of hope that something will change between them.

When you add suicide to this equation, it always means a premature death, a death by one's own hands, which is highly traumatic for survivors. Many of the same reactions that childhood and teen survivors experience are shared by adult survivors. Frequently the adult survivor has had a lengthy history of mental illness in the family, probably with the parent who took his or her own life. But there are other reasons why people commit suicide other than a long history of emotional turmoil. Sometimes financial situations start to feel so out of control that the parent decides there is no other way out. Chronic physical illness can still be another cause. Frequently the adult survivor has had to be the caretaker of this mentally ill, physically ill parent or the distraught parent who believes there are no solutions to his or her problems. At the time of the suicide, it is not at all unusual or abnormal for survivors to have a mixture of emotions. Relief felt by survivors is one of those common emotions in such cases, because the daughter/s and/or son/s may be physically and emotionally exhausted themselves. It is important not to feel guilty if you are experiencing relief, relief that your impossible task has ended and relief that your parent is no longer suffering.

Our participants have shared in this chapter the things which were helpful and not so helpful in getting them through the harsh event of parent suicide. We hope that through their candid and open confiding of feelings, emotions and messages, they have provided comfort and support on your own journey to recovery.

Survivors must take great pains to be gentle with themselves. Taking care of one's self is of utmost importance. Survivors may now find themselves in a position of supporting and taking care of others and might not find others to console them. A therapist and/or clergy may be of great value at such a time. Also, being very open and honest in telling friends and loved ones what is needed to help you get through this is essential. It may also help to share this book with those in need.

CHAPTER 4

Rebuilding
Shattered Lives

The death of a parent, whatever its cause, is difficult for sons and daughters. A parent's suicide complicates the grieving process greatly; when both parents take their own lives or when there is a suicide-murder, the emotional consequences for the survivors are immense. Seven of our participants have suffered such cataclysmic events. Four of our participants lost both parents to suicide either several years apart from each other or, in one case, from a double suicide. Two other participants experienced murder and suicide in their families. The other case is told by Roberta and Eddie, two people we interviewed. They share with us a sad commentary in which a psychiatrist ignored a plea for help after the attempted suicide of their son, the father of their granddaughter. The infant did not live to tell her story. Her grandparents do it for her.

When we interviewed these individuals who had experienced parental double suicide or murder/suicide, we found determined people with the courage to look at their own tragic experiences and decide that their mission is to break the cycle of suicide. After completion of the interviews, we realized that these participants were in the process of rebuilding their lives. We were inspired by their stories and we hope that you find inspiration as well.

As you read these narratives, notice the various and also recurring themes in each of them as well as the different stages of recovery that each participant is in. We want to caution our readers as they read these accounts, not to belittle your own losses. We can always find someone that we think has suffered worse events, and we can always look at others and say ours is worse. However, if we put such restrictions on ourselves and others, it would not be okay for any of us to go through the normal grieving process that each one of us sooner or later needs to progress through. Death is a major life event regardless of what the cause may be. All losses are important. Do not allow yourself or anyone else to say, "Look at him, he has it worse than you." Use these stories for inspiration and to learn more paths to help you move forward on your way to recovery.

Shelby's Story

Shelby is a single, self-employed woman in her fifties with an advanced college degree. Her mother died from suicide when Shelby was twenty-four, and her father took his own life five years later. After her mother's death, she became severely depressed. When her father followed suit, Shelby was drinking and very unstable. She made her decision to never have children after both parents had committed suicide. She went into intense psychotherapy after her father's death and continues to see a therapist once a week. She continues to grieve:

I lived with my mother, but on that Christmas Eve, I was on a date. When I returned home, I saw a police car, an ambulance and a hearse in my driveway. I jumped out of the car and went to the police car, thinking something terrible had happened but not having a clue that my mother was dead by her own hand. I went to the officer in the police car and asked, "What's happened here?" Then I heard my sister call my name, and she was there almost immediately, because she was waiting at the end of the driveway knowing I would be back soon.

We had graveside services for both funerals. Well, I think it was because we weren't really active in the church. We all were members, and we all went. But I don't think I got to participate in the decision about that, certainly not when Mother died. I believe I was just told. "The less fanfare the better" was perhaps the modus operandi approach there. The suicide no doubt was a factor.

Since my father was still alive, we didn't dismantle the house after my mother's death. After Daddy died, we did, and there was a business to be dealt with and about three years after his death we settled that part of the estate, and it resulted in my brother and me not speaking for about seventeen years. It was hideous and horrible. I have furniture and sterling silverware that belonged to my parents and also furniture that belonged to my grandmother and favorite aunt. It gives me a lot of comfort to have the history of the family around me. I can't imagine getting rid of those things. When my sister became ill last year, she wanted to collect pictures of the family and have them in her room in my apartment. She went away on a trip, and while she was gone I put up a wall of photos. I went through old albums that I don't think I'd ever seen before of Daddy when he was a one-year-old, Mother when she was a baby and I found myself just staring at some of those pictures and thinking how did it go so wrong. I'm really glad I have the pictures of them as children. But their deaths still mystify me.

During the years that followed, I have been back and forth trying to get my spiritual life in order, but then something would happen. I pretty much became un-enamored with God. I wasn't great with faith anyway, because I had been raised in a household with people who were intelligent and funny and crazy, but not religious. They were alcoholics, they put on a good show for the public, but they were crazy. They were wounded, deeply wounded themselves, and didn't know how to live their lives constructively. They didn't know how to raise children constructively or instructively. And therefore, I didn't learn how to do that either. And so, my disillusionment with all things to do with faith was born in a cesspool of chaos. And so my spiritual evolving came after both of their deaths.

I know that my brother harbored twenty years of tremendous resentment toward my mother. One of his therapists made the comment, "What a hostile act on Christmas Eve." So, only now after thirty years is he able to come to a sense of feeling sad for her. He was just angry for a very long time. I'm not sure I addressed her suicide either until I was in analysis. It was so much about me after this thing happened. Until I got into analysis, there was so much to deal with that I didn't even know how to ask the question. I didn't know how to look at life. I just tried to buffer myself with alcohol or pot or humor. It's so much easier for me to believe that I don't resent what they did, that I don't know what it felt like when I did resent it, if I did. I must have. But I have just profound sadness that they did what they did. I don't think I reached a point where I felt I had to forgive them. The one who needed to be forgiven by me was me. So I immediately took on the responsibility that forgiveness truly was about me.

I probably still think my father could have behaved better when my mother was alive. It was so obvious to me that he had stopped loving her. But the truth is so had I. She was so convinced that she was unlovable that she made that prophecy come true. She was difficult to love; she was difficult to be with. She was an angry, angry person, especially toward the end. And yet my heart broke for her that Daddy no longer had affection for her. He just ignored her.

After my father's suicide, my sister ramrodded me into going to a psychiatrist, and I fought it with all of my being. Finally just to shut her up, I went and met with the man. I said, "Okay, fine! My idea is that I will come and see you once a week, you know for a year." He said, "Well, that's not what analysis is." And I asked, "Well, then what is it?" And he said, "It's at least four times a week and we can't set a time limit." As it turned out, I was there four times a week for five and a half years. If my sister hadn't bullied me into it, I never would have done it. I believe that if I hadn't done it, I might not be alive today. I can't stress how important getting insight from a third party can be, a trained professional especially. Analysis is a whole different kind of animal. It's as if you are re-learning how to be. Since my older sister came to live with me five years ago, I have seen a therapist here on a weekly basis.

In regards to the analysis that I was in, we did quite a lot of "tell me your dream" and a lot of talking about dreams. I would tell my doctor constantly, almost for the whole five years, "You're so full of it!" He'd come up with something and I'd say, "Oh, please!" But what I know is that my dreams indicated that I felt tremendous responsibility, that I felt tremendous guilt; I felt I could have done something. And I left therapy knowing that was not the case. So, when I discuss analysis, I have to say that it is like wearing braces; it's not like wearing a retainer at night and then taking it off the next morning. You're there and you are wrenched, and it's like the onion is being peeled. One of the primary gifts I got from doing that was in being told that it isn't all about me, that Mother's behavior when I was a child was not about me and that Daddy's decision to take his life five years after Mother took her own life was not about me. I was still locked in the child's mind, and every child at one point feels that the things that are happening around the child and the chaos that is being seen has to do with something the child has done or not done. And I got clear on that. This has helped me in all my relationships since. It makes it easier for me not to take things personally when someone's a jerk or angry with me. I know better now. I protect myself better than I used to and not even consciously all the time. I am simply stronger because of therapy.

I don't believe that I have had any negative experiences in therapy. I'm sure there were things that were hit upon that made me furious. Within days or weeks, I'd realize it was so infuriating, because it was a truth that we hit upon that I didn't want to look at. I was lucky, because I know of people who go to therapists and don't like them and then don't go again. I got the best guy I could have gotten. He was very ethical, he was very steady and he was a nice man.

My mother's death—well both my mother's and father's—legitimized my status as a victim so that I could legitimately call out for and demand everyone's sympathy. I didn't deal with stuff. I didn't talk to people in a therapeutic way. I just announced the suicides to anybody I met. "Oh by the way, my mother killed herself." Analysis shot my acting like a victim down.

It took me about twelve or fifteen years until I could enjoy Christmas again. It became something horrible I just got through. Thoughts of my parents' suicides don't mess up Christmas anymore.

Krystal's Story

Krystal is a married woman in her fifties with children. At the time of her mother's suicide, Krystal was in her early twenties and was told her mother had died from a stroke. She learned the truth years later. When she was in her forties, her chronically ill father took his own life. Her story tells the silence many react with and shows so much of the damage that is done by lack of communication. Fortunately, Krystal comes to realize that keeping secrets is a cycle she would like to break. She does when she told us her story:

I was not living at home with my family when my mother died. My friends came to tell me of her death and to take me to my parents' home. They told me she had died of a stroke, and I never even thought that my mother might have died from anything other than medical reasons, because she had been ill with one thing or another for much of my life. She was always in pain and since one of my parents' close friends was a doctor, drugs were an easy thing for my parents to get. In fact, my dad gave her shots of a narcotic to ease her pain and eventually she had surgery hoping to stop her physical pain. She had a stroke during her surgery. She needed a cane or walker after that, which upset her very much. Evidently, she felt she couldn't live like that. It was more than a decade later when I found out that she, in fact, took her own life. I learned from my dad that he had known what she planned to do and had assisted her. He cried as he told me. I don't recall how it came up, but I remember thinking, and still do, how horrible it was for him to do that. I think he died when she did. He was sort of non-existent after his wife's assisted suicide. Later, in my forties, my father was diagnosed with a serious chronic condition, and he took his own life some years later, after having lived with it for several years.

At my parents' funerals, it was kept a secret about both of the suicides so friends attending did not know of either parent's suicide. I really do hate secrets and am thinking that I should discuss this with my adult children. I do not think that they know. Maybe they would understand me better if they knew.

My dad's parents came to our home after my mother's suicide, and they went through the house like a white tornado and took everything that had to do with my mother. It was terribly unfair, because I would like to own things that belonged to my mother. My dad had remarried before he died and his wife at the time had all the control over his stuff. It was horrible because I don't have things from my parents. I do have a scrapbook that my mother kept and I have my own baby book, so that is important. I do have a collage sort of picture of my parents and us on the wall, so I am happy I have that.

We weren't a communicative family, so we really weren't emotionally supportive towards one another, and each of us went into our own shells. We never talked about death or spiritual things and when our mother died, we never discussed that. I have seen families that talk about death and reminisce about the good times and sad times, but they do it together. I envy those families who get through death that way. We did not do that and it was everyone pretty much for him or herself. My sibling and I were not close, and although we are closer now, we weren't there for each other.

I have been to therapists off and on over the years and, of course, all the suicides come up. I do get depressed about all this and angry, because I had a mother, a father and a grandmother who all made choices that I believed to be weak and selfish. I refuse to follow suit. I don't wish to do that to my kids. I have chosen on purpose to be a different type of parent than my mother and my dad, and my relationship with my children is very good. But one of the consequences of all these suicides in my family is that when one of my kids becomes very upset, I always worry about how upset he or she is and whether suicide might seem like his or her solution. I can't imagine that this is in most parents' frame of reference.

Yes, I remain angry with them for what they did, so I guess I have not forgiven them.

I want to help other survivors and that is why I am meeting with the authors and doing this interview. As for suicide, I am determined to break the cycle.

Harriet's Story

Harriet, a college graduate and divorcee with children at the time of her parents' double suicide, was forty when we spoke. Her parents' suicides occurred when she was thirty-six years of age. With the suicides of her parents, there were no secrets. She tells what life was like for her at the time of and after the suicides. She says she is still in the midst of mourning:

I lived about an hour away from my parents, who lived in a small town and were highly respected in their community and across the state (my father, a retired minister and my mother, the organist). They had planned their suicides for a while and had driven to a motel that was in the same county so they knew who was going to find them. My story is unusual in that my parents left notes all around the room, even left a note to the sheriff, because they knew who was coming. After my parents' bodies were found, the sheriff of the town they were in got on the radio to the sheriff of my parents' hometown and told him that there were two bodies in the motel. The sheriff asked him who they were and the other sheriff said, "I can't tell you over the radio; you will understand when you get here." The sheriff went racing right over there and realized immediately. Their first concern was getting in touch with each one of us before other people started finding out.

My mother had called me a couple weeks before and was asking me questions about some of my friends and their phone numbers. My birthday was coming up so I thought she was just calling to ask me for that reason. She had left several pages of contacts and friends with phone numbers, the church we attended as well as the pastor's name and phone number. She even had written on one note, "Harriet is a single mother; do not call her at home." The sheriff called the pastors at my church who came to my office and told me.

My mother had typed three notes, one for me and one for each of my two sisters, and when we got to the house, there were three envelopes and baggies with our names on each on the bed. The baggy contained the jewelry my mom had divided up as well as cash. The notes said, "We know you won't understand what we have done. We had serious business problems that could not be solved either alone or together. If we could have, we would have. Please don't try to work out our business problems, because we couldn't. I think the children are too young to come to the service." That's all it said. Nothing was said that was comforting in those notes at all. I know in her mind, my mother was trying to make it as easy on us as possible. She even planned out the memorial service down to the details, like a reminder to pay the organist; this is who I want to play; this is who I want to sing. A group of ladies came from all over the state to fill the choir loft and sing. My mother and father asked to be cremated. They had bought burial plots just three weeks before, and they left notes saying, "If you can't bring yourself to cremate us, pick out the cheapest casket. Don't bury us with any jewelry. Keep my jewelry." They didn't want us to spend any money. My mother wrote another letter that said, "Read when only the three of you are in the same room, not anyone else around, not even your husbands." She said bizarre things like, "I think the piano has to go with the house, but make sure you get the Christmas sweaters out of the drawers." We did not know what was about to happen, if creditors were going to start coming and taking everything. As soon as the memorial service was over, we started cleaning out the house. I was physically, mentally and emotionally exhausted and totally incapable of making any kind of decision at that point. So I brought my two children and one of my sister's two children back to my house while my sisters got everything into storage, moved the piano to my house. The house was totally cleaned out in two days, because none of us could afford to pay the mortgage. Eventually I rented a U-Haul truck, went and cleaned out one of the storage rooms, because none of us had been able to deal with it even after all that time.

We had not a clue that my parents were depressed or that they had financial problems. Nobody did, only the two of them. They didn't discuss it with another soul. Their reality got seriously warped. I spoke with my mother on the phone three or four times a week and we saw each other if not every weekend, three out of four weekends. There was no preparation for what was to come.

I see forgiveness as releasing my parents from blame. I feel compassion for what my parents must have gone through. I became aware that my father probably had been clinically depressed for a very long time. I feel he's at peace now and he could not have faced the stigma of losing other people's money, because he always felt responsible for taking care of everybody. He would have lost face. That's the way he would have seen it. I certainly did not see it that way. All I felt was compassion.

My children were quite young at the time and were very close to my parents. I didn't tell them right away how their grandparents had died; I did not lie to them either. I waited for them to start asking very pointed questions and when it got to the point that I knew I couldn't avoid it any longer, I finally told them and it really hit my son the hardest. I thought I was prepared with everything that I read and with the pages that I had printed off the Internet. However, my son felt an enormous sense of guilt that he should have been able to stop it or that he should have known my parents were depressed. We were fortunate enough to find a children's bereavement counselor. She had never dealt with suicide before but did a lot of research, created puppet shows and even wrote a book. She helped my children a lot and, in the process, helped me a lot just by beingcompassionate. I believe it was not a coincidence that I found her. I call it a "God incident" instead of a coincidence. The counselor handled making sure that the children do not consider suicide an option and brought that up on more than one occasion. I think that once suicide is introduced in your life that all of a sudden there's an option where there wasn't before. The counselor asked to meet with me one day, sat there and cried with me, wanting to know how I was doing even though her work was with my children. Her mother had died, not to suicide, but she knew what it was like to lose a mother. I think that she was the most helpful of anybody I had been to because she sat there and cried with me.

Some people wondered, "Why can't you get over it and move on?" Some people avoided me. I found that my address book got totally rewritten and the friends I ended up with were surprising to me. The people who responded are the ones I never would have expected to respond. Other people just drifted away and I never heard from them again. One thing that struck me was that one of my mother's very best friends has kept in touch; she writes letters and puts me on her mail list when she travels out of town; she's made an effort to stay in touch. One of my mother's other friends called me recently, and I made the comment that some people didn't want to talk about what happened and I felt that one preacher wanted to sweep everything under the rug. She made the comment, "Well, people are just too busy to remember or make an effort." You know, people just don't have a clue. The suicides haven't controlled my life, because I just can't let them control my life but it's there and it never goes away.

I think the biggest thing that I have learned is to be more compassionate, because I had never experienced a loss before, much less one like this. It makes me realize how precious life is. I used to have perfect credit and this was very important to me. My credit is not perfect anymore but I know it will be corrected eventually. It would have seemed like the end of the world before, but when I see my parents died because of financial issues, it's just not that important. It changed my perspective. Since the suicides, I keep getting put in positions where I am around people who have had suicides in their lives, and I feel like this is happening for a reason. I reach out to these people. It's not easy. However, it helps to be around people who have experienced a loved one's suicide and understand, because nobody else could possibly fully comprehend unless they've been through it. It's different from other kinds of death.

David's Story

We spoke with another David who was in his thirties when we talked to him. Both of his parents took their own lives just seven months apart from each other:

My parents were the first big losses in my life; I lost them both within a very short period of time. I have several siblings, and we were very split in our relationships with our parents. My father and I had a distance between us that neither he nor I knew how to bridge. My siblings were much closer to my father, and in some ways I was my mother's "favorite," which also meant I was her target more than the others. Nothing I did was ever good enough for her. It was a very destructive relationship between us. After my father's suicide, I only saw my mother one time. We had a couple of phone/letter contacts, during which she continued to blame me and the same pattern of my not being "good enough" did not cease.

When my father took his life, I lived about forty-five minutes away. One of my siblings found my father's body. When I was called, my fiancée and I drove up there. By that time everyone was already at the house, and I talked to a cop. I didn't talk to the coroner or anything. Seven months to the day of my father's suicide, we got a phone call from my brother saying my mother had committed suicide. It was near Thanksgiving. My therapist had told me to stay away from my mother, because she acted in very mean and hateful ways. She said a lot of nasty things to me; my mother was very hard on me. My fiancée went out to clean up the house with some others and decided I didn't need to do that. I said, "Okay."

My father had been forced into retirement and thought he was financially broke. He didn't believe in divorce, but my parents' marriage was on the rocks. I believe he had an overwhelming sense of hopelessness and didn't know what to do. I don't think initially he planned to take his own life, but he became overwhelmed with lack of hope. Mother had mental health issues. She had begun to act erratically just before her suicide.

Our extended family, especially on my mother's side, completely disintegrated after the suicides. Inheritance issues became ugly. I don't have good relationships with anyone but my wife and stepchildren. To this day, I've never been close to my siblings or my parents. We're all in our late thirties and none of us has kids; I don't think any of us will have kids. I feel that says a lot about our upbringing.

What was most helpful to me was the support of a couple of my friends. I appreciated the people who showed up at the funeral. Probably the least helpful or the people I am most disappointed with are those who knew me, knew about my parents' suicides but never even attempted to talk to me about it.

I learned from reading books about suicide that if someone decides to commit suicide, this is his or her decision and the survivor is not to blame. What the therapist did was help me see some of the things my parents did when I was growing up and how it shaped me in my life. The other thing I learned was that in my family dynamics, I never learned to stand up for myself. I figured out just recently that if I don't stand up for myself, then no one will. All my life I guess I was waiting for my family to stand up for me and they never did. I was not happy with the way I was raised. I have never wanted children of my own. However, I have three stepchildren whom I am helping to raise. I don't want to repeat the pattern, so I try especially hard to listen when they need to talk and to give positive instead of negative reinforcements.

Andrew's Story

Andrew, a fifty-year-old college graduate and married man with adult children at the time we spoke, was thirteen when his mother killed his younger brother and sister and attacked him before taking her own life. He mourns the loss of his siblings and his mother and continues to feel guilt and self-blame. This happens to most survivors at the time of the loss of a loved one. Even when a death is caused by some serious medical condition, frequently we might think, *If only I had sent her to the doctor when she first complained of fatigue.* If not that, we say "if only" in regard to something else. Children often believe they can do what even adults in the same situation can not do. The fact that Andrew managed as well as he did is impressive for a thirteen-year-old. It is difficult for an adult, no less a child, to know that sometimes a person's life gets out of control, and there may be nothing that can be done to prevent a tragedy.

At the time when it happened, I thought I could have done more to prevent her from killing my brother and sister. I thought I could have been stronger, could have done something. I ran out of the house and ran to the neighbor's, and when I came back, they were dead. Maybe I should regress a little bit. The violence started out when my sister and I were lying on the couch in the front room; we were home sick that day and my mother came in carrying a baseball bat and hit me on the head with it. I staggered out the door and when I came back in the house she took the gun and held it straight to my head and pulled the trigger, but it misfired. I took the gun away from her and I ejected the shell. A few moments later, she grabbed the gun and ran toward the kitchen. That's when I ran out of the house to the neighbor's. I felt guilty, because I should have kept the gun. I felt like I should have been able to take it away from her instead of running out of the house. I felt, and I still do feel, I could have done this or that. The reality is I could have but I didn't.

We asked Andrew if he now knew a thirteen-year-old. "My grandson," he replied. Then we asked him another question, "Do you believe he could handle such a situation as that?"

"No, not really; it would be pretty hard," was his answer as he laughed.

At the time it happened, my mother told me she didn't want us to suffer anymore. We weren't really suffering, but she felt we were. She wanted to put us out of our misery so we wouldn't be suffering anymore. The truth was we were home sick, and we were not feeling good. But she overreacted. That was the way she was thinking. After she killed my younger siblings, she committed suicide. At that point, somebody was there. I don't know if it was the police or the paramedics.

When I got back home, the law enforcement wouldn't let me go inside. They asked me what happened and I told them. I had a big gash in my head, and they put a bandage on it. I went to the hospital. I don't know if I went by ambulance or how I got to the hospital.

I never did go back into the house. I suppose my dad took care of everything. I went to live with one of my sisters and then moved from sister to sister until I became an adult. It was difficult moving from one home to another. All of them went along with whatever I wanted to do. They were nice.

My dad lived with us for a while but then got an apartment while I stayed with my other sister. My dad came to see me every once in a while. He picked me up and took me to a drive-in for an hour or so. He seemed a little bit far away at that time. I can't really remember too much. I remember crying; I don't remember really feeling anything. It was kind of like a dream or just that it wasn't happening. My sister said they talked to me, but I can't remember that. I think I'm more withdrawn with people in my life. I don't really want to get too close. It's been difficult to make friends.

One time, my dad took me up to a place called Henry's Lake by Yellowstone Park and he was with his brothers at the time. My cousin and I were staying in the same room and he brought up the topic of my mom and wanted to know, probably out of curiosity, what happened and how I was feeling. I broke down and that is about the only time I ever talked about her suicide. After that, no one talked about it.

I had a mental breakdown five years ago. I went to a psychiatrist and mostly he just let me talk while he asked questions. He prescribed the medications that I am on now. I talked about suicide and I came close that night. He suggested I go into a lock-up unit at the mental institution there. In about three days, they moved me on to the non-secure section, and I had therapy there, which I felt was helpful. The medicine I'm on seems to be working real good as far as anxiety and depression. I think the psychiatrist chose well as far as my medication. I talk much more easily about it now than I did before.

At the time when I was in the hospital, I made a promise to God, well I made a lot of promises in the hospital, but I think that brought me a little bit closer to spirituality. I'm really not a very religious person, but I do believe in God. I made promises and I have kept them in the last five years, and I think that helped.

Without my wife, I don't think I could have made it through it all. She was at the hospital every day with me and she went through some of the sessions with the therapist and me. We talked out some things, too, between ourselves. We ironed out a few things. I told my wife not to call and tell my sisters, but she did anyway and they told her they were on their way. I thought, "Oh man!"

I'm glad my sisters came to see me in the hospital; they answered a lot of questions and told us a lot. I learned that they were feeling those kinds of feelings, too, and they kind of helped me get over it. They filled in quite a bit of what I didn't remember. I think it is a good thing to be more open after something like this happens. People need to talk about it even if they don't want to. My sisters were glad they came down; they were able to share some of their feelings as well. They felt guilty about not sharing their feelings with me before. It's pretty sad when you have to break down forty-some-odd years later and have something like my breakdown happen to get people to talk about it.

My sisters revealed that even before her suicide they felt something was wrong with our mother. They felt she was acting strange for some time, maybe a year. That's why they felt really guilty and bad. They even talked to her doctor who suggested that my mom see a psychiatrist, but my mom refused. Right before it happened, they said she came out of it; she was acting normal and seemed back to her old self again. I have since learned that clearly she was acting more normal because she was feeling better having made her decision.

We wish to emphasize here the observation made by Andrew. Characteristically when a depressed individual makes a decision about suicide (or in this case murder as well), it is typical that s/he may suddenly seem much improved and "normal" overnight in behavior. This frequently may warrant the need for intervention by a mental health professional to determine what is actually going on with this individual.

Roberta and Eddie Tell Their Story

Although this situation relates to the unsuccessful suicide of Bob (father of an infant), we are including it here. Roberta and Eddie, grandparents of this infant, tell about Bob, who reached out for help in his own way. He revealed to his psychiatrist he heard voices telling him to kill his wife and baby. His psychiatrist made a grave breach in judgment by his refusal to believe his patient, a tragic commentary resulting in the subsequent murder of Bob's family. This event needs addressing, because mental health professionals who do not pay attention to their patient's or client's threats to commit such an act are making a huge mistake. The patient or client who expresses violent thoughts must always be taken seriously.

Roberta speaks first:

My stepson, Bob, tried to kill himself. Our daughter-in-law called us and said that he had gone out for a newspaper and just didn't come back. She called about 11p.m., didn't know what happened to him or where he was. The police found him in a motel somewhere after an attempted suicide and transported him to a psychiatric ward. He spoke with the psychiatrist there that night and revealed that he feared he might kill his wife and child. A voice kept telling him to do that and clearly he wanted to be stopped. The psychiatrist told him that he was going to have to face the reality of what he was thinking and what he would do. He did not believe his patient would commit a violent act and told him so. The psychiatrist ended up releasing Bob the next day to go back home to his family. That weekend Bob murdered his wife and baby. I don't know if I could ever find any forgiveness in my heart for this so-called professional who was treating him.

When Judy spoke with this couple, they described more horror that followed. The nightly news spoke of the devastating event in their family for weeks. They dreaded turning their television on and avoided doing it as much as possible. On top of suffering excruciating emotional pain, society heaped more anguish upon them and into their lives. Roberta continues with their story:

We found out who our really good friends were. They were few in number and they were the ones who would just be there if we felt like talking, drop by to see if we needed anything. We did not get much support from my husband's family.

As a matter of fact, his relatives didn't even talk to us after this happened. Some of his first cousins didn't even come near us. People were speechless; our daughter-in-law and granddaughter's murder was such a horrendous thing. We did not have people breaking our door down to comfort us. Many people did not want to be associated with us, just didn't drop by. There were things that we heard later, people said, "We didn't drop by" or "We didn't call, because we didn't know what to say." What hurt more than anything is the fact that relatives, not on my side of the family but on my husband's side of the family, totally disassociated themselves from us. They devoured everything that was in the newspaper and the media. Every time you turned the news on, there were pictures of the murder. We had friends, too, who just stopped calling. Again, as time went by, if we came in contact with one of those people, we just kept getting the word that, "We didn't know what to say." It was just such a frightful thing. There were bad phone calls from strangers telling me I should be dead, because I gave birth to this child. Of course he wasn't my birth child, but it was horrible. We received some awful mail as well. We were so frightened sometimes from the calls and the mail that my husband kept the lights on twenty-four hours a day in the house and all the outside lights on all night. We had an alarm system put in. The news media was knocking on our door, knocking on our neighbors' doors. We didn't talk to anybody, certainly not the news media. They wanted to interview us personally but we wouldn't do it.

We went to a grief group that was being run by a place of worship. This turned out hurtful as well. We were told that maybe we should find another group to go to because the clergy facilitating this group said that our trauma was too horrible and upsetting for the group. He asked us to leave without any suggestions for us as to where to go for help. We found another grief support group on our own run by a different religious congregation and we were able to remain in that group. Everybody there was very understanding and supportive.

Later, we found a therapist who, above all, kept stressing and reminding us over and over that what happened was not our fault. She also told us that the pain does not go away, but we would learn to live with it and she was right.

Eddie interjects at this point:

The fact that others who we considered friends did not acknowledge what happened in our lives was difficult. I belonged to a club in high school and we continued to be friendly with members of this club after I married. I always thought we were friends, but after the murder happened, I heard from none of them and I knew they were aware of the tragedy, because one person in our group was at the police station when it all happened. I knew they all knew what was going on even without looking in a newspaper. They did not respond except for three people who didn't even live in the city. They are the only ones who asked us how we were doing and showed that they cared. However, I came to the conclusion eventually that there was no point in continuing my anger towards my former friends because in another fifty years, it won't make a bit of difference what they did or did not do.

Katherine's Story

Katherine lost her father to suicide when she was seven years of age and shortly after that witnessed her mother's murder:

My mom was murdered five months after my dad committed suicide. I think that some of my thoughts about both deaths blend together. I don't necessarily know that I am able to separate the two because the events were so close together.

My parents were divorced and my mom had married a violent man six months prior to my father's suicide. There is still a question to this day whether my father did or did not take his own life. As a family, it's divided between some that believe he committed suicide and some that believe that he was killed. He was really depressed, and on one hand, my brothers who were living with him at the time believed that he killed himself. On the other hand, he was shot in the right side of the head and he was left-handed. The coroner ruled it suicide, and legally, that is how the reason for his death stands in the community, but it is definitely in question. I vacillate between believing whether it was suicide or murder. I think I finally reached the point that I don't really care about the cause anymore. What I find painful is the fact that he is dead no matter how he died.

I believe that everybody around me talked about my dad's violent death, because it is something I just knew but no one to date has ever looked at me and said, "Your father committed suicide." I have newspaper clippings; I have death certificates. But as an adult, I have looked back over all that and have attempted to talk to my older brothers about what they saw, what they knew and what was occurring. I'm among the youngest of the brothers and sisters. My oldest sibling has a perspective of what was going on different from mine. He had almost an adult perspective of things, how he viewed the situation versus how a seven-year-old viewed it.

As far down the totem pole as I am, I am probably the most vocal of everyone about pulling out issues in our family system. Sometimes my family just puts their heads down when they see me coming. I have a great bunch of brothers and sisters considering all we have gone through, but they also know that I am the voice of the family and they are accustomed to that. I'm the one who is going to see the problem, voice it and put it on the table. I also have to be very, very respectful of their feelings. One good thing is that my brothers and sisters and I talk about our parents' deaths. I am not married. My siblings' spouses are not included during our discussions. I am the one the spouses approach and say, "You know, I have been married to your brother for ten years and he doesn't say anything to me." I am the one to include them and answer their questions.

I think it depends on where everybody is at a certain point in their lives and the fact that everyone has done a different amount of work on this tragedy. The older ones carry a lot of responsibility that doesn't belong to them and they don't let outside people into their pain. The reason why they let me and our other siblings in is because we share the same history and can understand. Their spouses have told me that my siblings' responses are, "You don't know what it is like; I won't tell you, because you have never had this experience and you won't be able to understand." But they share their pain with me to a degree and occasionally they say, "I cannot go there" or "I cannot talk about it." Emotionally they cannot deal, even all these years later.

I think I am generated by guilt. I mean, honestly, my dad had asked me to come live with him; my parents had separated and I said, "No." I am the only surviving witness to my mom's murder and nobody knew that for years. I felt at times that it was my fault that all of this happened and so therefore I must fix it. I tore the family apart; I've got to bring them back together again. That's what has generated my being the spokesperson of the family. With time, you know your perspective of the world changes, and as an adult, you see things a little bit differently. That's when I realized it wasn't my fault, but then I also realized that because I sought out healing, I am so many steps ahead of my other siblings and have a sense of responsibility to hand them a little bit of healing here and there.

I think that most of my siblings and I are very strong-willed; my older brothers talk a lot about how very determined and strong-willed I was as a kid. I think it was because my environment started out a little more secure even though it became rocky afterward. I was surrounded by a bunch of kids. I was talking to a friend of mine this week about her daughter going to first grade and how terrified she was, and I looked at her and said, "I had the opposite reaction. I used to cry and get mad at my mom for not letting me go to school; I am one of the kids who ran to my classes." I had all these older brothers and sisters who were going to school everyday where they were apparently having fun. I wasn't the first kid having to go to a strange place and separate from my mom.

My siblings and I became separated after mother's death, between one being drafted into military service, others going off to college and then each of the younger kids moving in with other family members. It's fascinating to see this huge family today, because almost all of us own our own businesses. We're all pretty strong individuals. The older ones initiated trying to find all their brothers and sisters and bring us back together again. The oldest were mature enough to stay in contact with each other. They found me and, of course, I had access to the rest of the family they were looking for.

As a child, I never told the police about what I had seen the night of my mother's death. They came and spoke with me, but I said nothing. I was scared. I was the witness so I knew without a doubt. I didn't tell the police until six years ago and it did not make any difference six years ago because my stepfather was dead anyway. I learned he committed suicide twelve years after killing my mother. I thought, "What a coward!" Part of me felt good, because evidently what he had done bothered him. My stepfather never was convicted of my mother's murder, because there never was a body found. Everything was at the crime scene but if they couldn't find the body, there was no crime. They never found her. This is how bad it was. We just wish we could find and bury her.

The suicide and murder have affected my relationships with men. It dramatically affected my life. I'm older now and have gone through this healing process, but it's almost too late. It impacted me severely at an important stage in my life. It made me extremely determined to become financially independent so I would never have to live through the issues my mother had to experience.

I was an extremely spiritual child. We didn't go to church all the time. It wasn't that, so I'm not necessarily sure where I got my God concept as a kid. But as an adult looking back I remember I prayed every day. I was terrified of the man who lived on the corner, and I had to walk by his house on the way to school. I prayed to God every day not to let that man kill me. Lo and behold, it was the man in my house that I should have been worried about. But as I look back on it, I wonder if my own prayer didn't save me, because my stepfather could have killed me as well. After all, I was the only witness. So spiritually, I really do think this prayer just kind of went with me. I have spent a great deal of time reading books and trying to understand God. It has impacted my relationship with God because back then I thought God hated me and that this was my punishment. For the longest time, that had to be restructured; I had to learn a lot more about grace in my life. I didn't have it. Yes, spiritually, this did have an impact.

But everything was like a really nightmarish dream. My oldest sister saved everything and among all her stuff were my little drawings showing my stepfather killing my mom. Nobody picked up on it. Looking back at what I was like as a kid, I can say, "Oh my God." I remember doing little rituals with my dolls. I had the dolls, you know, that you pulled the string and they would talk. When they started to fess up, they would have to die and I would bury them.

It really boggles my mind that nobody bothered to get any of us counseling. If a murder-suicide happened in my family today, I'd be the first one saying that the child is going into counseling. I have a different view of grief than most. My view is you don't ever get over it. It doesn't ever go away. It's not like I'm going to wake up one morning and go, "Oh gosh, this loss, this feeling of loss that I have in my heart for my mom and my dad is gone." It's like having a huge scar on your body after an accident; this scar is not going away. The books I have read about suicide don't say that. At times you don't notice it. Yes, years later the intensity of the feelings isn't anywhere as great. My best friend of thirty years lost her father recently. Her pain of being without her father brought mine up. It reminded me that I don't have much pain anymore but it reminded me, "Ah, I don't have a father." I am not saying just lie on the floor and be unable to work for the rest of your life; I don't believe that, but I think it's false thinking that the pain goes away completely and normalcy comes in. Every time I go to a wedding, when somebody has a baby or at family gatherings, it's really apparent to me that I have no parents. My parents are grandparents and great-grandparents and don't even know it. That still comes up and is rarely expressed.

As far as children, I feel people think all too frequently that if no one talks about what happened, then it won't be painful for the child. In reality, the child needs to be able to talk about the tragic event. I had a huge need to talk about what happened. I also had huge nonverbal and verbal information coming back that you don't talk about this. I learned real quickly that what I needed was considered unacceptable. The message was not to talk about my parents' violent deaths with my friends or their families and that my family didn't want to hear about it either. I learned that if I told a child who in turn told his or her parent, then I would find myself without a playmate.

The only thing I haven't said is that I pretty much raised myself. I remember thinking when all of this happened that I needed to close my eyes and get through the next ten years and then I could take charge of my life. I told myself that eighteen was the age. Because I lost my parents, I trusted nobody else and forbade anyone to touch or get near me. Their murder and suicide changed me in that way. It also made me really, really determined to raise myself, to get an education and take care of myself.

Judy reveals, "I too decided that all I had to do was to survive, remain sane and grow up, that my life would get better. And actually, I did just that. I had a whole lot of work to do, but my life got considerably better and has continued to do so."

Mia tells, "That was my experience too. I believed that once I could get in control of my life, then I could control whether it would be happy or not. Until that day, I would wait and wait and wait. First, I earned a little control at sixteen when I got a car and that was a little bit of freedom and then at eighteen I became responsible for myself."

Overview

Earlier, we discussed the ramifications of the death of a parent and then proceeded to explore the additional hurdles that children of suicidal parents have to overcome. Among the important topics we've focused on are trust issues and the stigma afflicted by society upon the survivor.

In this chapter, we discussed the feelings, attitudes and issues faced by the survivor of suicide of both parents and murder/suicide. This chapter looks at these instances among all ages of survivors, from childhood through adulthood. The trust issues and stigma the survivor must face in the case of multiple events such as those brought up by survivors of doubly tragic events is enormous and, in many instances, lifelong. The amount of chaos and disruption imposed upon families and friends when a single suicide occurs multiplies when we discuss suicides of both parents or murder/suicide. In some families, there were multiple suicides including parent and child/ren or aunts and uncles, grandparents etc. However, we have concentrated on two types of events: parent suicide of both parents and murder/suicide with the exception of Roberta and Eddie. We included their story, because it stresses the necessity of listening, hearing and taking seriously the words of a clinically depressed, distraught or mentally ill person.

Through survivors of multiple tragedies, we see that the situations are shattering. Those who tell their stories here have gone beyond survival. They are rebuilding their lives and have made the choices to not repeat the legacy that was passed on to them. They are either already thriving or working towards that goal. We believe these stories are an inspiration to others.

■ ■ ■

PART II

Immediate and Later Consequences

■ ■ ■

Whether the suicide of a parent is revealed to a son or daughter immediately after it has happened or when that child is confronted with the information years or decades after the incident, there are usually dilemmas and traumas to be faced: Who can I turn to? Where do I go for help? Does anyone really care? What can I do to survive this? Children of any age who are faced with the suicide of a parent are presented with so many conflicting emotions, directions and suggestions that they are in some ways separated from the world and their own sense of logic.

These questions are not answered easily, but it is our hope and intent to guide the shocked child (at any age) and to find people who will help him or her to feel acceptance, solace and security.

It is frequently not until some time after the act of suicide that offspring can realize they are not alone and that this has happened to others. For survivors, they tread on a vast and tangled road until they can accept that their parent's act has changed their lives and their future. The demands and restrictions on how to act, what to say or do and who to confide in is colored by the fact that they were "abandoned" by someone who was supposed to be there to provide love, care and guidance.

It is not until after we have gone through a trying and complicated situation and had time to reflect on it that we see how each and every important incident in life has in some way made us the person we are now.

My family experience did not include suicide but it did include two great losses: the deaths of an adult son and an infant daughter. These were not planned nor created incidents but a part of life. They influence both me and my family and help us to understand that these happenings occur.

Harold Servetnick

CHAPTER 5

The First to Respond

For most survivors, the shock of learning of their parents' suicides (either by witnessing it or hearing about the act from someone else) is something that remains forever locked and active in their memories. Frequently, shock causes survivors to respond without any emotion attached. They can talk in great detail as to the specifics of when they first found out their parents had taken their lives. The smallest sensory detail of a particular smell, sight and/or sound is what sticks in the mind of the survivor, very probably a lifetime. Thus, we believe it is crucial that those anonymous individuals we call "first responders" (coroner, chaplain, firemen, paramedics, sheriff, detective and police), who are at the initial scene, be trained professionals who can be sensitive and responsive to survivors who are present.

When we talked a second or more times to our participants, we asked if they dealt with any first responders. If they did, we wanted to know how they, their family or whoever was at the suicide scene experienced it. Almost three-quarters of the survivors said they either weren't at the initial scene, they were too young and it didn't apply to them or they felt indifferent to the whole experience. Of our remaining participants, half felt they were treated sensitively and the other half felt they were not. The first to respond on the scene of a suicide has an enormous task, we feel, to assess the situation thoroughly, while simultaneously addressing the needs of whoever is present. It is an emotional and tragic event for all involved.

Ambur, fourteen years of age at the time of mother's suicide, reveals:

When I was in the police car, I kept asking the policeman what happened, can you please tell me what happened, and he wouldn't tell me. He just said, "We will get you home, and the people there can tell you what happened." I was absorbed in my own thoughts, my own imagination until we actually got to the house. I don't feel like he was trying to shut me up; I felt like he actually was uncomfortable. He was a neutral figure. I felt like I wanted his answers, but he was like this blank wall just sitting there.

Elsie, forty at the time of her father's suicide, tells her reaction to the first responders:

Very blunt, no compassion or caring or kindness. Very cut-and-dried answers, sometimes I felt like there was some secret, something they didn't want me to know. I felt as if we were taking up their time. As far as they were concerned, suicide was the only word or information we needed.

Lorraine, twenty at the time of mother's suicide, states:

All I remember is that they seemed very business-like and were all about taking care of business, collecting the suicide notes, asking perfunctory questions and asking if we would want the gun she shot herself with... that wasn't too pleasant.

Shelby, twenty-nine at the time of her father's suicide, says:

I know that in the instance of my father's death, the police told my sister, "We have the gun here if anyone wants to pick it up." Then they told her, "We are ruling this an accident. We liked your father a lot." I think they were trying to do something nice that I knew wasn't true. I knew they were making an effort to do something nice for my dad's family because they liked my dad. And so it was printed up in the newspaper that it was an accident.

Cara, thirty at the time of her father's suicide, discusses her feelings:

Family never spoke about the law enforcement being upsetting or anything. I think that whole thing was a sort of a blur to them. Even though I wasn't there, I can say that one thing that isn't helpful on the part of law enforcement is that they left the mess there for us to clean up. They come and investigate and then leave with all the mess for family to clean up. At least they could help to make some arrangement to take care of that and not leave that for the family to have to do. Friends of ours cleaned up the mess. I don't think that is anything that any of us had to do.

On the other hand, Erin, age nineteen at the time of mother's suicide, felt differently from Cara:

A detrimental and bothering experience came from the initial talk with the chaplain involved with my case. She returned the call the day that it happened, and when we started to talk, her main concern was how I was going to clean up the mess that my mother had left when she shot herself. The chaplain was concerned with me hiring a service in the Yellow Pages that would clean the bathtub. She was letting me know the prices of like three hundred to four hundred dollars. I could have cared less about the bathroom at that time. That was some advice that she should have given only if I had asked for it. That was very uncalled for and made things more gruesome for the moments that I was on the phone. I thanked her for her time and never called her again.

Survivors have different needs and expectations from first responders. Some may not want law enforcement to cover up the suicide for the family's sake and someone else might wish for the first responder to do so. There are those who want help with the cleanup and others who resent it. Some first responders are more sensitive than others. Obviously not any one person can do their own job and always satisfy, or even partially satisfy, the survivor as well. The job of the police is to assess and determine if in fact the death was a suicide. Then they must preserve the evidence and control the scene. We don't feel that it is necessarily their job to assist the survivors with the emotional realities of their parents' suicides. We advocate that on any suspected suicide call that's received through 911, a staff psychologist is also sent out on that call to specifically handle the family members. In addition to this, we propose that policemen and women receive some basic training in the ways to answer questions of family members at a suicide scene and also be prepared to direct them to the appropriate community resources.

Lastly, we believe it would be best if the family did not have to take responsibility for the cleanup after a suicide. While it might be the family's duty to pay for this service, we hope that the survivors could be given a list of resources of whom to call and perhaps some assistance in doing this from a police department trauma counselor. Many police departments have a staff psychologist or some other such person who is trained to accompany first responders who can be of assistance to survivors. We found one such national organization currently operating in sixteen states. Crime Scene Cleaners, Inc. was established in 1996 and operates twenty-four hours a day, seven days a week. They are licensed, bonded and insured and state that they "can handle problems quickly, properly and discreetly with full attention to health, legal and regulatory issues." Across the country, there are other firms that offer similar services.

Helpful Experiences
Two participants appreciated the empathy of the coroners involved.

Allison, forty-six at the time of her father's suicide, says:

The male coroner who came to my home left the female coroner at our house and he just left. She was there all alone for the majority of the evening with us. It was after hours and she was very, very good. She asked us if we wanted a chaplain to come in. She did certain things for me that I asked. I wanted my dad's ring, and she went in and got it. She also gave me her telephone number, and I did call her afterwards once or twice. I saw the male coroner again because of the way I am in wanting answers. I got a court order to get into the records at the police station and to be able to view everything. And one time when I went in there, he happened to be the one who waited on me. He recognized me as I did him. He sat there for over an hour with me in one of the rooms and went over everything. He answered questions and went over all of it with me thoroughly. This helped tremendously. Not only that, but I still have his phone number. We have a group called "Surviving Our Loss After Suicide." He came to our group one night and spoke.

Cynthia, twenty-five at the time of her mother's suicide, tells:

The coroner was very nice actually. I can remember him. He asked how I was doing, and "This must have been a hard thing for you to go through, sorry you have to come here and see this and release this gun, but you know it's part of your property now, as your mom's property, and we need to know if you want the gun or if you want to release the gun." I said I didn't want it. And he said, "Well, you can sign this release and what we do is destroy the gun." I remember at the end after I signed it, because I was a little bit emotional and everything, he said, "You just remember to take care of yourself, okay?" He was real nice.

Interview with a First Responder

We interviewed D.T. Amos, who was a Criminal Investigator for the state of Texas and is a retired Chief Investigator for the Leon County Sheriff's office. We asked him about his training, his experiences of suicide calls and if and how he could address the needs of the survivors. The actual interview of D.T. Amos is cited because we believe this is the best way to relay his information.

In your education as a police officer, did you receive preparation to question people who have lost a family member, friend or neighbor to suicide?

People desiring to be a police officer must first attend a police academy and complete required training hours. Dealing with suicide is not one of the areas included in the curriculum. The law enforcement academy alone is simply to give the tentative police officer all the information and education that he needs to pass the exam to become a police officer. There is a lot of education available after that in terms of training classes and courses. They are given by various groups (hospitals sometimes; chaplains; others dealing with suicide and/or family death). The training is available in larger departments; but in the smaller departments, there is not much training at all.

Are any of those classes required by your department?

None are required. Most of the required courses in training are going to deal with police activity; how to process a crime scene, for example.

So they would be voluntary if an officer wanted to attend?

Yes, and there are a lot of courses out there and training classes like that for police officers. Academies will give those and they will put out newsletters of where, what and when, and they can be taken for credit.

What would you like to see the police academy offer in the

investigation of suicides and homicides?

They offer homicide investigations, but remember an academy goes across the whole spectrum of law enforcement, all the way from what we would call here in Texas the Penal Code, the Code of Criminal Procedure, traffic laws, all of that. The academy acquaints you with that, juvenile laws etc., basic crime scene investigation techniques. But in terms of what it really takes to investigate homicides and suicides will never be obtained in the academy. Of course, training courses are available. That is done through years of experience and on-the-job training, training courses that you can take and classes that you go to. Basically within the academy itself, there is probably very little that trains you to investigate homicides and suicides.

Do you think the academy should change that policy or include some sort of mandatory training?

No, I really think it needs to stay like it is. There are introductory courses. In other words, when you are going through the academy, you will get to see an autopsy. To do a homicide investigation or a suicide investigation, it takes a lot of in-depth type of training. Every suicide that I have investigated, I treat first as a homicide. I have over two thousand hours of training above and beyond what's in the academy: the training of how to investigate homicides, things to look for, what to do and what not to do. To come to the conclusion of a suicide is usually the last thing unless it's quite obvious.

How common is it for family members to try to get police officers to cover up and determine another cause other than suicide, i.e. life insurance issues or cover up for any other reason (clergy suicides)? Does this ever occur and how do you handle it?

Part of that is because of the stigma attached to suicide. The answer is, "Oh, yes." In my own investigations, I have had requests to reopen a case. I have had lawyers contact me to reopen a case, for example, to see if there isn't another conclusion. Maybe I didn't cover all the bases; maybe there are extenuating circumstances; maybe there are things I overlooked. In some instances, yes, I've had that.

How do you handle that?

As gently and as firmly as I can at that point because there are those who would question your ability to do the investigation. The insinuation seems to be that I don't know what I am doing or that I don't know my job. I never took it that way, but when the request comes you have to handle it. I had one case in which the person shot himself, but his wife was in the room at the time. That was one of those situations that I was 99 percent sure it might have been a suicide, but there was a question that it could have been a homicide. There were a couple things that were not quite right. After it was over and we got the autopsy back, my report said self-inflicted gunshot wound, and when the autopsy report came back, it said the same thing. You look at a lot of things for forensic reasons. In the case I spoke of, the wife claimed that her husband did shoot himself, but that it was an accident.

When a suicide happens, what part does law enforcement get into and not get into with respect to cleaning up after the scene?
When we get a report of a suicide, EMS will get the same report. But they will never enter a suicide scene until law enforcement goes in first, particularly if there is a gun involved or any situation where there has been a weapon involved. One of the reasons they do that is because if there is any kind of a crime involved, such as a homicide, people in there can corrupt a crime scene. So EMS will always wait for law enforcement to get there. The first responsibility is to secure the scene, keep people out who should not be in and make sure no one else gets in to corrupt the crime scene. We also want to get photographs: photograph the position of the body, photograph where the weapon is if there is a weapon, what it is, where it is and any other things that are around. That is the first thing that we do, and as soon as the scene is secure and there is no danger, EMS will come in. If there is any attempt to do any kind of medical assistance to the victim, then they will do that. As far as cleaning up on the scene, we never consider that our responsibility. We will clean up our part, but as far as cleaning up the mess as one of the participants said in the survey, we don't do that. Our primary function is to treat the scene either as a crime scene or a suicide and do our function as law enforcement, basically determine the cause.

We've heard about this national company, Crime Scene Cleaners. We contacted them (the Chicago company), and they sent us their brochure. Do you have any agencies in Texas that you know of that you would contact to clean up the scene if there was a homicide or suicide?
I don't know of any. We knew of no one who would do that. For one thing, cleaning that part up, some of it needs to go with the remains to see if there was any reason for it as they go through all that. Basically, it is family members and whoever they want to get to clean up the scene. Sometimes we don't want

the scene cleaned up right away; we are still doing the investigation. We may come back the next day when it is light and we want to take some pictures. If something happened at night, we want to get some pictures. We will tape it off at the crime scene and we will go back the next day with our cameras and with other forensic equipment.

Because participants spoke of that as traumatic for them, and obviously it would be, we asked for further information. In Mia's mother's situation, she wasn't found for several days so there was some cleaning up to do after she passed. Do you think it would be appropriate and beneficial for first responders to give family members a pamphlet of companies who offer a cleaning service?

I think so. I think something needs to be done that way, because one thing we do for family violence is that anytime I have been out to a call where there has been some violence to the victim, we leave them information as to who they can call, safe houses, child advocacy centers, where they can get help, also the victim's help that comes from the state. There is state help for the victims. There are brochures put together that we have to give to the victims at that point. I think a brochure like that that would give help and assistance would be in order to hand over to the victims of suicide. The victims are the ones who are left behind. We just never put one together and didn't really consider that our basic responsibility to do that.

What approaches do you use in an investigation? How do you obtain the needed information with as little trauma to the survivors as necessary?

Everything is different. One thing, as we look at it, we want to get as much information as we can as quickly as possible, to get statements of what happened while it is still fresh on someone's mind. In one particular suicide, I went there and the boyfriend was there and there were some suspicious things about that, a lot of drinking going on and other things. I said, "I need to get statements," so while she was in the emergency room, I sat him down and told him I needed him to write out a statement. I asked him to put his thoughts down as they came to him and told him to tell me what happened. I didn't want to put words in his mouth; I can't do that. So I told him to tell me what led up to this. So I got a statement from him right away and that is the first one that is there. Down the line, they may change it. In fact, he did. We got another statement that didn't quite match up to what he had said to begin with. Also, then we questioned other people, "Did you know this person? Did you have contact with them? Did you have any inclination that they were having difficulties or whatever?"

In another situation, a strange one where the wife was there, the husband had planned a fishing trip for the next day with a friend of his, which was unusual. The friend said the deceased called him the night before and said tomorrow afternoon he wanted to go fishing, where he wished to go and they made plans. I got a statement from the friend. Now, is this reasonable for someone who is planning a fishing trip? That evening in the house there were some arguments going on because the man had made a video of himself in bed with another woman and the wife found the video. There were arguments going on and, this is one of my premises that I think, she pulled the trigger. I got statements from her and statements from others as quickly as I could.

Again, each situation that I go to is totally different. There is no ABCD to follow. I had to treat that situation a little bit different from the person who found them. "How did you find him? Where were you coming from? What led you here? Was it a phone call or do you usually visit here that time of day? What made you come here?" You want to get as many witnesses as you can, if there are witnesses to it, to find out all the details because that will have a bearing on whether it will be investigated further as a homicide or a suicide. Talking to family members is difficult. A lot of it depends on the age. This one particular lady, she was absolutely angry with him because of the video that she found. She found herself in an interesting position that she had a motive. We had to get a statement from her and then his daughters from another marriage who were there. Then we start putting all this together.

As far as dealing with the grief, we try to be as gentle as we can. My approach is I always take someone with me; sometimes depending on the situation, I will take a female deputy with me. Usually one will ask the questions and the other one sits and takes notes as you do it. We start out with the verbal end of it. We never take a piece of paper and shove it in front of somebody. You sit down and gently start talking and say, "I know this is extremely difficult for you to go through all this, with the trauma that you faced. It's important for us to find out all the details at this point and we really need your help in doing this." You begin to talk to them, and then I would ask them, "Would you be willing to put this down on a piece of paper? Would you be willing to do this statement?" If they say, "No, I just can't do this now," I say, "Well then let me ask you some questions" and the other deputy, while I am asking the questions, is writing information down. "What time did you find this person? Where were you at that time? What were you doing?" We get times and dates and then the other deputy will be writing that down. I'll be asking the questions or I will write them down if they are not comfortable with writing on a piece of paper. The reason you take two is to get away from the business of "he said, she said." That is a real critical situation at times. I always try to get something on a piece of paper simply because if I do a report from notes and if it ever comes into a court situation, the person may say, "I never said that." "Well yes you did." "Well, I never said it. You put it down that way but I didn't say it." To me, getting a written statement is crucial in any kind of an ongoing investigation, even when it appears that it is obviously a suicide.

In one instance, we got a call for a suicide; the guy had run out in the morning and he was sitting on the edge by the driveway. He had been drinking beer and he had taken a 9mm. semi-automatic, put it in his mouth and pulled the trigger. His sister found him that afternoon about five so the question at that point was did he really do that? Is there somebody else that was there? When the gun went off, where did the shell go? We looked for that; we know what kind of an ejection takes place out of a weapon. We look for the angle of that. Each one is different. But being with the individual itself, we just try to be as gentle as we can. That is why we are very concerned about who does the interviews in suicides, because some of them can be pretty rough.

How would you approach children in questioning them about the apparent suicide of their parent?

There are two ways to do that, depending on whether it is a girl or a boy. Little girls are tending to be intimidated by uniforms. As an investigator, I always wore street clothes. When I left patrol and went to investigations, I never wore uniforms; I wore street clothes. I always had a gun on and a badge, but street clothes are not quite as intimidating as a uniform. Sometimes, we would take the child to a child advocacy center, which are normally focused on child sexual assaults, but they are trained people who know how to deal with children in a comfortable environment. We would tape them. The difficulty is with trauma of children and their having to tell their story over and over and over again. This is very traumatic for a child. So we take them to a child advocacy center and would go to a room where there are teddy bears and it's just a comfortable family thing like that. The session is videotaped. We watch the video on both sides and they don't know we're watching it and we can also do the audio. We put on ear phones and the person who is doing the interacting with the child will gently go through the questioning of the child and what happened. They are trained to do that with the children and I am not. I am trained to mostly go for the throat. After that is done, then the child has told the story one time and it's on tape. That becomes part of the investigative package. If the child is older and they are willing to talk, then it is a little bit different. But you get a four or five or six-year-old who sees somebody blow their brains out, it's not pretty. It would take specific training for a police officer to be able to deal with a child who has actually seen it happen. There may be some officers who can, but there are other ways to deal with children. Female officers are very good at that.

Does all this require different training?

Absolutely! A lot of that is specialized. When one goes through the law enforcement academy, everything is general. I have had special training in homicide and child sexual assault. I guess I have two to three hundred hours of training just in homicide and that much, if not more, in investigating child sexual assault. That takes specialized training and when that happens, they get on your pager with "We need you." Dealing with adult children and spouses is difficult. You do the same where one officer talks with them and the other takes notes. The deputy taking notes is unobtrusive so that there is no distraction as to what he is writing down because you are focused face–to-face with the one giving the report. For this technique that you learn, again it's a call of what the scene is, what the situation is, who is there and who is not there.

What would you include in a list of what to do and what not to do for a police officer/detective for questioning survivors?

It depends a lot on how the person views law enforcement and how law enforcement views their function. Like, "Lady, I am here to do a job, get out of my way." Some of them are like that and there is not much you can do about it, because in agencies, that is there. My advice would be that they have special people in suicides that they call for the investigation. Normally in larger departments, it would be part of what they call CID (Criminal Investigations Division) to do this instead of sending a street deputy whose primary job is wrestling drunks and doing drug busts. Don't send them to the suicide because they are not really equipped to handle this. This takes special training. That would be my advice there. Any advice that I would give to an officer going in is, "Secure the scene." Make sure no one gets in and no one gets out until we get there and begin to forensic the crime scene itself. That's my advice, as well as to not even talk to the survivor. Leave that up to the people who are trained to do that and the investigations, the criminal investigators. Don't start taking witness statements or anything like that. If they want to do that, say, "Ma'am or Sir, I am here to do this. We have some people coming that will answer your questions for you at that point." A lot of times they come up and ask us, "Why did they do this, how could they do this?" Our job is not to answer that. That's when the officer should say, "We have some people coming that can answer these questions; right now my responsibility is to do this. I'm so sorry."

I know one person who died from a tractor accident, and his wife was DRT (dead right there). When we got there, he acted like almost nothing happened. He was in shock. He didn't know what was going on; he was talking and there was his wife out there underneath that tractor. So violent death hits different people in different ways and the training that you have, I think it is important to read that and pick your response on how you deal with that. We had the statements in hand, and he was in no condition at that point to give a statement. Down the line there's got to be some kind of advocacy for the survivors. "Who can we call, who can help us? Who understands suicide and homicide?"

What specific questions might you ask in determining whether the death was a suicide or a homicide?

It isn't particularly asking the questions. We get statements and then we start putting things together. We get statements and start asking questions like, "Where were you? Where was he? What were you doing at the time that this happened? Where were you standing? Where was your child?" We get the immediate information first. Then we begin to forensic the scene and start looking at angles. If the gun had not shown that there was a contact wound on one person, I would have gone for homicide but there was a contact wound. We start looking at where the body fell, blood splatter and where pieces of that went. How tall is the man? We check out the angle where the bullet hit. Label where the holes are from the bullets. When we look at the angle and where things hit, then we can determine exactly where he was standing and how he was facing at that point. "Does that match up with what the person said?" So as we forensic the scene, we start putting all these things together. Then we start asking the questions. We begin to see some inconsistencies and things like that. When we are first there, we want to know who, what, when, where, why and how. Then to determine whether it was either a homicide or a suicide will come after we do the forensics and do other statements, other investigations and then come to the conclusion at that point. We wait for the autopsy report with the pictures. We want to get that back and see if there was anything else involved. What was the alcohol content of the body? Was this guy drunk when he did that or did he have any alcohol at all? Did she say they were drinking? Did she say he didn't have any alcohol in him? How many beers did he have? Those questions of determination come at a later point. Match up the story with the facts. Was it really suicide? There is a whole lot more work to it than is seen on TV. We then question what hasn't been done.

Do you have any comments about our participants' experiences? (Criminal Investigator D.T. Amos had just reviewed responses to our questions concerning first responders on our participants' surveys.)

Every agency handles violent death differently; I don't know where these surveys came from. I remember one that said law enforcement never showed up; that was a strange one. However, I think it is pretty typical of law enforcement people who don't have a clue on how to handle homicide/suicide situations.

What questions should we have asked that we did not ask?

Do we like to go to those things? No. No we don't, because we are dealing with death a lot of times and we are dealing with trauma and victims. We are around fatalities and accidents. We are around a lot of dead people in all kinds of circumstances and situations. Everyone has their own niche; it's sort of an intuitive thing. To be an investigator, one needs a lot of patience for the long-run and it is boring; it's boring in terms of doing the investigation. We get a lot of phone calls and take some abuse but that is part of the job. It's putting the thing together and is a lot of writing, a lot of reports and a lot of thinking. That's why it's always good to have a team to work it through together. We both catch what the other misses. It is very, very precise. On one suicide case, there were a lot of phone calls made, and we started getting phone records, the timing on the phone records. He says he called at eight and the phone record says six, so what was he doing during those two hours? Was it light or dark? If one is a good chess player, then that person would make a good investigator.

Overview

In the situation of a violent death such as suicide or murder, usually the first to arrive at the scene of the crime are police officers. Certainly others respond as well, such as the EMS, but they never enter a suicide scene until the police go in first, to prevent corrupting the crime scene. It is important that first and foremost the police are there to do a criminal investigation. Survivors to whom we spoke went through the gamut of experiences with these responders, ranging from bluntness and no compassion to business-like to sensitivity in their ways of dealing with survivors. It became evident from our interviews that many survivors expected various responder services that simply were not realistic.

D.T. Amos, the criminal investigator to whom we spoke, revealed what police look for at the scene of a violent death. He states that first and foremost he starts out the investigation of suicide as a homicide. The scene needs to be secured and information needs to be obtained as quickly as possible. As difficult as it may be for survivors to be questioned at the death scene, it is necessary that the investigation begin immediately. In the case of children, the most ideal situation is for them to be taken to a child advocacy center where there are trained professionals to gently question them and videotape their interviews.

Though the tasks of first responders differ, and we need to be aware of these, the need for sensitivity in handling survivors should be a major consideration. The first effects of a parental suicide on survivors are traumatic and long-lasting. Our hopes are that first responders will be responsive and effective in carrying out their duties but also sensitive to the feelings and needs of those directly affected by the tragedy of parental suicide.

CHAPTER 6

Life in a Fishbowl

■ ■ ■

Toward the end of her aunt's life, Judy asked her aunt to describe what she could recall about Judy's mother's funeral. It was not a story Judy had heard before because her aunt had always refused to even talk about the suicide:

You know what bothered me after your mother's funeral? After the funeral, nobody made a cup of coffee, there was nobody to make a tray and they didn't bring food in. It was so awful. Usually when someone dies, I think you have to have food when you come back from the cemetery; you need something good, you know what I mean? No one made anything. And I always felt so bad about that. Anyway, I still remember people sitting on the balcony on the porch, you know, sitting on the banister watching. Not a soul came back to the house to see us afterwards and all that, not even family. They went back to their own houses. The whole thing wasn't good. When there is a suicide, people don't bother with you much. First of all, they don't know how you are taking it so they don't show up.

Judy responds:

My aunt passed away one month after this conversation, three days before Thanksgiving. She was buried the day before Thanksgiving, and I was fortunate to catch a flight to Pennsylvania on a very busy day for airlines to attend her funeral. My aunt and I concluded our conversation through her final act on her funeral day. The reception after her funeral was to be held at my cousins' home, and when I made the offer to contribute financially for the reception dinner after her funeral, I learned that my aunt had already attended to this matter. She had made provisions with her attorney to provide money from her own estate for trays and, of course, many cups of coffee after her funeral.

Mia recalls the day of her mother's funeral:

After my mother's funeral, friends of hers and my father returned to his condominium for a reception. But later that night, he returned my siblings and me to my stepmother's house for a party with her friends. In my mind, people seemed to be celebrating that my mother was finally gone! It was an extremely surreal experience to have seen my mother's coffin that morning at our church, left it at the cemetery and then to be surrounded by strangers in my stepmother's house who were listening to loud music, laughing, drinking, smoking and acting like it was any other weekday.

My father had gotten married eight months prior to my mother's suicide to a widow whose three children had played with my siblings and had baby-sat me while we were growing up. We lived around the corner from their house. Obviously, my father and she were not planning on sharing seven children when they agreed to marry. But here I was with my three older siblings literally on my new stepmother's doorstep. The history between her and my mother was a tumultuous one, and my stepmother was not exactly pleased to have my mother's children under her roof as constant reminders of my father's deceased ex-wife.

My stepmother refused to allow me to put up any pictures of my mother in my room, because she didn't want a "shrine" to my mother in her house. Six months after I moved in, my brothers and I expressed an interest to go to an annual convention of the society my mother had started to be there when they presented the first award in her name to one of their members. My stepmother thought that was ridiculous and told us it had been six months, we needed to stop mourning and get over it.

My next six years of living in that house were filled with drugs and alcohol being consumed by everyone around me; my parents, my siblings, my step siblings and me. We all had our own private pain, but couldn't share it in a healthy way, either alone or with each other. The anger, denial and lack of empathetic emotions in that house suffocated me. I couldn't wait to leave at eighteen and go to college. So, I put off dealing with my mother's suicide until then. I didn't have any other choice. It was all I could do to get through those six years without really hurting myself.

Suicide is a reality from which most people would like to run as fast as they can, never turn back and have to look at the tragedy again. It is an incredibly agonizing event for many family members and others who were close to the person who committed suicide. However, this need to escape makes many members of our society not console or help the survivors in such times. Oftentimes, the survivors are ignored and treated poorly as they try to cope with a loved one's suicide. We like to see ourselves today as more evolved. We like to believe that society does not shun the families and friends of the suicide victim as was done generations ago. We believe we have moved forward in our sensitivities toward sufferers of tragedy, and in many ways, we have. However, in many ways we have not.

While it cannot be honestly claimed that our society is free of the stigma of being a survivor of suicide, we certainly have come a long way from past generations. Property and possessions are no longer seized from the families of suicide victims as was done in centuries past. In most cases, suicide victims are no longer buried outside the cemeteries. Society as a whole tends to be more sensitive towards family survivors of suicide victims instead of condemning them and ostracizing them from their social groups. Still, on some occasions, as experienced by some men and women with whom we spoke, and Judy and Mia as well, they have suffered many situations in which this punitive attitude arises when a family member kills him or herself.

In this chapter we will discuss:

- Results of our survey about the people in our participants' lives who were supportive, and also on those who were not supportive, of the survivors after the suicide.

- People in the lives of our participants whom they are able to talk to when their need arises to share their thoughts and feelings.

- What was said or done by others that was both helpful and unhelpful for the survivors. These findings include family, friends and acquaintances, with the exception of clergy, therapists and first responders, since they are discussed in separate chapters.

Most Supportive Elements and People

We asked our participants who in their family and community were the strongest support to them after the suicide.

- Twenty-six participants were students at the time of the suicide and many spoke of their teachers. Jill W. was one person who brought up the positive teacher support she received:

During my eighth grade year, I had a history teacher who I liked. She was also a coach for the girls' basketball teams. She knew that there were home problems, but we did not discuss them in detail. She always made herself available to talk with me if I wanted. I think she saw me as having potential but also as an "at risk" child. She asked me to be the manager for the basketball teams. We stayed in touch while I was in high school. When she heard of my mother's suicide, she called me at the funeral home and at my grandparents' house. We could not leave the country for about a month after my mother's death because of the air controller strike, so she drove out to my grandparents' and took me on day trips to the park, shopping, her house, etc...and let me talk. She went out of her way to make herself available to me. She also wrote to me regularly while I was in Denmark, and our friendship developed more through the years. While I was in Denmark, I became friends with my French teacher. She was also tremendously supportive and helped me deal with the extremely difficult adjustment of living with my father. I am still friends with both of these teachers and think that both were the major influences that helped me get through all of the grief and change.

- Twenty-two of our participants were married or had partners when the suicide occurred. One-half of them found their spouses very supportive. Of the eleven who were not supportive, the survivors indicated that their marriages were suffering prior to the suicides. Jennifer, one participant, speaks of her own relationship problems after her mother's suicide:

My fiancé (now my husband) and I nearly dissolved our relationship after my mom's suicide. He was extremely supportive until I became involved in alcohol and recreational drugs to "escape" my pain. After two years of alcohol and drug abuse (such as marijuana and cocaine), Craig offered me an ultimatum— either get help for my problem or he would have to leave me. That was the best thing he could have done for me. I'm clean and sober and have been for years. We have a happy, loving marriage.

- Fifty-six of our participants had siblings and twenty felt they supported one another at this time.
- Fifty-seven had a parent living at the time of the suicide; fourteen felt they received support from their surviving parent. No one commented on stepparents being a support, but later when a parent remarried, one participant reported that the new stepparent was very supportive.
- Six participants found an aunt or uncle supportive and seven found support from a cousin. Eight had grandparents who were quite supportive emotionally. One reported her sister-in-law strongly supported her.
- Fifty of our participants were over age ten. Twenty-one of them found strong support from at least one friend. The youngest survivor to receive support from a friend was age eleven.
- One person was given support by a family doctor.
- Approximately twenty-five participants held jobs and one reported his employer gave support. Three people reported gaining support from co-workers.
- Thirteen survivors reported that they wanted support, but no one was available to them. Thirteen said they had to support others at this time. Three participants reported that they did not feel the need to discuss the suicide.
- Six survivors received assistance from a support group.
- One participant said she felt support in dealing with the suicide by "talking" with the parent who took his own life. She said this helped even though it was a one-way conversation.

Non-supportive Elements and People

When we asked our participants, "What did people do that was helpful?" we found it surprising as to the large number of survivors who replied, "Nothing." Frequently friends, acquaintances and/or family members do not know how to deal with suicide. So when the suicide of a parent occurs in one's community or is shared with a friend or acquaintance, common responses from such individuals include silence, pretending that he or she did not hear what was said, abrupt change of subject on the part of the individual who just learned of the suicide and/or finding an excuse to leave. None of these responses are useful to the individual who has just made him or herself vulnerable by sharing such information.

However, the type of silence that is not helpful needs defining. Silence without compassion and/or appearing not to hear what was said is quite painful for the one who has just divulged this information. On the other hand, do keep in mind that a person can use silence to show empathy. Facial expression of shock, sadness but clear engagement either in conversation with the person telling the news and/or appropriate nonverbal communications such as a hug or a comforting hand on the person's arm is very real and helpful. Words can be used at such a speechless moment such as, "I don't know what to say. I wish I could comfort you with just the right words." But comforting physical gestures of communication can be an effective form of silence even though no or few words are spoken. One can communicate in ways other than speech. The following are some of the things that are harmful responses to a survivor of suicide.

Silence is toxic when an individual responds in any of the following ways after a survivor has shared information about his parent's suicide to that person: appearing not to have heard or clearly indicating that he or she wants to get away as soon as possible.

We believe though religion can often be of great comfort and if one is a believer, there are some invocations that should never be said to survivors of suicide. Several participants spoke of the platitudes they were subjected to. We feel it is arrogant and grandiose to believe that any of us can speak for God. Regardless of what one's beliefs are, preaching and such comments are not at all helpful, according to those with whom we spoke.

Among the comments our participants did not find comforting or helpful were:

- "It was God's will. Your mother's suicide was all in God's plan."
- "God never gives you more than you can handle."
- "You know your father is burning in hell, don't you?"

Ben, three years old at the time of his father's suicide, comments here:

I've heard it said all of my life that people who commit suicide go to hell. This has really scared me, because I always worried that I would not be able to get to know my father when I die. It also has been troublesome for me to consider that a God of forgiveness would not show mercy to those who commit suicide. After all, He is the God who said, "Come to Me all you that are weary and burdened and I will give you rest." As an adult, I have read the scriptures, and I cannot find where it definitely states the final destination of people who have died from suicide.

- "Everything happens for the best."
- "Time heals all wounds."

Giving reckless advice and telling the survivor what he or she should feel and what to be grateful for is a violation of the survivor's boundaries. Such comments prolong recovery for the survivor, do not indicate support to the son or daughter of a suicide and are not comforting or empathic.

Among the remarks we heard from our participants:

- "Get over it; it's been a year already. You shouldn't feel this way."
- "The past is in the past. Leave it there."
- "Quit crying and get yourself together or you will end up just like your mother."
- "Be happy that at least your father left you money."
- "You should not talk about how your mother died."
- "Just be glad you have a roof over your head and three meals a day."
- "Be glad your mother didn't take you with her."
- "Just be grateful that your parent is dead and not in an asylum."

Cynthia, age twenty-five at the time of her mother's suicide, tells of the pain heaped upon her from two of her aunts:

Immediately after Mom's suicide and for the following year, my two aunts became critical of me and didn't want to discuss the suicide or listen to me share my feelings. They also excluded me from some family events, such as birthdays and anniversary celebrations, and would make excuses for not inviting me. My aunts also were critical of my mother, blaming her for her choices in life and criticizing her after her death. My aunts and I have rebuilt our relationships and resolved some of our problems in recent years. We are somewhat closer now, although some resentment still exists.

Lori, twenty-three at the time of her mother's suicide, tells of a survivor of parent suicide who was the least helpful of all. When a survivor becomes this insensitive, it is clear that he or she has much unresolved anger over the person's own parent's suicide.

I worked with a girl whose mother committed suicide and she was the least helpful person of them all. She was really judgmental, because I was struggling. She confronted me with these words: "My mother killed herself and I just took care of everything. Then I was just right back at work. What's wrong with you? Why are you being like that?" I found this shocking, because it came from a person from whom I least expected.

Blaming, criticizing and/or judging the deceased parent or the survivor is incredibly counterproductive to the healing process. We cannot and should not speak for the one who died from suicide. We do not know what the survivor is thinking or feeling and cannot speak for them as well.

Here are some unhelpful comments reported by those to whom we spoke:

1. "She just wanted to hurt you" or "What a selfish thing to do."

2. "Oh my goodness, that took so much courage for your father to do that."

3. "It's your father's fault that your mother killed herself."

4. "You shouldn't have said that to your mother this morning. You really upset her and that is why she is dead now."

5. "I know just how you feel."

The fact is that no one knows just how someone else feels, not even another survivor. This is important for survivors to understand. They need not become defensive with those who are trying to offer some words of support and say the wrong thing or just don't know how. We should try to understand that the acquaintance or friend really is at a loss for words. However, it would be better for this person to express, "I don't know what to say." Telling the survivor, "I know how you feel" is a conversation blocker and deters any talking on the part of the survivor who is suffering. If you are trying to comfort another person, it is best to refrain from claiming that you know just how the sufferer feels, but empathy is always good. Rachel, fifteen at the time of her father's suicide, was aware of this even as a child:

This one girl really meant well, but came up to me the first day of school after winter vacation and hugged me and said, "I know just how you feel." She didn't, but nonetheless, the gesture meant a lot. She didn't avoid me.

On the other hand, making cutting remarks are hurtful.

6. "You know you are now a high-risk person for doing the same thing."

It is cruel and unnecessary to suggest that the sons or daughters might follow suit. Kate, sixteen at the time of her father's suicide, addresses this:

A lot of hurtful things were said during the time. Right after his suicide, my step-dad said to my brother and me, "You two better not pull that shit your father did." This was about three weeks after my dad died. Some kids at school made fun of us, acting like my dad's suicide was a funny event. That was probably the worst.

Judy saw a counselor when she became an instant mother to her husband's two daughters:

I went for some advice on dealing in a positive way with my new children, ages five and nine. After a couple of sessions, the social worker questioned me about my own parents. When I revealed my mother's suicide, she became very alarmed and said, "Oh my gosh, I should have asked you this right off. You are high-risk for doing the same thing." Her agitation and comments were quite unnerving to me, and I had no intention of any self-harm.

More often than not, our participants reported that one of the most painful aspects of the immediate period following the loss of a parent through suicide was their friends or relatives doing or saying nothing. So many survivors experience a variety of negative responses:

1. Being avoided by friends, acquaintances and family.

2. Changing the subject or suddenly having to leave when the survivor brings up the topic.

3. Ignoring the suicide as if it never had happened or assuming that the survivor doesn't want to talk about the suicide.

4. Never mentioning the parent's name, as if he or she never existed.

5. Looking at the survivor with a blank stare and saying nothing.

6. Making it apparent the person doesn't want to be there and listen to the survivor.

Allison, forty-six at the time of her father's suicide, tells of her difficulty in finding a compassionate friend:

I went for a long time wanting to talk about my father's suicide. A lot of people in my family didn't. My father was an alcoholic and the family wanted to shove the whole thing under the carpet. I was told not to talk about it. There were friends of mine and family members that I would bring the topic up with. I wanted to discuss certain times and certain incidences in order to try and figure out things in my mind. No one would want to listen. I would be told to get over it, move on and find closure. What I was doing was trying to reach that point and find closure. I couldn't do this if I remained silent. This was frustrating and very difficult finding people who would listen to me. For most, it was a closed chapter in their eyes. That was my process and struggle that I experienced.

What Can Friends, Acquaintances and Family Do that is Helpful to the Son or Daughter of Suicide?

Friends come with different skills. There are the friends who are particularly good listeners; others are great at cooking up meals; some like to go out and have fun; while still others might want to stay home and watch a good movie. The list can go on and on. All friends can make different contributions that will be helpful to the survivor. If someone close to you loses a parent through suicide, consider the suggestions from our list and think about what your strengths are that you might offer to your friend, family members, co-worker or acquaintance in his or her time of need.

1. Above all, be observant and sensitive towards the son or daughter of suicide by giving loving and comforting gestures. Judy, whose main guardian took over her care when Judy was seven weeks of age after her mother's suicide, tells her experience:

After my open-heart surgery, I was struck by the fact that this was not the worst thing that ever happened to me. My collapsed lung after my surgery was particularly frightening to me, but a new awareness came to me after all this. I was surrounded by love: my family, friends, rabbi, religious congregation, therapist from years past and medical personnel that were caring for me and, of course, God. I was not alone and received nurturing and excellent care. I felt carried throughout this event, thought about the poem "Footprints in the Sand" and could visualize only one set of footprints at that time.

A strong contrast to this was the harshness and insensitivity of those who showed no empathy towards me when I was two months short of age three and suffered a severe loss when the only person I knew as my "mommy" was no longer to be my caretaker. I cried a lot throughout my childhood. My family was tired and angry because of my crying. No thought was apparently given to why I was so very sad. When I cried, I heard from a family member that if I could cry, then they all could do so. My despair was followed by ridiculing me with my family making crying sounds at me.

Another such instance of being in pain was frequently at social gatherings. I was yearning for my "mommy," often at such moments of what ordinarily might be times of fun and happiness. People were laughing and having a great time and I would feel most invisible as my longing for my loved substitute parent escalated. My pain and I went unnoticed during these get-togethers or at least that is how it appeared to me. I am not saying not to laugh or to enjoy good times, but it would be helpful for parents and others to notice the child and acknowledge the awareness that these times tended to be more difficult for the son or daughter. Being so alone at these times was by far the worst thing that ever happened to me.

2. Being there and listening was the most frequent participant response that we received from our interviews. You do not have to be a survivor yourself to be able to say and do things that are helpful. Listed are suggestions as to how anyone can be helpful, along with a condensed format of our participants' experiences. The authors wish to remind you to not put yourself in the role of a therapist. Be empathic and kind without giving advice and/or trying to analyze. We can simply be understanding and non-judgmental.

- Even if it is not comfortable, which most definitely it may not be as suicide is not a comfortable event, surround the survivor with caring and kindness. It is respectful to listen to the survivor's feelings even though it may be difficult. It is tough to hear and very painful to experience the loss of a parent through suicide. It can be healthy to move outside of our own comfort zone and listen to something painful. Sometimes, for one reason or another, there are those who can't deal with this. They can be helpful in one of the other ways.

Allison, forty-six at the time of her father's suicide, says:

Right after the suicide, the most helpful thing from others were their phone calls, visits and just their being there for me. That meant a lot. Actually, after the suicide I truly found out who my real friends were. They were the ones who came around. That was the part that astonished me. Some of the ones that I thought were my best friends turned out not to be after my family's tragedy. There were those few I never had considered as friends prior to the suicide who came around, followed up with me and were not afraid to do so. They turned out to be the ones that I would call my actual friends. My father's suicide rearranged my friendships.

- Knowing and saying the right thing to the survivor of parent suicide does not necessarily come with the wisdom of age and experience. Mostly it comes from the sensitivity of the individual. Judy's nineteen-year-old granddaughter, Michelle, responded enthusiastically when she heard Judy was writing a book. Then the inevitable question came, "So what is your book about, Grandma?"

Michelle knew that my mother had died when I was young, but the topic never came up as to how. So I started by discussing my mother, how depressed she was and how back in her day, helpful medications such as anti-depressants did not exist and mental health care was nowhere near what it can be today. I explained that she believed that her only way out was suicide and that sadly she acted on her belief. Michelle listened intently and then replied, "What a terrible thing to happen to you, Grandma. You never knew your mother." She became pensive for a few more moments and then reflectively continued, "You know, you turned out really well, Grandma, in spite of all that."

- It is very reassuring to be available to the survivor at times when he or she needs to talk. However, if you say to call at any time of the day or night, make sure you are able to handle such calls.
- People need to hear themselves talk out loud after a suicide and hear what is going on inside them. Be tolerant and understanding of

rambling, repetition, emotions and anger. Unless asked, don't be quick to offer advice.

■ Survivors may need to tell you about the appealing and delightful qualities of the parent who committed suicide or may need to express the distasteful and objectionable side of the dead parent. Either way, be non-judgmental of what they need to talk about.

■ If at an appropriate time you decide to suggest that a therapist is someone who might help, recommend this in a sensitive manner, e.g. "When I went through a difficult period (divorce, job loss or death of someone close) I found a therapist really supportive and beneficial. I was just wondering if this is something you might want to consider."

■ Give validity to the survivor's feelings and be respectful and caring. Sometimes a friend may need to protect a survivor if there is any self-destructive behavior. Cynthia, age twenty-five at the time of her mother's suicide, tells how her close friends supported her:

Two of my closest friends were very, very helpful to me. I could call them and talk to them at any time. They would come over and get me out of the house. They were very understanding. They were willing to listen to me talk about it without changing the subject or judging me. I feel so lucky to have had my two friends. They would be right there for me on the phone or come over to my house. I was in denial much of the time; I would go out and get drunk. They would make sure I didn't drive. I would really recommend a support group for a survivor who doesn't have friends who will be there for you as my two friends were. Also, it helps to get a therapist who specializes in grief therapy. It's too hard to get through this on your own.

■ Many people say they do not visit or call the survivor simply because they don't know what to say. We would advise not to get too hung up on whether you are doing this perfectly or not. Speaking kindly and sincerely is a good guideline. Carla, eleven years of age at the time of her father's suicide, says:

It's hard to remember specifically what anybody said that was helpful at the time. I would say that the most helpful thing was just their being there. People find it so difficult to find the "right" thing to say at such times. Having been on both sides of it, I have found that for the most part, we say things that are not really right or really wrong. The most important thing is to be there.

- There is a definite line between being nosy and being genuinely interested. If you are close to the survivor, then you might know how much to ask. If you feel uncomfortable saying or asking something, then don't say or ask it. If the person is not able or willing to talk, then don't prod and definitely don't dig for details. People frequently just talk and tell you what they want to say. We hear from Jill M., twenty-seven years of age at the time of her father's suicide, on this issue.

I appreciated the people that would hit it straight–on, like asking, "What happened?" or "What's wrong?" or "Are you okay?" They were my good friends, people who knew me well. They didn't beat around the bush; they weren't "mealy mouth" about it. "How can we make things better for you?" I appreciated that approach to some degree from people who were close to me. From others, maybe a silent understanding was better for me than someone trying to express something they had no idea what it would be like.

Ambur, fourteen years old at the time of her mother's suicide, discusses this as well:

My extended family were sad, those who lived afar and some of those close by as well. When they would ask me questions, I felt like they had other motives, as they seemed more interested in having the story to tell people and in gossiping about it. I never felt that these particular relatives really cared about me. I couldn't talk to them. They just wanted to get the inside scoop, so to speak.

- Say things only if you know them to be true. If you have something good to say that was true, then say it; otherwise leave it unsaid. Ben, age three at the time of his father's suicide, discusses this:

I can remember my mother and my maternal grandmother telling me that my father loved my sister and me and that he had planned things well for us (for my sister and me) to be taken care of financially. Also, they have always said that he really missed out on a lot by not staying around to watch us grow up. Because of that, I have never doubted that he loved and cared for my sister and me.

- It is not unusual that a survivor might not tell anyone for weeks or months about the suicide. It is possible you may learn that your friend has gone through a parent suicide years or decades after the fact. When he or she does share this tragic event with you, the person may need much the same type of help and support as someone who recently experienced this trauma. Be as loving, attentive and considerate as possible to the survivor in the years after the suicide. This is a trauma that people frequently find more painful, lingering and long-term than a death from other causes such as medical illness or natural causes.

Candice, twenty-two years old at the time of her father's suicide, addresses the issue of secrecy surrounding her father's death:

One of the things that made my experience a very lonely and even more painful one was that no one knew my father's death was a suicide. The cause of death had been portrayed as a heart attack. Besides me, only my mother, my siblings, their spouses and my fiancé knew the truth. Thus, what people said at the time of his death was what would be said to someone mourning a death from other causes. "It must have been his time." "God must have some need for your father." "Just think of all the wonderful memories you have of him" (like the memory of finding him in his bed not breathing?). After seventeen long years, I could keep the secret no longer, and I would say I cracked.

Once I had told what had really happened, I seemed to have a need to tell it again and again. I could no longer keep a lid on the reality and the pain. I had numerous very close friends and, little by little, I began to share the real story of my father's death with them. They were all shocked and stunned. Several of them knew my father as their pastor when they were young. For the most part, they reassured me that I wasn't crazy for being distressed and despondent. They listened and allowed me to talk with them, even though so many years had passed. None of my friends were critical or said, "Aren't you over that by now?" At this same juncture, none of my siblings or my mother mentioned the nature of my father's death.

- It may help the survivor to hear another's own personal tragedy when appropriate and comfortable. One might say, "I don't know how you feel, I never had that happen to me, but I do know what pain feels like because my best friend died suddenly in a car accident."

Karen, twenty-four at the time of her mother's suicide, reveals:

It was comforting to have people who had experienced suicide come to me with their stories. I found it thoughtful when people in my life shared a loss of a parent or brother to suicide.

- Those who have maturity in years and have experienced tragedy can frequently be consoling to the survivor of suicide.

Patricia, who was twenty-two at the time of her father's suicide, says:

The most supportive people were a few generations in age ahead of me, maybe those who had challenges with their own parents or experienced the loss of a parent through whatever means that might be. Really what I found most helpful was talking to those individuals. My boss, who was in her mid-forties, at that point was especially helpful. A very close friend of mine, who was a close friend of the family and had small children, was very helpful also. She was in her late thirties. Those who tended to be more helpful were people who had more life experiences, had been through some type of similar situation or had experienced death more so than the average person in their early twenties. They were able to talk to me without it sounding threatening or overwhelming to me. It wasn't even always so much what they said but the fact that they weren't afraid to talk to me.

- Survivors of parent suicide, as a basic rule, require a longer recovery period. It is important for friends to still be there when the suicide is well into the past.

Cara, thirty at the time of her father's suicide, tells about her understanding friends:

One of the most helpful things was their willingness to just be there in whatever capacity that I needed them to be there. If I needed them to just listen, needed to go out and not even talk about it and just enjoy some time, whatever it was, just their physical presence and willingness to be there, not just right after it happened but along the line, you know, as things progress. You know, it's really hard right when it happens but you are still kind of numb, too. Sometimes you even need them more a little ways down the road, like when it's been six months or a year, or probably for me it was the first two years that were the most difficult.

3. After a suicide, accept what a survivor must do to survive, providing s/he is not destructive to him or herself or anyone else. Here are some suggestions to help the reader with this:

- Don't judge their thoughts, feelings and, in general, how they are handling grief, unless of course their manner is harmful to themselves or others. Respect the survivor's need for time alone. Sometimes survivors need to be alone and avoid public gatherings after the suicide, and at other times they need to get out and be around others. Understand this and above all, be kind. Grief is extremely individual. Shelby, who, during her twenties, lost both her parents to suicide, explains her feelings:

After my mother's suicide, which was on the morning of Christmas, 1971, there was an outpouring of people gathered in my hometown, so there were an awful lot of people there. I know that on New Year's Eve, I, twenty-four years at the time, went to a party at the country club with a friend of mine. I did not know how people were going to react to my being at a New Year's Eve party six days after my mother's death. A woman who I didn't really know particularly well came up to me, specifically to say how brave she thought that was for me to come and how good she felt that I was able to do that. This always stuck in my mind. I may never see her again as long as I live, as I have never seen her since. But I remember feeling so heart-warmed by that. In retrospect, I probably wondered if people might not have thought that I was weird for having done that. But she was supportive of my just getting out of the house and doing something, which of course I had to do to remain sane.

- The survivor may want to decide which activities he or she wants to do or may tell you that he or she is not up to making a decision. You can offer suggestions or make a choice for the both of you if the survivor asks you to decide. Survivors might wish to attend an informal get-together or be with others shortly after a suicide, and others may desire to be alone. One of our respondents said:

I felt good at school. That is where I needed to be! Maybe it was the outlet. I had a professor who was very nice to me in the very beginning when I was in an excruciating amount of pain. He said to me, "If you ever need to talk, please, my door is open." I could tell he was very concerned and that I had an open invitation to talk if and when I needed to. This went a long ways with me. That could have been a defining moment for me.

4. There may be day-to-day tasks which the survivor needs to have taken care of. Friends may volunteer to take over or assist with these. Here are examples of some of these:

- Keep the family's mail organized.
- Keep lists: such as phone calls received, visitors who brought food or other items and friends who helped in one form or another.
- Keep track of commercial services, bills, cards, newspaper queries and notices.
- Offer to help with the documentation required by an insurance company; this usually requires a copy of the death certificate. The insurance agent will tell you what else is needed.
- If survivors are children, pay special attention to the young people, as the remaining parent is grieving and may be unable to meet the needs of his or her children. Much of the time, survivors of suicide need very practical and immediate help with their children. This may be needed at the time of the funeral and for months to come. Allow each child to express as much grief as they are feeling and are willing to share but do not exert any pressure on the child. Offer to take them to school and pick them up.

Harriet, thirty-six at the time of her parents' double suicide, states:

I'm a single mom. People prepared meals for me. I play the piano at my church and my choir just gave me an envelope full of money and said here, just use this to eat out and feed your children, whatever you need. As far as my work place, I had been at the same company for seven years and they just said take as much time as you need and we will pay you; they did not rush me; they were wonderful. There must have been at least twenty people that drove an hour-and-a-half to come to the funeral in the middle of the day. They came to my parents' house. They were very supportive. It was an unusual place to work.

Offering to make phone calls for the survivor can be a very helpful thing to do after the event. Sharon, forty-two at the time of her mother's suicide, tells about the thoughtfulness of her husband at that time:

My husband called my best friend as soon as he brought me home. He called for her and she came over and she just sat with me and we cried together.

- Sons and daughters may need help in handling practical matters: packing and cleaning up the parent's home and the financial and funeral arrangements. It is a good idea to ask the survivor which items of their deceased parent are important to them that they want to keep. If the survivor wants to discard something that he or she might have second thoughts about at some later date, it might be a good idea to put such things in storage.

My family was really helpful. Afterwards, the rest of my family, Mom's sisters and brother were willing to help handle all of the things after my mom's death: notifying friends and her landlord and taking care of creditors, the bank, financial arrangements, the funeral, going to the apartment and packing all of her stuff, the furniture, things like that that you can't even think about doing after it happens. They helped with that. I couldn't go back in that apartment. That was where she did it. They came in and helped me handle all of that, the necessities. They helped to sell her car and gave me the money from that. The only thing that I do regret about not being there is that I didn't go and say exactly what I wanted of my mother's. I didn't get some of her coats, her fur coats that she had wanted to give to me and some of her old clothes. She used to have all her clothes handmade. Some of my baby stuff was lost in the shuffle for example, the outfit that I came home from the hospital in. I don't know where all of that stuff went. That was hard but I got over it.

- If the family has pets, you might offer to help with them until after the funeral. Eddie, whose son murdered his wife and baby, said this was helpful to him and his wife:

People offered their sympathy, definitely, in different forms: cards and phone calls, offering to help my wife out with different tasks while things were going on. We were members of an obedience dog club and there were 150 members and many of them called to ask if they could take care of our dog. Also, one of the things at the church services, a couple actually came from our dog club.

5. Whether child or adult, the son or daughter of parent suicide is likely to have memories triggered should there be another suicide that happens after his or her parent's event. Barbara tells about the mother of

her best friend committing suicide later in her childhood:

I was in junior high school when my best friend's mother committed suicide. I remember my dad and my step-mom being real concerned about how I felt about that; telling me I could stay home from school if I wanted. So, they were being concerned and watchful. After they told me about my best friend, they were more open to me asking questions and this was helpful to me. My dad was always very positive about it. He was always real adamant that my mother didn't make this choice to leave me, that she had tried several times to get better and that she was sick. They told me good things about her, like her being very smart and stuff like that.

I remember him being available to answer my questions. It was the first time I really got to talk about the suicide and my birth mother.

6. As was brought up earlier, school teachers can be helpful in their own individual ways. Some survivors receive comfort and therapy through the arts. There is more than one therapy for treating grief. John, sixteen at the time of his mother's suicide, found his music teacher helpful in this way:

The most helpful thing for me at that time was my relationship with my music teacher, because I was still languishing in my interest and this helped bring it to the forefront and actually tapped into my soul artistically. He knew Mom very well, and he never really dwelled on her or offered too many things, but he did help me kind of find my musical soul. That was very good therapy for me because I became really committed to the arts after this happened.

7. The grieving son or daughter may need extra sleep and/or may be unable to sleep. Many may find it difficult to get the rest that is needed. Going through grief, death and suicide is exhausting. Sometimes if the survivor has children, it is helpful to offer to baby-sit them while the parent gets rest or has time to take care of his or her needs.

8. Be more attentive to the child survivor than ever before.

- Above all, when there are children involved, we certainly don't want to cause additional pain, just as we hopefully would choose not to do so with adults. Even younger children, when they lose a parent to suicide, are very frequently shunned after the event from the family and community for a variety of reasons. People do not want to think about suicide or those who have taken their own lives. However, it usually is very uncomfortable to see young children left without a parent, not to mention if they were left because of suicide. For those close or even not close to the one who died from suicide, there may be guilty feelings about their relationship or lack of relationship with the deceased. To avoid feeling this, people may also avoid the child or children.

- When you are dealing with child survivors, it is helpful to give them a small, meaningful or comforting memento or gift that they can keep with them, or something to help them express their feelings. In addition, it might help to have the older children do something physical such as run, swim and go on outings with you. Shelley was sixteen at the time of her father's suicide, but was seven and one-half when her father abandoned her:

A girlfriend and her parents gave me a little gift that I kept as a memento. I was very young at the time and didn't know them too well. It was the "Story of the Rose" in a little two-inch by one-inch book form that I carried with me for a long time. These people were friends of my dad's parents. Their acknowledgement touched me very deeply and meant so much.

- It is especially important to allow the children to continue the right relationship with the deceased parent's family. If for any reason the family is abusive to the child, then the visits must be stopped right away. Always, decisions such as this are to be made in the child's best interest and not for any self-seeking reasons of the surviving parent or stepparent. The parent's discomfort of the child's involvement with this family is no reason to discontinue this relationship. The child has already lost a parent and the additional loss of that parent's family only exaggerates the child's pain. Barbara, six at the time of her mother's suicide, tells how important and necessary this was for her:

I don't remember specific things that people said because I was about six years old. I basically remember the feeling of my paternal grandmother just surrounding me with her love and being very nurturing, leaving me feeling very protected. She probably babied me a little too much, but that was a positive and a pretty good thing as well. So, it was more of a feeling than something someone said. The other thing I remember is right after my mother died, taking a trip with my maternal grandmother and my aunt and her children and having a connection with them.

Handling the Trauma of Parent Suicide

Sometimes survivors develop thinking that makes them very difficult for their family, friends and co-workers to deal with, therefore complicating their relationships. Keep in mind that having a parent who opted out of life is a shattering event. However, although survivors have experienced a tragedy, this does not give permission to be hurtful and overly demanding of others. If you are a survivor recovering from the shock, be aware of attitudes that may turn away others.

Becoming very bitter may eventually cause the alienation of friends and family. Pay attention to your verbal responses to people. Here are some of these destructive thoughts:

1. The world owes me something.

My needs all need to be met by those around me. That includes my wants as well. You need to overlook it if I get ugly with you. If I step on your toes, know that I am in great pain and you also need to ignore that because I have a good reason to be mean and to hurt others. I need to vent my feelings and if my anger targets you, so be it; I expect you to understand.

Survivors must be careful that they do not adopt the attitude of being displeased no matter what others do. Everyone has his or her own style of offering support, and frequently people may not know what the survivor actually wants. It is important to remain open to positive support and be appreciative.

2. Tiptoe around me.

Be aware you may have conflicting responses:

Don't tell me of your sadness and pain, because I have my own. Watch what you say! Don't make me mad! Don't send me flowers, because I don't want them. Why aren't people sending flowers? I don't want company; why are people bugging me by calling and coming over? Why are people staying away? Don't tell me what is going on with your father. I don't have one and I don't want to hear about yours. Don't cry to me that your mother died; my situation is sadder.

Survivors may become so self-absorbed that they might forget that others also have their own lives and issues. There are many different types of tragedies that people endure during their lifetimes. Although one might feel like he or she is the only one that this has happened to, it is imperative to remember at some point that others have had their own tragedies and that they are important as well.

There comes a point sometime after the event when survivors need to take an interest in and care about others even though they continue to grieve. If as time goes on they do not consider others and share in their sadness and happiness, they lose friends. If they attempt to make others feel bad or guilty that the survivor's father or mother has taken his or her own life and expect all individuals to be watchful of every word spoken, they will eventually be left out of their friends' lives. Overlook when others say, "I know how you feel." Refrain from becoming angry and saying, "No, you don't." Often others are reaching out and groping for the right words to say. The comment said by some, "I am so sorry" does not literally mean that the person is saying that it is his or her fault. It can be interpreted as, "I am sad that you have to go through this." There is no need for a survivor to say, "Why are you sorry? You didn't do anything." We can recognize how we feel without verbally acting upon our feelings.

3. People should just know what I need and want.
People have different wants and needs after a parent suicide and what comforts one person may have just the opposite effect on another. Here are quotes from five different participants about their needs:

- For me, one of the things that really angered and bothered me was others coming to our home and sitting there with me. There wasn't a whole lot anyone could say or do to comfort me.
- People avoided me and stayed away. I needed people around me and they weren't there.
- Don't send flowers! I cannot stand anything that so much as resembles a carnation.
- People are imposing food on me and I don't want food.
- Other things that were helpful are obvious, like bringing food and comfort.

Others cannot read minds and automatically know what is needed and wanted by the survivor. If an individual says something in a loving and caring way, it is not any misdeed if the person makes an error in reading your needs, wants or concerns. Use sensitivity towards the person who is trying to be helpful. When asked what people can do, honesty is best in telling them directly what might help, for example:

- "I need people. I would appreciate hearing from you more frequently for a while."
- "Would you keep our dog for the day and night of the funeral?"
- "I don't feel like eating. If you can bring dinner and eat with me, that would be wonderful."
- To someone close to you, you might say at times, "I need silence and just to be held by you."

Sometimes what is needed is to be left alone. After asking for this, do not complain when someone respects that wish.

Survivors need to be watchful that they do not get stuck in this mentality just discussed; don't get stuck there. Survivors can become very difficult to be around and most unpleasant if they assume this kind of victim role, expect that the world owes them something and want others to tiptoe around them. Remember, friends and family cannot read your mind.

4. I have to live with this; that's tough if you can't deal with it. Sons and daughters of suicide might be in shock for a very long time after their parents' suicides. It is good to be aware that what happened might be very upsetting to others as well. Not everyone is equipped and/or trained to listen to the details of the suicide. Other people can go into shock simply by hearing the particulars of the actual suicide. It's called *secondary shock*. This is another reason to share these specifics with a therapist who is competent to cope with the trauma of what one has gone through. This does not mean that the authors are advocating to keep the suicide a secret from others. Many survivors (even long after the suicide) occasionally continue to tell anyone, no matter their age or relation to them, the entire story with all its details. This should be reserved for a trained professional who knows how to address and treat suicide survivors. When one becomes too colorful and graphic with their language and telling people all the facts about the suicide, he or she might be trying to shock them. A clue that the son or daughter might be doing this is when s/he is habitually blurting out what happened without any preparation. If you find yourself consistently saying things such as, "You should have seen her jaw drop" or "What a look I got from him; he turned white," then figure this is being done for shock value.

In such cases, we need to examine our own motives for this behavior. Are we getting some satisfaction in seeing others shocked? We believe one reason this is done is to be noticed and to say something that would capture the attention of others. Perhaps one is trying as well to obtain some sympathy and/or to evoke empathy in anyone who will listen. Still another reason may be anger. The attitude that may be prevailing is I had to live with this; that's tough if you can't deal with it. Sometimes survivors give details for reasons other than shock value. Mia said she would tell anyone her story to try and get them to want to become a nurturing caretaker for her, to replace her maternal figure and to fill in for an emotionally void family life. Whatever the reason for this action, it does not produce the desired effect of building a healthy support system. Rather, it might alienate the son or daughter from those who could potentially be the friends s/he is seeking. When one needs to discuss all the details of the suicide, this needs to be done with a psychologist, social worker or other such qualified mental health professional.

Overview

We have been discussing how members of society who will interact with the survivor—be it a work friend, close friend, extended family member or casual acquaintance—can help the survivor. It is our hope that those who read these suggestions from survivors will take them to heart.

We have also reflected on ways our society can become more sensitive to what survivors are going through. Frequently, people and institutions do not know how to and/or don't want to cope with this type of tragedy. They may avoid and reject the survivor. Some may not reflect compassion and we should enact better measures to help survivors.

However, the survivors should not expect perfection from others in their expression of sympathy and caring. People do the best they can when they come forth to offer condolences or help. It may be difficult for some to find just the right words to express how sad they feel. In the midst of grief, both survivors and those around seeking to comfort them must not expect perfection and must be forgiving of faults. It is okay to make clear what your needs are: "Right now I need alone time. Could you come another day to visit?"

For survivors, one last group of people that needs to be addressed may be someone whom you least expect to come forward to offer support and help, someone you barely ever noticed, someone you never considered to be a prospective friend. Be open to new friends. Many of our participants commented that after the suicide, a strange phenomenon occurred. They found out who their true friends were and may even have had a complete overhaul of friendships and new relationships that are of higher quality and depth to them now.

CHAPTER 7

Reclaiming Our Lives

Andrea Michael, a licensed social worker and psychotherapist, discusses some of her personal and professional observations:

Suicide affects all who are left behind: friends, colleagues, children, family and neighbors. It's often impossible to put all the elements together and figure out why this happened. Often people are left with not knowing very much about why this tragic event happened. My personal experience with suicide was not a parent of mine but my niece, who killed herself at age sixteen. Nobody knows what was really going through her mind. We have her writings done months and years earlier. She had counseling in the past. Nobody knows whether she really intended to kill herself or if she was just checking out how to do it, experimenting with would this work or not. Perhaps the roughest part of making peace with all this is that we can't explain it because the person who did it can't tell us. They're not here. The not knowing is often the hardest part for people to grapple with. Why would someone do this? There isn't an answer that fits for everyone. Sometimes there is deep depression and you know it because it is clearly obvious. Sometimes it's an angry response to the world: "I didn't get my way. Life isn't treating me fair." Sometimes it's a cry for help and suicide was not intended. There are so many components to why someone would take that step, if they actually intended to take that step or if it was an accident. I think that happens often with teenagers and with older people. It is the "not knowing" part that is so tragic and hard for many people to make sense of or to come to a sense of closure and peace.

At some point in the journey of suicide survivors getting their lives back and understanding what their pasts mean and what their futures hold for them, many of them have sought out the help, advice and counseling of people in the mental health professions and perhaps clergy. Frequently, the suggestion is made by someone—a family member, friend or co-worker—to talk with a "therapist" or someone from your church. This is positive advice for most people to suggest when a friend or loved one has gone through a crisis. It's also, we believe, a worthwhile effort to undergo, providing the counselor is a mental health professional or counselor who is a good match for the survivor and who meets certain criteria discussed later in this chapter. Ultimately, the final decision of whether or not to seek counseling belongs to the survivor.

Anticipatory Grief and Catastrophic Thinking

Critical issues our participants have gone through during the shock and grief process have been shared with us. Anticipatory grief has been brought more to the public's focus today because it has been occurring among United States military families who are in danger of losing loved ones. There is an overwhelming sense of anxiety and impending grief that military families constantly feel that at any minute there will be a knock at their door with the news that their husband, wife, brother, sister, son or daughter has been killed in action. Kristin Henderson speaks of this at length in her book, *While They're at War*.

Much information on anticipatory grief is available online as well as from results of several studies and research papers. Although military families suffer this, the term has mainly been associated with families of terminally ill individuals whose deaths are inevitable. The Medical Center of Central Georgia (www.mccg.org) defines it as:

Similar to the normal process of mourning, it occurs before the actual death—in anticipation of the death.

The Association of Cancer Online Resources (www.acor.org) says:

The term anticipatory grief is most often used when discussing the families of dying persons, although dying individuals themselves can experience anticipatory grief...These aspects have been identified among survivors: depression, heightened concern for the dying person, rehearsal of the death and attempts to adjust to the consequences of the death.

One of the most common outcomes of anticipatory grief is an early separation from the dying person.

Suicidal individuals and survivors of suicide also experience and exhibit the characteristics of anticipatory grief. For example, generally suicidal individuals are depressed over a long period of time. They may rehearse their death either in actuality by attempting suicide or mentally by making plans for their actual act. Quite often they gradually detach from close and/or intimate relationships, either peacefully or with what appears to be irrational anger.

In the cases of sons or daughters of suicidal parents, they function in constant fear of receiving a call or coming home to their parents' houses one day only to discover that their mothers or fathers have successfully taken their lives this time. Many of our survivors we interviewed told us of how they were shocked when it actually happened but not surprised that their parent had committed suicide. Many of these sons and daughters had spent several months and/or years taking care of a mentally ill parent. After the event, they had to come to terms with their relief as well as their grief.

The connection of anticipatory grief to sons and daughters who survived their parents' suicides is most interesting. The Association of Cancer Online Resources makes a clear distinction between the grief following an expected loss and the unanticipated loss:

Unanticipated loss overwhelms the adaptive capacities of the individual, seriously compromising his or her functioning to the point that uncomplicated recovery cannot be expected. Because the adaptive capacities are severely assaulted in unanticipated grief, mourners are often unable to grasp the full implications of their loss. Despite intellectual recognition of the death, there is difficulty in the psychological and emotional acceptance of the loss, which may continue to seem inexplicable. The world seems to be without order, and like the loss, does not make sense.

For us and for the majority of those survivors with whom we spoke, this feeling of chaos about our world is always with us to some degree. We believe parents are supposed to give us many things: unconditional love, security, safety, a sense of our own history and psychological stability. When a parent takes his or her own life, all of these constants are put into question. We see our world as unpredictable, very unfair and full of potential tragedy. In this mode of anticipatory grief, we often feel that those we love (our remaining parent, siblings, husbands, wives, children, loved ones or friends) might be taken from our lives as well, whether through suicide or other cause of death.

Mia, age twelve when her mother committed suicide, recounts:

Over the years, I've had many dreams about my father dying. I've even woken up sobbing because I'm so convinced that it had happened and I've become one of my worst fears: an orphan. Other irrational thoughts that reside in my subconscious are that my siblings or my husband are going to be killed at an early age through a terrible accident. Whenever my husband travels for work, I'm full of worries of visions of his plane or his rental car crashing. I drift off into these fantasies without knowing it and have to do some serious self-talk to bring myself back into reality. It's gotten worse since I became a mother four years ago. I often think that my life couldn't go on if my son died. What fuels these fears is due to my mother's suicide, because unfortunately I know now that anything's possible.

Judy, age seven weeks at the time of her mother's suicide, tells:

I am presently gazing at the photo of my mother with me as an infant taken just two days before her suicide. Her detachment from me is quite evident to any observer. Since she was certain of what she believed she must do, she could not allow herself to become bonded or attached to me.

This detachment followed by her suicide so early in my life started a cycle of complex trauma for me. (Complex trauma is a term used to describe a person who has experienced multiple traumas over a long, drawn-out period of time.) Especially for children, these multiple traumas often intermingle together. As a child, the abuses, multiple losses and rejections that I experienced became one prolonged, confusing, blended event for me. I knew my mother had taken her own life and I always thought that the nurse who cared for my brother, Stan, and me until I was almost three years of age was my mother. She loved me and I loved her. No doubt I had moments of feeling anger at her for one reason or another. I confused all of this and believed that the mother who cared for me was hurt because of my anger and committed suicide. In actuality, the woman whom I considered my mother died fifty years later of old age. She left our household for reasons I could not make sense of and, of course, was not my birth mother.

Anticipated grief became a way of life for me. Without realizing it, I engaged in catastrophic thinking: What is going to happen to me next? When I grew up and married, if my child or husband returned home late, I was sure that tragedy had once more visited me. Fortunately, thanks to effective psychotherapy, I now only infrequently experience unrealistic anticipated grief.

Health Problems for Survivors of Parent Suicide

We asked all of our participants: "Did you experience any unusual health problems just prior to or after your parent's suicide?" What we discovered was that parent suicide makes many sons and daughters of all ages (from infancy through adulthood) physically and emotionally ill.

Thirty-five survivors with whom we spoke reported that they suffered from multiple physical and/or emotional symptoms or illnesses. Nine participants reported that they were too young to remember. Some of the most severe illnesses (physical and/or emotional) occurred in those participants who either chose or were instructed to be silent and secretive about their parents' suicides. At least twenty-one participants admitted to some form of emotional illness. These conditions included major depression and/or anxiety requiring medication, alcohol and/or drug abuse, serious sleep disturbances, insomnia, flashbacks and panic attacks. One participant developed a dissociative disorder after a childhood of severe abuse from her father, which then ended in his suicide when she was nine years old. One young woman developed anorexia after she was firmly instructed not to discuss the suicide and to tell others that her father suffered a fatal heart attack.

Sixteen survivors reported having physical illnesses: stress related digestive problems (ulcers, vomiting and severe abdominal pain), kidney problems, increased cold and flu episodes, mononucleosis, significant weight loss or weight gain, back pain, recurring subconjunctival hemorrhages, migraines, vertigo, difficulty breathing and intense chest pain. For two participants, the severe stress of the suicide may have exacerbated serious chronic illnesses. One woman was just recovering from a series of surgeries when her father took his own life and she suffered a serious medical setback. A seven-year-old female child quit eating and required hospitalization for one and a half months after her father's suicide.

In addition to these illnesses, almost all of our participants revealed suffering numerous other emotional problems resulting from the suicide ranging from abandonment issues to relationship difficulties as well as fears of self and family members becoming mentally ill and/or possibly suicidal. If you have experienced any of these physical and/or mental problems for what feels like a long period of time, we strongly recommend seeing your primary care physician and/or a trained mental health professional who can treat and help you cope with these problems.

Determining which Therapist Meets Your Needs the Best
Judy tells how her need for therapy was experienced:

I did not receive any counseling until my adult years, other than for several months as a six-year-old at a child guidance clinic where my stepmother and father took me. Speaking of my past was prohibited; anytime I made an attempt to do so, I was reprimanded. I became a "silent" child and eventually started to forget. Counseling in the nineteen-forties and fifties was nowhere near as highly developed as it is today and with the exception of my speech therapy, I feel more harm than good was done to me. Since I was restricted by family as to the topics I was allowed to talk of and had lack of trust in all adults, I simply did not speak at my Child Guidance Clinic sessions. My silence was construed to be from lack of intelligence, not from trauma. This judgment made by the counselors was communicated to my father and stepmother. Their and other family members' negative attitudes towards me and my presumed aptitude were conveyed to me for many years to come.

As young as seven or eight, I remember thinking that if I just waited until adulthood, I could then choose to take control of my own life and get the counseling that I needed and that is, in essence, what I did.

As an adult, finding the right therapist and the right type of therapy was a task that I accomplished by trial and error. This is a common experience and it is important not to give up hope as you search out the best suited professional to guide you. After the first two that I had been with for a period of time, I used a new technique to find a therapist. I started meeting with and interviewing different therapists for fifteen to thirty minutes. The fourth one I spoke with and interviewed I knew was right for me; a therapist who was skilled in using many different techniques in doing therapy, including bioenergetics.

Bioenergetics therapy combines talk therapy and body work. The theory is that while one cannot consciously remember certain things, the cells in one's body do not forget. Andrea Michael describes Bioenergetics Analysis as "a method of psychotherapy that incorporates the body in working out the emotional, cognitive and spiritual issues of the individual." Although this approach works for clients of any age, it is especially effective to use with clients who have experienced trauma during the pre-verbal years.

Over time with effective therapy, I made huge strides in my healing process. Only after I understood myself on a broader level and became grounded did my life begin to change in wonderful ways, including my ability to accept and give love, to know joy and to experience a wider range of emotions. I changed in so many ways. I knew when it was time for me to leave my safe haven of therapy. When I was ready, I told my loving and skilled therapist that it was time for me to "fly." She grinned. The good news is I am still growing and healing. I can do it on my own since I have discontinued therapy.

Some Questions When Interviewing a Therapist

1. What is your approach?

   a. Do you explore the background and the childhood of your clients or do you stay right in the here and now? (Andrea Michael, LCSW believes one really needs to look for a therapist that does look for childhood issues and childhood influences.)

   b. Do you always use one approach or do you try many different ways of getting at a problem? (Again, Andrea says it is best to have a therapist who doesn't have just one method for working out all problems. There are a variety of approaches that a therapist can use to help a client to work out an issue.)

2. What is your training? How long have you been practicing? What are your special areas of interest? Do you have any specialty areas?

3. Have you worked with the kinds of issues that I am bringing? (Andrea points out that the issue that the client may bring to therapy might be other than the suicide of a parent. In fact she says, "I don't think anybody I worked with really brought that as the primary issue." They might be bringing issues of employment difficulties, grieving someone else or something that has happened in their lives or feeling a sense of dread, catastrophe or great anxiety.)

4. Do you do grief therapy? Do you have knowledge especially of survivors of suicide and how to help them?
5. Is your schedule flexible in that you would generally be available to see me at times of crisis? How might it be arranged if I felt I needed to see you right away?
6. If there is something that prevents me from coming to your office, could we do a phone session?
7. How much do you charge per session? How long are your sessions? Do you accept insurance or do I have to pay in advance? How much time do you require for a cancellation?
8. How long do you think I might need to see you?

Further Therapist Considerations for Survivors

Three additional subjects our participants mentioned while discussing searching for a therapist are important traits for individual survivors in choosing their therapist, ways in which therapists made a difference in their lives and warning signs that a therapist may not be the one for them.

Our participants felt that the most important and essential traits for any effective therapist are the qualities of being a good and non-judgmental listener with empathy, compassion and sincerity. Specifically, a non-judgmental counselor does not place blame; they help you to understand yourself and others.

Candice, a survivor, got to a point in her life when she knew she needed professional help. Candice's father was a minister and her mother was afraid that his family and parishioners would be devastated and think differently of him if they knew that he had taken his own life.

Candice, twenty-two at this time, tells:

She insisted that if anyone knew about the suicide it would undo all the good that Daddy had done. All the love and spiritual support he had given to others would be questioned. I was confused, because I did not believe that Daddy's final decision wiped out his dedication to God and to his family.

Candice eventually sought the help of a therapist. Her depression due to life with an alcoholic spouse precipitated her awareness. She had no idea at the time that her father's suicide was contributing to her depression. Her therapy story points out the importance of a wise and caring therapist:

My first experience with therapy was very unhelpful. I had gone because I was married to an alcoholic. My two children were being negatively affected by his behavior, and I was very depressed and anxious. He declared that I was well put together.

I did not give up, however. I found another therapist who was not so fooled by my collected exterior. I don't know what it was about this therapist that gained my respect and trust so easily. The first session I focused on my life with an alcoholic spouse. Although his alcoholism did affect my life, it was clearly a distraction from the real issue behind my depression.

On the second session, my therapist started to ask questions about my family so he could draw out a family map. He asked about my mother and if she was still living. No problem there. When he asked about my father, I became extremely anxious. My heart began to race, my thoughts were frantic and my face felt hot. I became speechless. I had told the lie so many times about my father's "heart attack" that I had almost believed it. But here I was, not able to talk. The therapist very kindly and very gently told me I didn't have to talk about it at that time. I could talk whenever I was ready. He didn't know what was going on with me but he could see that I was in distress. I kept repeating, "My mother said never to tell." My therapist was very patient. I finally knew that I had to get it out, that I couldn't leave that session without speaking the truth.

Finally, the words came from my mouth: "My father killed himself." I began to cry as I had never cried before. I had no clue that this issue was so present. I had successfully packed it away somewhere for so many years. I know it was this particular therapist's patience and empathy and the fact that I must have been ready to tell that allowed me to unload the burden. He was loving and supportive, yet I was sure that he would judge me for allowing my father to die. That judgment never came.

When I left his office that day, I panicked. I knew my mother would be angry with me...and she was. To this day, Mom has not told anyone about my father's suicide, not even her sisters or closest friends.

The professional needs to be a patient individual who is centered, emotionally available, grounded and attentive. S/he should be a role model by taking care of her or himself.

Donna tells of the counselor who helped her and the difference he made in her life. She was fourteen at the time of her father's suicide, but was in her later twenties when we spoke:

The most amazing part about my recovery was when I was in college. I went to see a career counselor, and the one who I was to see was gone. Another counselor who did not do career counseling said, "I can take her." Well, it didn't matter to me. We went into his office, and there it was on the wall of his office, a picture of the bridge. Staring at it, I was stunned just to see it. He asked, "What's wrong?" I said, "Nothing," He continued, "Does it bother you? I can take it down. Do you want me to take the picture down?" I said, "No. It's fine." He said, "Okay." I asked, "Where did you get that?" He said, "Well, I was a public speaker in this area and received it as some type of appreciation for doing the speech." I said, "Oh." He said, "Is that okay? Do you want me to take it down?" I said, "Well, no. It's fine. Don't worry about it. Just leave it."

He was curious about why I had such a hang-up about the picture. We would do career stuff and then he'd go back to the picture again. This happened several times; he knew I didn't want to talk about it. I'd answered all his questions but I was curt with him. He questioned me as to where the bridge was, which I answered, and then he asked, "Is there a reason that you know that? Honestly, no one's even looked at the picture. It's a pretty boring picture. Look at it. It's a black and white picture of a bridge. Pretty boring!" "Well, yea, but my dad jumped off it," I replied. He looked shocked and was quiet, then said, "Do you want to talk about it?" I said, "No."

He said he'd like me to return to go over the results of my career counseling, which I did. He somehow brought up my father once again. I continued to answer his queries but I didn't volunteer any information. He wanted to know the story so I told him as if it were someone else this happened to, not me. I continued to see him on and off and eventually he did all he felt he could.

He thought I needed closure. He believed a good way to attain that would be for me to see the police report. He thought that by seeing proof maybe I could accept that the suicide had happened and believe it. I was always saying that I didn't know for sure that it happened. I didn't know that my father was not alive. There was no body found, because it was wintry and icy. In fact, my father's body was never found in the spring when the ice broke. There was no death certificate, no funeral and no headstone. So, my counselor took the afternoon off, which is beyond the call of duty. He didn't have to do that. He phoned all over the countryside to find out where the missing person report was filed. Turned out that it was at the police station a block from the college. So he phoned and somehow talked his way in. We walked over to the police station; he got the police report of my father. They gave us tags and name badges to walk around, and then we went to a meeting room. One of the officers had the report with him. Then, we had to decide. Did I want to read it or did I want him to read it to me? Anyway, he looked at it, and I think he read some and then I looked at it because I wanted to see if it was actually the right name, birth date and address. The report showed that there were witnesses. I was able to have closure.

After this day, I was able to go on and live my life. A month later, I met my husband and we started dating. I wasn't so cold anymore and no more did I hate men.

John, seventeen when his mother took her own life, clearly points out how important a therapist's listening skills are to a survivor. He explains why professionals must check out what the client is thinking and not to assume anything. He tells of a therapist who was not on the same wavelength with him. Then he goes on to tell of a mental health professional person who was extremely valuable in his recovery:

I was seeing a therapist before Mom's suicide and that time before her suicide was a very hard time for me because I was suffering quite a bit myself and had some of the same feelings that Mom actually acted upon. It was very strange to continue therapy afterwards with this man because he thought that now since my mom succeeded at suicide, that I was at a much higher risk of doing the same thing. However what he failed to understand was that in my mind, I didn't feel the same way about it anymore. I had gotten over the thoughts of killing myself with Mom's one act. He would treat me as if I was very fragile, extremely disturbed and stressed and suffering from a lot of trauma, which was not entirely untrue. However, his approach was wrong; he was totally off-base because I no longer wanted to kill myself.

Fast-forward ten years from that time. I saw a therapist for about a year. He was the antithesis of the person that I saw ten years earlier. He had the experience and skills that I had never had up until that point. He really helped me. In that short eleven, twelve month period, I felt like I uncovered a lot of the layers of pain that I had never explored and dealt with… He listened to me more acutely than I think anyone in my life ever had. He took notes on everything I said; then he'd review what I had told him and uncover things that I'd said, analyze my words and come forth with insights that changed my thinking totally. We would end the therapy session with an agreement as to what we discussed and what needed thinking about. I would leave there knowing that my mind was expanding and I was really growing emotionally. I felt like I was meeting with an oracle or the wise man of the village. I felt like he was giving me the good medicine. It was an amazing and positive experience. I dealt with Mom's suicide. I finally got to the point where I didn't feel responsible for her act and got to the point that I understood that there was nothing I could have done to save her.

Some participants appreciated their therapists giving them assignments to work on and reflect on in between their sessions. For those survivors, this approach fit their personalities and learning styles.

Mia tells how homework was most important in her recovery:

My most recent therapist was very successful with me because she gave me assignments to complete in between sessions. They ranged from writing activities to reading articles to doing some serious thinking on a specific question she would ask me. I found this approach really beneficial because in between the days that I saw her I could in essence continue our therapy and be ready to discuss new topics when I saw her next. I never felt like I was wasting my time.

Cynthia's experience illustrates that different survivors benefit and recover by different therapeutic techniques used by therapists. At age twenty-five, she lost her mother to suicide:

Her assignments that she gave me right from the beginning of therapy were a valuable part of my therapy. She took my history at first and we talked about different ways of dealing with my feelings. I was to keep a journal: specifically to write down my one-word feelings each morning when I woke up, log what I did during the day in just a couple of sentences and write one-word feelings again before I went to bed. At the end of the week during our session, we would look back and recognize what I did that helped turn my negative feelings into positive ones. Each week I would try to incorporate more positive activities. I eventually learned how to turn my negative feelings into positive ones. In addition, I wrote a gratitude list by finding something to be thankful for in my life each day and jotting it down. One important thing that she called the Grief Letter of Closure was where I wrote and said goodbye to my mom.

There were times right after her suicide that I wrote, "I love you, Mom. I'll see you soon." That was my mind-set at that time. I felt like I was going to go do the same thing. Then as time went by, I got better. Later on I wrote such things as, "I love you. You're not physically in my life anymore but you'll be with me always in my memory, but I'm going on with my life." Now I find it so interesting to look back, see how I was at the beginning and how I have progressed.

Nurturing therapists who validate their clients are especially important for many survivors. Others mentioned appreciating straightforward therapists. Almost all our participants had comments on this topic.

Mia, who at age twelve lost her mother to suicide, has this to say:

At the time of my mother's suicide when I was twelve, I was already seeing a psychologist to help me deal with my parents' divorce three years earlier. I continued to see her until I was sixteen. In my early twenties, I saw three different women, each for less than one year. (There were other issues that led to therapy, but eventually my mother's suicide was always discussed in depth.) In the past six years I have seen two different women, again for about one year each, altogether six different therapists during my lifetime. With the exception of one therapist, I would say that I benefited from each one and certainly left therapy each time a bit more healed. What made the one woman unhelpful was that her style was so clinical and sterile. She sat in the same cross-legged position the whole hour, rarely talking to me or asking questions. She only responded to me with a "Yes" or nodded her head. I found her approach incredibly awkward and uncomfortable. I continued to see her only because my older sister recommended her and I was eighteen and at a really low point in my life. The other two women I immediately clicked and felt secure with, always knowing that their attention and focus was on me the whole hour.

Shanna, twenty-seven at the time of her father's suicide, prefers an approach that is both nurturing and straightforward. She says the most traumatic part connected with her father was not the suicide itself but the abandonment she experienced by him as a child.

I think it would have to be someone who could be straightforward enough to get through enough of my history but also could have compassion and show that he cared. The therapist that I worked off and on with was cut-to-the-chase and matter-of-fact in his approach with me. Yet he was able to deal with my emotions as well. For me, this is what I needed.

Ambur, fourteen at the time of her mother's suicide, points out:

The best thing that my therapist did was to help me identify the place and the point in my life that the suicide had an impact on. She was able to make connections and point out to me how something seemingly unconnected could be related to the suicide.

After I had been seeing her for some time, I was feeling satisfied with the way my life was going. Then one day I said to her, "You know, I have done a lot. I think that when I really look at what I have been through, survived and have had to deal with, I think it's pretty incredible. I must be a really strong person to have done this. You know I never really sat down and thought about it." She said without hesitation, "Absolutely." She validated that I had been through something that was very, very difficult, that I did constructive things to help myself and came out of my tragedy in a positive way. That was something that I always remembered because no one in my family, none of my friends, no one I had ever known had said this to me.

Candice, twenty-two at the time of her father's suicide, speaks of her struggle:

My therapist told me that my father's suicide was not my fault. I didn't believe him at first. I really believed that the only way to say "I'm sorry" to my dad was to join him. There was a sense of inevitability that I would follow my dad. After working with me, my therapist realized that I was equating myself with my father. He assured me over and over, "You are not your father. You may have some similar traits, you have depression, but you are not your father." It was then that I realized that I didn't have to make the same decision my father had made.

Joan, nine years of age when she found her mother's body, reveals the importance of the therapist not being timid about discussing suicide with a survivor nor avoiding crucial questions:

I went to a psychiatrist whom I worked with. He put me on medication for that period of time and he was the first person ever who asked me what I saw as a child. "What happened? What did you see? How frightened were you?" It took fifty years before I was ever asked these questions. What happened and what I saw that day is the mental picture that I see forever, and yet I was never asked that question until that day.

Joan discusses what she saw:

It was Saturday morning. I don't know why I always remember this but my mother the night before had told us to put all our little tables and chairs on the railing of the porch. She was done cleaning the porch. That wasn't really unusual. I don't know what time it was, probably eight o'clock whatever. I was telling the little ones to get dressed and I called over to her that I couldn't find socks for my brother. She said look into the drawer, and then I heard the door, I heard her go out the door. So I thought she was going out to feed the chickens or whatever she was going to do. So after we finally got everybody together and went downstairs, she wasn't there. We started looking around and couldn't find her and went across the street to her friend and to see if perhaps she was there, having coffee or whatever. The friend said, "I saw her go up the street." So I don't know how many of us children there were (probably everyone who could walk). I remember this little parade going up the street, to the corner shoe shop and barber shop. We stopped about every place and they said they had seen her but she had gone back. So we turned around and went back to the neighbor's house to get the neighbor who said she would help us look for her. She came back with us to our house. We looked around, in the chicken coop and all over. Then somebody got the bright idea of opening the garage door and she was in there. I can still hear the neighbor scream in my right ear.

Just last week, I was speaking with a young man about my mother's suicide. He had no experience with suicide and he came out with these words of wisdom, "Everybody is found by somebody. No matter whether it is an adult or child, it is shocking and never forgotten."

Sharon, forty-two at the time of her mother's suicide, found her therapist's candid approach most beneficial and healing:

Actually the therapist that I had at that time I was already seeing when my mother actually took her life. He already knew me, the kind of issues I had in my life. He was the one who brought up to me the element of a sense of relief. I didn't think of that myself until I started to talk with him. I had been to the emergency room just the day before because my stomach was in so much pain; I had so much abdominal pain and I'm sure it was a stress reaction. When he introduced that element, I was able to look back and say, after I thought about it, that there was a sense of relief here because I have been worried about my mother all my life. She already had a prior suicide attempt when I was about ten years old; I always felt like her caretaker.

It is important that the person you see be qualified and licensed to do therapy. However, it is the skill, empathy, values and steadfastness of the therapist which are of critical importance to the survivor.

It may not always be a mental health professional whom one sees in an office; it can be a fellow survivor who reaches out to the person in pain. Joan, nine at the time of her mother's suicide, shares this experience:

While watching TV one day, my husband and I were watching one of the morning shows that featured an author who wrote a book about his mother who died from suicide when he was a young college student. Eventually, he was talking about the gift of her suicide and at first I was shocked by that. Then I realized that I started to feel that way because without that experience, I wouldn't know what I know. What I have learned from my mother's suicide has been helpful to other people in several ways. For example, one friend of mine said she wanted to kill herself after her husband had died suddenly. She had three children and said she planned to kill herself when her youngest finished high school. Five years later when I ran into her, she was still talking about killing herself. I asked her if she started writing her letters to the children yet. She said, "What do you mean?" I said, "You can write that you are committing this act for mental health reasons or your kids will never understand why you feel that's your only option." So we talked quite a while and six months later, I got a letter from her saying that she had decided she wasn't going to take her own life and that she didn't feel that way anymore. She said she thought a lot about what we talked about. As difficult and tragic as it has been for me, I created my own gift from my mother's suicide.

Karen's statement points out that credentials, though important, are not a guarantee for a favorable therapy situation. Karen, twenty-four at the time of her mother's suicide, tells of her experience:

I probably would recommend what I actually found the least helpful in a therapist, a lot of credentials. I still think it's the best policy. The psychiatrist that I talked to was probably the least helpful person I ever talked to. As an example, one time he started talking about penis envy and I don't even know how we got there. He was trying to put some real plastic, maybe Freudian interpretations in there that didn't even belong. I do tend to talk better with women so maybe I should've gone to a female.

The gender of the therapist, according to our participants, might be an important factor for some survivors. For individual reasons, some prefer male therapists, others female therapists and yet for others gender is not a factor.

Judy tells why she found it so important to seek therapy from a female therapist:

My mother was psychotic when I was born and then took her life when I was seven weeks of age. The nurse who took care of my ailing grandmother also parented my brother and me; I thought she was my mother. Then she left her job two months before I turned three. After that I had a cruel female caretaker for two years. Then my stepmother came on the scene. I did not have good luck with mothers. Although my relationship with my father was not a loving one, my need was more pressing for a therapist who was female and maternal in her approach.

Although grief is an individual and subjective matter, with a suicide death there are many other complicated issues such as abandonment and loss. Some of our participants believe that only a therapist who has experienced a suicide or some sort of traumatic loss could possibly understand and be of help. We feel, and others with whom we spoke also concurred, that this type of personal experience does not need to be a prerequisite for a therapist to be effective with suicide survivors. It is important for the mental health professional to have knowledge of the grief process and to understand about suicide, survivors of suicide and mental illness. The therapist needs to have a great amount of sensitivity and patience, because surviving a suicide death, most of the time, is unlike death from many other causes and generally is more complicated in the way of recovery. Also, therapists need to try to comprehend how the survivor feels about the suicide and not presume that they feel a certain way. There is no certain pattern that every survivor feels in response to a suicide.

Katherine, seven at the time of her father's suicide and almost eight when she witnessed her mother's murder, speaks of what she found important when she sought out a therapist:

I think that the therapist needs skill in dealing with clients who have loss or abandonment issues, because one of the things that I suffered from is constant, intense fear of people around me dying. When I developed a relationship with my new therapist, I would become extremely fearful that she was going to die too, because of my previous life experiences. I had a particular therapist who was detached and had a fear of people becoming close to her and so that fed into my fears of losing those close to me. I quit seeing her. My next therapist was not fearful of my abandonment issues and when I would tell her that I am terrified of her dying while on her vacation, she understood me. I could then take a deep breath and feel reassured that I wasn't some sort of "freak person" who was walking around. Her attitude enabled me to work through my intense fears.

Cara, thirty at the time of her father's suicide, gives another example that having experienced a suicide does not need to be a prerequisite for being an effective therapist:

I was already in therapy when my father took his life because I had problems with depression myself before the suicide ever happened. This was a good thing for me because I had already established a relationship with my therapist and the suicide had such a major impact on my life. She had not been exposed to suicide in that she did not experience it firsthand herself. She was very easy to talk with and wanted to know what was going on with me. She was open to hearing if she wasn't taking something in the right direction or understanding what I needed. She was very good about getting a handle on what I really needed from her.

Many felt the age of the therapist was important. There were differences of opinion on this subject. Some older clients preferred a professional with many years of life experiences who had been through parenting, marriage and losses and knew something about the era they grew up in. Some younger clients wanted someone closer to their own age. Others wanted someone older who would be a parental type for them.

Betty, fifty-three at the time of her father's suicide, speaks of the importance of age if she chooses to see a therapist:

I think that if I was looking for a therapist I would get someone more my age so they could understand what I was saying, someone who could be aware that times and attitudes were truly different back then. If I got a much younger one, they wouldn't know that when I started working, I could not wear pants to work. That's a small example of how we lived in our day verses how we live now. People with children are very different than people without. I would say that I would look for a therapist who had children.

Therapist/Survivor Matches

After your interview, consider the following in determining which therapist is right for you. Remember you must listen to your inner voice to guide you as to whether or not you have found the right individual.

- Do you feel safe, emotionally and physically, when you are with this mental health professional?
- Do you feel cared about as a person?
- Does it feel like your therapist is genuine and honest with you?
- Is your therapist listening to you and able to relate back to you what you are saying in a way that is meaningful to you?
- Does your therapist conduct him or herself appropriately at all times with you?
- Does the therapist act with genuine empathy towards you?
- Are you comfortable in discussing all your issues with your therapist?
- Is your therapist calm with your crying or verbal expression of emotions?

Therapeutic Measures

Here are some things our participants found helpful to receive from mental health professionals:

- Good feedback, support and validation.
- Hearing that the suicide was the decision of the parent, not the daughter's or son's fault.
- Just talking and hearing yourself talk about the suicide and getting it out in the open with a safe person.
- Recommendations of good books to read and a support group, either a grief group or a suicide survivors' group.
- Peaceful visualizations in therapy.

- Just being told that the sadness might not go away completely but that survivors do learn to live with it and do gradually feel better.
- Being given space to rant, rave and cry with a kind and patient therapist.
- Assignments to work on in between sessions with follow-up the next session.
- Analyzing dreams to understand one's feelings and thoughts as well as the ways that the suicide is impacting one's life.
- Being instructed to do nurturing things for one's raw emotions after therapy and to try to arrange not having to return to work if necessary.
- Medication to help with coping after a comprehensive evaluation by a good psychiatrist. Information about medications, both verbally from a pharmacist and through an easily understood written insert.
- Counseling before and after prescribed medications are used.

When Therapy is Not Successful

For the overwhelming majority of our participants, therapy (individual and group) was a positive experience; most of the therapists they saw were helpful and caring. In general, many are very competent at what they do but unfortunately, there are those who are not. We believe recognizing and admitting one's own limitations in handling specific issues is part of being a competent psychotherapist. If a counselor finds that he or she cannot for any reason work with the son or daughter of parent suicide, the responsible way of handling this situation is to admit this to the survivor and to assist the client in finding a new therapist or group. This should be done in a professional and kind manner and not in one which brings further pain to a survivor.

Roberta speaks of her own and her husband's pain over being rejected by a grief group when Bob, her psychotic stepson, murdered his infant daughter and wife:

We had an unsettling experience with a group that was run by a professional facilitator. After a couple of sessions, he told us that what had happened to us was so horrible that it was upsetting the others in the group. We were told that we needed to find another grief support group to go to. He made no suggestions as to who might be able to help us. Fortunately, we were able to find a compassionate and understanding group with a facilitator who welcomed us.

Here are warning signs that you might want to change therapists:

- If the psychotherapist is distracted and/or doesn't appear to be listening.
- If he or she takes phone calls during the sessions.
- If the professional is defensive or avoidant about answering questions about his or her approach and qualifications for your therapy.
- If the boundaries of the professional are inappropriate or questionable.
- If the therapist avoids certain subjects saying, "Well, we won't work on that. That doesn't seem important" or "I only work with this one way."
- If the therapist lets you do all the talking. This might not be the best approach for the suicide survivor who is troubled by the suicide of a close family member such as a parent.

Some therapists or doctors use the approach of remaining silent most of the time and allowing their client or patient to do all the talking. The doctor or therapist speaks as few words as possible to assist the client or patient in their own search for insight. This is called the Freudian approach. While at one time this was the popular approach to therapy, fortunately today there are many other approaches used by psychotherapists that are practiced quite frequently.

Suicide is a tragedy that many people don't want to talk about. However, silence becomes a real plight for many survivors. Frequently the survivors choose silence as well. One male participant said that he had a psychiatrist who just sat and didn't say a word. He just wanted his client to talk and speak of his discomfort. He had been through a tremendous amount of pain as a survivor and this approach felt cruel to him. Unfortunately, there are mental health professionals who use this approach as a crutch when they don't know how to handle a situation or when they are uncomfortable with a client's emotions.

- If the professional doesn't take the patient or client seriously.

Occasionally a mental health professional seems to react as if the client's problem isn't important when the person shares his or her thinking or what he or she is planning to do. An example of this is Bob, whom we discussed earlier. He is the one who attempted suicide because a voice in his head kept telling him to kill his wife and infant child. The psychiatrist with whom he spoke did not believe him and released him the following day. This story ends tragically when, two days later, Bob murdered his wife and child.

- If he or she doesn't seem to understand or be interested.

Candice, twenty-two at the time of her father's suicide, was quoted earlier on a very good therapy experience; however, she did not initially start out with the help she needed. Her first experience was with a therapist who avoided the topic of suicide and was not okay with getting into the emotions and issues surrounding suicide.

For the sake of his client, he should have referred Candice to another therapist who could discuss her feelings and the topic of suicide. She explains:

My first therapist never explored my background. He tapped into my intellect and not into my heart or into my dad's suicide. I could dialogue with him all day long on a cognitive level. He knew I was going to Al-Anon; he said I had good support from friends and family; he said I was very well put together so he released me. I felt on the one hand kind of accomplished, because I had achieved looking like I was well put together, but very frightened inside. I thought if I'm well put together, who's going to help me?

Leann, thirty at the time of her mother's suicide, tells of her traumatic session with a psychiatrist:

I had never gone through a great loss in my life until my mother's suicide. I probably did what others without health insurance would do. I went to see my university health center to see the staff psychiatrist. I sat with him for maybe an hour or so and spilled my guts out to him. I am sure things were coming out from everywhere in my brain. He looked at me after I shared my deepest pain. Do you know what he had the idiocy to say to me? "Well I'm not sure what it is that you want me to do for you." You know, I went there feeling like everything had been beaten out of me, and here is this doctor who is supposed to be there to help me. I just felt like banging my head against the wall right there, just saying, "Oh my God, I can't win! I can't even get help!" So I left the psychiatrist's office feeling even worse than I did when I came in.

- If the therapist is insensitive and/or makes judgmental comments.

Elsie's father committed suicide when she was forty and shortly thereafter her brother committed suicide. She describes her painful experience with a counselor after both events:

I went to a Christian counselor after my father's suicide; I thought a Christian would understand me better. I went for my second session about two weeks after my brother's suicide. We spent the first ten to fifteen minutes chitchatting, catching up. He asked me if anything new had happened in my life since November. It was very hard for me to tell him about my brother, not because of the suicide but because my sister had said to me, "You know this is your fault; you are the cause of his dying." (I was afraid the counselor would agree.) He went totally silent, didn't even speak for possibly one minute; it felt like ten to me. I looked at him as I realized he had not said anything. He was completely shocked; the look on his face at that time, I have not forgotten, even today when I think back. He only asked, "Why?" I explained some of my brother's life and things that had occurred in the time since my dad's death. He got up from his chair, took my elbow because I was standing up walking from my chair to the window and back. He moved me toward the chair and said, "You call me if you need me." I left and never called; I needed him or I would not have been in his office to start with. He made me feel unworthy of his time, like he did not want to be in my presence. I have never sought or looked for or expected any kind of love, understanding, acceptance or kindness from a person since…I shut myself up and talked only to God.

Therapist's Individual Viewpoints and Approaches
Some of the therapists with whom we spoke offered their own individual approaches with adult clients who have lost a parent to suicide and their advice in seeking a mental health professional.

Dr. Leslie Knutson, Ph.D., from Milan, Italy, told us:
Clearly, every client is unique. Any client who has lost a loved one through tragic and unnatural circumstances first needs time to feel comfortable in therapy before they can really start the hard work of working through the raw and unfinished emotions related to this death. As clients become more familiar with therapy and how they feel when their emotions come out during the hour, I might begin to gently probe them about their memories surrounding the death. I would then carefully try to have clients understand how their past associations with this death are connected to their present-day circumstances

(i.e. relationships, sense of mental health well-being, sense of future.) The goal for this client would be to place the suicide in a psychological context that is appropriate for them today so that they can live today without serious social, emotional or relationship complications because of the suicide. I do not believe that there is a "right way" or a "wrong way" to do therapy with a client who has lost a parent through suicide. Every client is unique in how they feel about their loss and in how they feel vis-à-vis disclosing, talking about, crying about and resolving this loss in front of a third person. A good therapist will be attuned to what it is that a client needs to do emotionally during their path to resolution of this loss. A good therapist will know when to push the client to look further at their issues and, similarly, when to pull back from pushing too much painful exploration at once.

Finally, a good therapist will be sensitive to the client's needs for reassurance that what they are feeling—whatever that is—is understandable. I guess I would just like to reiterate that if a client does not feel comfortable—say after two to three sessions—with his or her therapist that s/he should trust in their instincts and not continue with that therapist. I want clients to have a sense of empowerment about trusting in what is right for them. Unfortunately, not all therapists are equal. Some are better at handling painful and over-whelming issues than others. In summary, there should be the freedom for the client to leave therapy if the situation does not feel helpful. Staying in therapy if a client does not feel safe can be a critical mistake. If one is not sure about whether they should stay in therapy or not, they should seek a second opinion from a trusted medical or mental health professional immediately.

Andrea Michael, LCSW, CBT, bioenergetics therapy, gave us her approach:

First, I want them to tell their story: talk about what happened, how they felt about it, how old they were, who took care of them, who was there for them, how the family dealt with it and how the story or reactions changed over the years. I really want to hear the whole story and go from there. I'd want to know if they have worked on this in previous therapy.

It may be that the emotional aspect of it is closed off from the client. I'd work with them using gestalt or bodywork techniques to help them get into the feeling level. Gestalt therapy is a form of therapy that may be used in one-on-one therapy and couple or group therapy. This therapy may engage role-playing, such as a client or patient talking to an empty chair as they envision and talk to the parent or other person with whom s/he has the unresolved issue. The client imagines that the individual is responding to the words that s/he expresses. This approach helps in gaining insight and feeling the emotions connected with the person sitting on the chair. To help some clients in safely expressing his or her anger towards the imagined person in the chair, a soft and safe object such as a towel or padded stick can be used to beat on the cushion or a chair. Frequently, the client may discount the experience. The therapist may hear the client say, "I was an adult so it didn't matter" or "I wasn't that close to my father, hardly saw him anyway." So I would work with them in getting in touch with what they did miss and whatever part it is that they are not able to deal with. These might be the emotional, cognitive, spiritual or physical aspects.

There are many ways of working with these issues. Sometimes I will help my client create an altar or memorial for the deceased parent or a ritual whereby he or she could talk to the parent at different ages. So much of the therapy is in the moment, what feels right intuitively with the client. I wouldn't push the client to talk about it over and over again but would encourage it when there were appropriate times or other losses. Recently I had a client who lost a pet and she was very, very upset about it. After we dealt with that, I could relate that back to the loss of her father and she saw that she was grieving him as well as the pet. I try to stay very much in the moment and connect well with the client throughout this process.

Support Groups as an Option

Some of our participants attended support groups and many found them quite valuable in their recoveries. Erin, Amanda, Cara and Candice speak of their individual experiences with support groups.

Erin, nineteen at the time of her mother's suicide, tells of her positive experience:

In my support group, we had discussions regarding the feelings that we shared. It made us all feel better to be around people who had been through something extremely similar, like I was not the only one that this had ever happened to. I felt less like a weirdo that way. Also, I became extremely sad for people who lost their children. In a way, I would feel less bad about my situation, at least for the moment. That sounds strange, but it helped me to put my life in perspective when I heard others' sad stories.

When I spoke of myself and my story, I noticed that people would notice me because I was one of the youngest in the group. When it became my turn to introduce myself and my situation, people would cry and would share my sorrow with me. I was nineteen when I attended the group. Many people would come and talk to me about what had happened and how my just attending the meeting would give them strength, even though I had not lost a child as some of them had (perhaps because I was close to being one still). It was sort of like being in a line for a roller coaster. You are scared and you begin to look at the people in line ahead of you. You notice children younger than you in line and on the roller coaster and you think well look at them; I can do it, I know I can get through this.

Amanda, seventeen at the time of her father's suicide, chose an internet support group:

I encountered a support group online, "Survivors of Loved Ones' Suicide." Well for a few weeks, I lurked, I read and I realized that I wasn't the only person that felt partly to blame for a loved one's suicide. So I realized for the first time that I wasn't the only person in that situation. That was helpful for me.

Cara, of whom we spoke earlier, was thirty at the time of her father's suicide. She talks about the acceptance she felt in her support group:

I went for the first two years after Father passed away. I think I did find it helpful because it is easy when something like that happens to feel so alone. None of my friends experienced anything like that. They might have experienced a death but not a suicide of a parent. This decision made by my father was just extra baggage to have to deal with. It was just really reaffirming to go there and hear people talk and know that even though experiences vary, that there are survivors who think similar things and to know that this is something that impacts you greatly and that you learn to live with it. It was really good to have a place where I felt like I could say what I felt without censorship or I could just sit there and take it all in, if that is what I needed to do. It was all okay in our group.

Candice, twenty-two at the time of her father's suicide, said she had gotten involved with a Survivors of Suicide support group and also attended several conferences geared to suicide and survivor reactions. She shares:

I told my secret when I went to a Survivors of Suicide support group. It was somewhat helpful but I only attended about six meetings. My experience was so different from the others because of the delayed onset of my grief and confusion. Their loved ones' suicides were very current. The hardest time for me was at the eighteenth anniversary of his death. I felt so alone because it made no sense to the others that I was reacting as though it was the first anniversary of my father's death. Even my siblings and mother did not share in my pain. I guess all the prior anniversaries had just been tucked away in some hidden place within me.

Andrea Michael, the therapist who earlier shared her ideas on finding the right therapist, goes on:

For the people who are left behind, I encourage them not to make a saint of the person who died nor should the survivors make a demon of the person either. Instead, strive to see them in all their humanness as someone with positive traits as well as a being who had problems, issues and weaknesses.

It is important for the survivors to recognize their own strengths, how they are different from the parent who committed suicide and to strive to live their lives in a happier fashion. The survivor needs to know she or he has many more options and can live happily. I've always thought the best revenge is to live a good life. Not that this is revenge, but it is the best outcome to live beyond the suicide.

Overview

For the sons and daughters of suicide left behind with a multitude of issues, among them grief, catastrophic thinking, physical and emotional health problems, abandonment and unanswered questions, finding the therapist that is the right match is of utmost importance and needs careful consideration. Empathy, honesty, genuineness and appropriateness are all important traits for a therapist to possess. When searching for a therapist, interview each one as you might do so with anyone who is applying for a job with questions about their approach, experience, flexibility of schedule and charge. Ask if grief counseling is one of their special skills. Also look into grief support groups as well as suicide support groups. Above all, pay attention to your innermost thoughts and feelings as to whether the therapist, facilitator and/or group is right for you.

Some survivors choose to see an individual therapist; others prefer a group; many choose to experience both. Still others talk with friends and/or family to help in recovery. Some are silent and tell no one. When we choose to be silent, the pain remains raw and recovery does not generally happen. When we speak of our experience and express and accept whatever emotions that come forth, we are in the process of reclaiming our lives.

PART III

Hope Persists and Recovery Emerges

It needs to be recognized that the suicide just doesn't go away. When you talk about the nature of forgiveness, you can forgive but what happened doesn't go away; it is still there. I think there are some other traumatic experiences in life that do recede in time. Certainly this recedes to an extent; it is not an everyday reliving but it is always in the background. It is something that you need to know. A suicide survivor is similar to a holocaust survivor in that both survivors have to find a way to deal with this event as being a fact of their existence and to make their life then work. At some point, God willing, they may even draw on this experience to enrich their own life. The idea of being a survivor of that event has to be elastic. It is just not continuing to exist after the event is over, it's really having that event be part of your life, hopefully some time in a positive way.

Rabbi Alan Freedman's reflections on the recovery process

■ ■ ■

CHAPTER 8

The Clergy Speak

■ ■ ■

Mia tells us about turning to religion for comfort:

I went to an Episcopal church until my mother's suicide. The priest was an older gentleman who was kind and loving to my whole family. He made Sunday services and Sunday school enjoyable because he welcomed us and made me feel some sense of normalcy in our lives. He passed away a few years before my mother died and a much younger priest took over. This newer priest was kind and eager, but not yet seasoned with the years of experience that made our first priest so sensitive and wise.

My experience with the new priest when I was twelve was neither successful nor helpful. I telephoned his secretary to make an appointment to discuss my feeling of disillusionment with God and my church. Sitting down to talk with him felt unfamiliar and difficult. I asked him how God could have let this happen and many other questions. His answers were meaningless to a twelve-year-old. Being young and unfamiliar with suicide and counseling an adolescent, he resorted to what his training had taught him about dealing with terrible events. He gave me the same vague responses my father and other adults had given me. He never engaged me in any dialogue but instead talked in generalities about how God doesn't make bad things happen. He may have felt a bit guilty, because my mother had gone to him a few times in search of guidance and comfort; then she ended up killing herself. Maybe because he knew my siblings and me, he couldn't handle the pain he felt for us. Whatever the reason for his inability to help me at that time, I still believe it wasn't his fault that I felt angry with him and the church. Along with my church, he represented what was safe, consistent and comforting in my life. I believed in the teachings of my church and wanted him to answer questions that had no answers. My older brother Stephen summed up how I felt at that time. He said, "The suicide felt so unfair to me. I considered us as pretty decent religious people and believed that Mom's taking her own life was maybe a sign that there was no spirituality or at least that it didn't play an important role in making my life better. I felt abandoned by God and therefore I turned my back."

Mia and other participants tell us how clergy's responses to survivors, knowing what to say, how to speak and to whom they are speaking in order to give appropriate guidance to children and adults after a catastrophic event such as a parent suicide; all of this is very important. In this chapter we turn to Christian, Unitarian and Jewish clergy to discuss such issues as their education and training in dealing with the surviving family members, heaven and hell in relationship to those who have taken their own lives and types of funerals their faiths advocate in such cases. We also cover both the positive and negative experiences that our participants had with clergy and their own religious congregations when survivors' parents took their lives.

Grief Training of Christian, Jewish and Unitarian Clergy

We asked the clergy to whom we spoke about their educational training to deal with family survivors of suicide. The majority said, "None." Three commented that they received "limited" preparation. Mostly they received the traditional education that was given to clergy: philosophy of education, theology and some general knowledge on dealing with people. We concluded that individual clergy have to educate themselves or find some type of continuing education after leaving the seminary in order to handle complex family situations. In some cases this type of knowledge is acquired by experience. One clergy replied that he had explored resources available at the seminary on complicated death issues and found very little.

New clergy, we found, often have to confront difficult situations within their congregations without adequate preparation. They may find themselves uncomfortable dealing with such situations. They do the best they can. However, as you will see from our participants' commentaries, some actually do harm to the bereaved and shocked families. Sometimes a clergy member has experienced a personal suicide loss, which may help in dealing with parishioners who have gone through a similar loss. Providing there is sensitivity and caring towards their parishioners, a clergyman's actions may be therapeutic even though experience or a personal connection to suicide is absent.

Clergy have many duties: being a preacher, doing premarital and marital counseling, dealing with the bereaved, organizing religious educational programs for all age groups and managing many business aspects of their church, temple or synagogue, to name a few. Religious congregations ask much of their clergy, frequently too much. In our interviews of participants, we heard of several instances where the parent who lost his or her life to suicide was either clergy or someone practicing some form of ministry.

A few of the clergy we interviewed had undergraduate backgrounds in psychology or had taken courses offered in psychology. Three clergy who more recently graduated from the seminary said they had received some clinical pastoral education. They learned therapeutic counseling measures, including: practicing active listening, expressing empathy, helping clients to self-probe their own experiences and feelings, guiding survivors to discover possibilities for the future and assisting them to set goals and make choices. We found some had attended classes covering some instruction on family systems where they studied different events that affect family setups, and suicide was occasionally mentioned as one of these. The information received, however, is limited. Nevertheless, it was clear to the clergy with whom we spoke that suicide is a traumatic event and attention needs to be paid to the family who has lost a member to suicide.

One clergyman we interviewed, Minister Davidson Loehr, Ph.D., expressed his view concerning his education in the seminary:

In one or two courses in divinity school, and in many group discussions among staff chaplains, I learned well that the trump suit in both life and counseling is authenticity. This involves naming and facing fears, demons, owning our pain, growing around the holes that significant losses create (rather than pretending that we can "get past" or "heal" such losses). There is both wisdom and healing in simply being with people, letting them talk, not judging, being a caring presence. And I do think seminaries teach this—not in a course, but through the general pastoral atmosphere that attends schools preparing people for ministry. You have to have dealt with some of your own fears about death or you'll be unlikely to be more than "technical" support. Like so many things, a depth of character is required; authenticity in the minister is required. And that can't be taught.

Participants and Their Experiences with Clergy

As we spoke with participants, we were struck by the finding that only seventeen reported having interactions with clergy concerning their parents' suicides other than prior to the actual funeral service. Of these seventeen, eight reported very caring, supportive and valuable help from clergy.

Positive Experiences

Carla, eleven years at the time of her father's suicide, speaks of her powerful interaction with the priest in the church she attended:

Our priest was phenomenal. The first question my sister asked him was: "Is our Daddy in hell?" The mere thought of it destroyed me, and our priest looked at us and said, "No—I don't believe he is. Your daddy was a good man and he loved all of you and led a good life. I don't believe he's in hell." I did not then nor do I feel now that he made that statement to make us feel better. Looking into his eyes, I knew he meant every word of it. The idea of my father being in hell was and is completely unacceptable to me, and I'm so very thankful that our priest settled our fears immediately—that was truly a gift.

Kris, who at age thirty-one gave birth to her baby just one week before her mother's suicide, expressed her positive connection:

Yes, they were helpful. Although the pastor that I was closest with at the time of my mother's death is no longer at our church, I still maintain a friendship with him. I see him a couple times a year. The other pastor that replaced him at our church came shortly after my mom died; she and I became very close friends. She was a great support as well, even though she did not know my mother. I could not tell you one thing that they did or said that was not helpful. I just have to say they knew just how much to ask and never asked more than they thought I wanted to talk about. It's been an incredible journey since then, trying to figure out how God plays into all of this with me, because when my husband started getting sick again, my first question was, "God, why are you doing this to me? What didn't I learn the first time? Are you trying to teach me a lesson?" You know, I felt like I was the one who was being tested. And so, I had very long conversations about faith and about my journey and about how God does or does not work. I would definitely go to clergy before I would go to a professional counselor.

Billi Sue, age fifty when she lost her mother to suicide, discusses her clergyman's attention:

My rabbi and his wife came over that same night I learned of Mom's death. I did not know she died from suicide at first. What was really strange was that my rabbi's first thought was suicide and he said the word. They knew my mom and my step-dad. He knew her and I said, "Oh gosh, she wouldn't do that." Anyway, the rabbi had such a way of making a person feel good. He would hug me. He tried to help me plan for what was expected. I had never been to a mortuary; I had never been to a funeral before. Well I had been to one; my friend's mother had been hit by a car. That is the only funeral I ever attended. When I was a child, my mother would say, "Funerals come soon enough. You don't need to go to funerals when you're little." My rabbi helped prepare me for the kind of questions that would be asked and what it would be like. I remember asking him if it smelled in there. He helped prepare me for things that I would experience going into all this. The rabbi made me laugh; he would interject a little humor. I was laughing and I just found out that I lost my mom. Then I would cry. He would talk about when his dad died, and I would have to say the rabbi was fabulous.

We got to San Diego the next day and found out it was suicide. I called my friend and her job was to call the rabbi and my network of people. I told her to tell it was suicide. Do not tell anyone that my mom died and don't tell anyone that she just passed away. She said, "Alright, but I'm not comfortable." I said, "It's not supposed to be comfortable but it's a fact." I asked my friend Paula at school to tell the principal and told her the same thing. The rabbi called me in San Diego to check in on me and after I got back into town to ask how I was doing and he spoke with my husband, as well. He was always attentive when I attended services. He told me neither to feel that my mother committed a crime nor to even think that she was not worthy of being placed in sacred ground. She chose to be placed at the family plot, which is in North Dakota. He told me not to allow anyone to "make" me feel guilty, to belittle me or to try to take the dignity out of her death by suggesting that she was less worthy because she did this. Actually, no one did. There was a time when Orthodox Judaism would not allow anyone to be buried in the cemetery who had committed suicide. It was considered a sin against God.

Harriet, thirty-six years of age at the time of her parents' double suicide, recalls her pastor:

My pastor at the time had lost his father to suicide. His wife had lost her mother and that was a very defining moment in her life even at forty-one, so they both understood. They called and kept in touch and just never gave up. My pastor was unable to say anything. All he could do was sit there with his hands on my shoulder while the other pastor told me what happened. He was so distraught because my mother had played the organ for a couple months at my church, so they knew her well. After they told me what had happened, they drove me to my house to pack and then they drove me to my parents' house in rush hour traffic. It was a ride that was never over, you know, a trip that takes an hour and fifteen minutes took three hours. They knew how I felt and they didn't treat me like an alien. I felt like an alien in my own skin. They didn't treat me any differently. They understood what it is to mourn and that it's not an instant thing that you get over. Their wives did as well. That was so helpful. They were just there for my numerous questions and gave me scriptures that I needed.

Josephine, age nineteen at the time of her father's suicide, tells us about the minister who aided her:

After my father's suicide, I needed help spiritually. This was a long process and I'm sure I will continue to work on this. It began with the realization of how destructive my anger was, which led to therapy which led to all sorts of feelings. It finally came down to the realization that unless I gave this anger and resentment up, I'd be the one hurt. My minister and I did some healing work and Holy Communion together and this was where the grace happened—that and lots of prayer (both alone and with others). I did a lot of spiritual work, even got a theology degree. I continue to use clergy for spiritual direction.

Tammie, age two years at the time of her mother's suicide, discusses her clergy's helpfulness:

I always resented churchy people because I thought they were too perfect. I thought they were too polished, too untainted to understand my dirtiness, you know, my situation. That is not what I found out. The longer I was around Godly people, churchy and spiritual people, I found a real humanness to them, which I needed to relate to because I needed to connect. I started to realize that I belong to the human race no matter what my upbringing had been. I found it real helpful, because they related to me on a human level with all their faults and their imperfections. They guided me and they were there for me. They took me in like an orphan little kid. I sort of felt adopted.

They are human. It's not perfect; the church is not perfect, but it's not hell either. It's like the light in the world. They have their faults like anybody else. That was a harsh reality because they were like my saints in my life, and I had to learn that the saints in my life had imperfections and shortcomings. Some of the reasons that they understood me were because they had experienced losses too; they had made mistakes; they had defaulted against each other. So that was one helpful realization, because I idealized them in the beginning.

Joan talks of the priest who played a valuable role after her mother's suicide (when Joan was nine) during her adolescent years:

We were practicing Catholics and so I went to a Catholic high school, which is the school my mother went to. My father insisted that we all go there. We were out in the country and the school was in town.

I used to spend a lot of time in church writing letters to my mother. It was a little country church and it wasn't very far from where I lived. I'd just go there; it was quiet; it was dark. Our house was chaotic most of the time, and it was nice to have a place to go that was quiet. I used to go look for quiet places. Eventually there was a priest who became a very dear friend to me. I had a lot of conflicts about a lot of things, obviously. But one of the things as I got older was the fact that it was beginning to look as though I was going to be the designated caregiver. One of my sisters was married, a brother was married, another brother was in the Coast Guard and my youngest sister was going to be married. I was not. I was living back at home after nursing school. I was living and working at home and it looked like my grandmother was getting older and it looked like there was no way I was going to be able to get out of there. I had a priest who was very empathic and a very good friend. We talked and talked and he helped me through many of my conflicts during my years of growing up. It was really because of him that I had the courage to break away. I joined the Air Force so that I had someplace to go, could get paid and have something to eat. Spirituality has been much more important to me in later years than it was in the early years. Actually, I knew a lot about religion but I didn't know much about spirituality.

Negative Experiences

Kate, sixteen at the time of her father's suicide, reveals sad memories:

We had a memorial service two days later in a church other than our own. Our church refused a religious service for him because he took his own life.

Elsie, forty years at the time of her father's suicide, discusses bad experiences:

I asked my preacher for the name of a Christian counselor. He gave me the name. He never asked me any questions, if he could help or if I wanted to talk with him. Nothing! He never asked me if I had made an appointment or if I was better. He did not show me that he cared about me. He had been preaching at the church where I went for over ten years at that time.

The other members of my church did not ask me if I was okay, if I needed their help in any way or if they could visit and talk with me about my daddy, nothing. It seemed that people were afraid of the word suicide; they think it might touch them in a real way.

Jill W., sixteen years at the time of her mother's suicide, seeks but doesn't find comfort:

Our minister and other church members never tried to reach out. What was most hurtful was that at the funeral, a different minister did the service and basically said that my mother would not be forgiven by God for the suicide. The minister made a point of saying during the service that he usually does not do "these" services and that under the circumstances, when the cause of death is suicide, a traditional funeral is not given because it is not God's way. My own belief is that God is not going to condemn someone who was ill and tried desperately to get help.

Lori, twenty-three at the time of her father's suicide, bitterly remembers:

The service could not be in a church, and our pastor refused to do the service. He could only have a very brief graveside service without clergy. My father was buried in the cemetery; he was buried in the family plot, not outside the cemetery, not in the fringes. All of us stood around and there was snow on the ground. It was bleak. My husband gave a brief speech and that was it.

Olivia, twenty-two years of age at the time of her father's suicide, sadly recalls:

I called the preacher at our church and asked him to come over because I knew my dad was upset and the preacher was busy doing something else. He apologized and came over later in the evening after it was too late. I know he felt bad and if he had known what was going to happen, he would have come over quicker, but it was a negative experience that I had to get over. Many of the people from our congregation came over with food and support for about two weeks following his death. We found this to be very helpful. After that time period however, when grief really started to hit, few people seemed to come around.

Participants Who Were Unready or Unwilling to Get Support
Sometimes clergy are willing and ready to be open, supportive and helpful but their attempts may not be accepted by survivors.

Caryn, thirty years at the time of her father's suicide, discusses how she sought comfort:

I was already involved in church and Bible study, strong faith in God. There were days of feeling like I would be doing well to get out of bed and put one foot in front of the other. Even if my friends didn't know what it was like, I had a sense that God at least knew me and that I always had someone who always understood what was going on for me. There were days that if I didn't have that faith and if I couldn't talk to God, that I would have fallen apart. No, I really didn't speak with any clergy. They knew and they were involved at the funeral; clergy were open but it was something I didn't take them up on.

Angela, nine at the time of her father's suicide, discusses her distrust:

My father sexually and physically abused me; I believe his abuse was spiritual as well. I always thought there was no way that God would ever accept me because of what I had been through or because I was so dirty. This has affected my trust in God. As for getting help from clergy after my father's suicide, keep in mind that my dad was a preacher. It is not easy for me to trust clergy.

Funerals and Comfort

We found that perhaps the most important start in the recovery and forgiving process for the survivor might very well be the actual funeral, eulogy and the compassion and sensitivity of the clergy. When Judy's mother took her own life in the 1940s, it was common to refuse funerals and eulogies to those who committed suicide and to bury those who died from suicide outside the cemetery, outside consecrated ground. The prevailing attitude at that time was that suicide was a shameful death and undeserving of a religious ceremony. Funeral practices were, and some still are, changed because of a suicide death. Sometimes the religious service is held in the chapel, because clergy will not or cannot hold the service in the main sanctuary due to their religion's rules. Sometimes clergy refuse to do a religious service at all; there might only be a gravesite service, and this may or may not be officiated at by clergy. Other times there is only a memorial service. Although the stigma continues to live on, fortunately there are clergy and religious congregations as well that are sensitive, supportive and helpful during these times.

Sometimes funeral practices need to be changed for reasons other than policies of the church. For instance, it may be the desire of a particular family to have the casket open for viewing, however often this cannot be done in the case of suicide because of body disfigurement. In the case of one of our participants, her father's body was never found, because he had jumped off a bridge into a river; the suicide was witnessed by several people. In this situation there never was a funeral or memorial service, and it took many years before the person could be declared legally dead, which made the grieving process longer and the suicide harder to come to terms with.

Two participants had fathers who were clergy die from suicide. Both mothers in these families swore the adult children to secrecy as to how their fathers had died. These adult children whom we interviewed developed eating disorders. Their physical and emotional health suffered seriously from being forced to keep such a secret. Both these survivors felt that no one came forward to minister to the clergy's family.

Clergy Discuss the Eulogy and Funeral When There is a Suicide

Father David Hoster of St. George's Episcopal Church talks about his church's philosophy:

In the Episcopal Church, the way that I come at it, every funeral service is different. There's always some way that it is addressed to that particular person. Some of our folks are ritually minded in terms of the church, and we stick pretty close to what the Prayer Book says, but there are other times when we write other prayers, when we invite family members to speak, when I speak in different kinds of ways. If I were performing the burial for a person who committed suicide, I would be very alert to the family's state of mind about that. If it were appropriate to bring that into the service in some way, we would because I find that funerals themselves are tremendously important, therapeutic moments for folks. If you do something right, it can help the healing. If you screw it up and do something wrong, it can impede the healing and give them something to be mad about for years. Ignoring it completely may be just the wrong thing to do; it may create the feeling that the church is in denial and couldn't deal with this. You have to talk carefully with families to understand what their needs are.

Folks and churches often support denial. They have a very rosy picture of what a church is supposed to be. I mean, God is all about being good; everything is supposed to be good; Heaven is all about harps and clouds and everything is supposed to be peachy, and so when you come to church, everything is supposed to be peachy and that is what the minister might be expected to do, which completely denies the difficult hard and dark aspects of life. If someone committed suicide and this is left out, that means basically you're coming into church and having a whole dimension of a person's life denied. This communicates to all attending this funeral, the message being that the person who died from suicide isn't connected to God somehow and neither are you because you are feeling the way you are. Absolutely ignoring something like that is not just neutral; it sends a message.

Rabbi Richard Zionts gives his ideas and practices:

Funerals for people who died from suicide are basically the same as for anyone else. I say a lot of prayers of comfort. In the eulogy, I try to give them a feeling of comfort and try to allay any feelings of guilt or anger. There is a wonderful eulogy written by one of my colleagues called "Do not judge this violent death." In other words, don't rush in to judge that type of thing. Suicide is still a complex phenomenon, still a lot of unanswered questions. Sometimes it's not even possible to tell if a person is suicidal. Suicide notes can be full of ambivalence. Sometimes it is a cry for help. It depends. I think the best thing to do is not to have a long, lengthy service. In some cases people like to speak, friends and family members like to speak. I try to tell them in situations like that, it is better not to do this; it is better to make this as painless as possible. It is better if I as the rabbi just give a eulogy and that's it. When I speak with children, the important thing is to assure the children that it wasn't their fault, they aren't responsible and it was nothing they did because children could be in terrible agony and guilt.

Father Larry Mattingly of Cristo Rey Catholic Church states how his church handles services:

Last year, we had sixty-five funerals ranging from shootings to suicides to natural deaths. There were some real tragedies along with the natural end of life moments. But as to suicides, certainly we welcome that funeral here in the parish. When a funeral is arranged, we do not ask about the cause of death. Funerals are not different because of the way people die. However, it is helpful when preparing the homily to know the cause of death and say something appropriate about the cause. I speak to the cause of death, especially if it is a tragedy. Everyone in church knows what happened, and not to mention it would leave them wondering. But after making reference to the cause of death I move on quickly to the message of God's love. I want the family to know that God loves them. I try to be honest in a gentle way. I hope they will feel supported at a difficult time.

Rabbi Alan Freedman of Temple Beth Shalom has a different way of handling services in such cases:

You don't refer to the death having been a suicide. You talk about all the good qualities of the person, and you may make a reference to the fact that they spent the last few years of their life in turmoil. You can use some euphemistic language but in a eulogy, particularly a Jewish eulogy, you only mention good characteristics. Everybody has something nice that can be said about them. If it isn't nice, you don't say it at all. They might have been wonderful to the kids; you can say that but you can't lie. On the other hand, you do not go out of your way to be hurtful. It's generally conceived that suicide remains in our society as a negative and you don't want to go out of your way to point it out.

Minister Davidson Loehr, Ph.D. of First Unitarian Universalist Church tells of his own ways of handling these funerals:
When conducting a memorial service for someone who has taken their own life, the mood in the room is different. I do talk about feeling angry at the one who killed her/himself and say it is all right to feel angry with them, with God, with anything or anyone. It is almost impossible, though, to wrap the memorial service in any celebration. It's a loss, almost always a dumb decision, an angry and misguided act, the loss of a life and of the differences that life could have made. So the act of suicide itself changes the whole mood of the memorial service.

Questioning God
We asked our participants how the suicide affected their spirituality. We heard about anger toward God and that the presence of God is often questioned after a suicide.

Amanda, seventeen at the time of her father's suicide, expresses her devastation during her interview with us when she was twenty-nine:

I prayed every night, and up until he died I was praying for him to get well, for him not to kill himself, because I knew he was going to. I was also praying that he wouldn't take me with him. I woke up one day and he was gone. I didn't comprehend how God could allow that. There are horrible people in the world, criminals you see on the news. Why not one of them? That's how I had justified to myself my anger towards God. Why my father?

I immediately had a very distinct anger at God for allowing this. I didn't voice my anger towards God to anyone. My mother raised us to be high-spirited; we were raised Baptist. I didn't voice that I was angry with God because that in and of itself is a tremendously guilt-ridden statement. It is something I had to work through. It is taking a long time to work through that.

I was a child when my father committed suicide. I grew up literally overnight. The person I was no longer exists, and I will never be that person again. I will never look at the world in the same optimistic way. My soul, my spirit—whatever it is that's inside of us and makes us who we are, was broken, and I believe will never be healed.

All my life I've been told that God does not give us more than we can bear. I just don't buy that anymore. My father's suicide "broke" me and for the remainder of my life I will be broken. I've accepted that this is the best that I can hope for in my life as a survivor. I struggle every day to see how this experience has made me a better or stronger person. For the life of me I can't see how it has.

Angela was nine years of age at the time of her father's suicide:

I've split how I view God, punitive on one hand and loving and merciful on the other hand.

I did receive contradictory accounts of whether or not my mother might get into heaven. Some people believe that if you commit suicide, you do not go to heaven. I don't know the answer to that question but I definitely lost some faith over the issue.

Clergy Discuss Questions of Faith

We posed the question to clergy as to how they might respond when a survivor questions, "How could God have let this happen? I don't believe in God anymore. I am leaving my religion."

Rabbi Steven Folberg of Congregation Beth Israel says:

First of all, I would listen, really listen. Then I think about Harold Kushner, who writes that when somebody says, "How could God let this happen" what they are really saying is, "This is terribly unfair." You acknowledge it and say, "Yes, this is about as bad as it gets." You legitimize what the person is feeling. When a person is that angry, I think you just let them have their anger.

I think what they are expecting is that you will be terribly threatened by what they are saying about doubts about God. In Judaism, doubt is a part of faith; it is not antithetical to it. If you open up the book of Psalms, you see these Psalms where the Psalmist is saying, "God, where are you? Why have you abandoned me? When are you going to come and take care of me?" You say, "If that is religious literature and if religion is about faith, then why is that in the Bible?" The answer is that this kind of pain and doubt is part of the human experience. I think we need to be able to say to somebody that doubt, misery and being distraught are a part of Judaism because they are a part of the human experience, so there is a place for all of that. Being angry at God does not put you outside of the Jewish tradition; it puts you firmly within Judaism. Someone said that throughout history, Jews have affirmed God, denied God, been in love with God and been furious at God. One thing Jews never have done is to ignore God. I can't tell you who said it. It is okay to say, "God and I are on the outs right now. I am not talking with God."

Minister Davidson Loehr, Ph.D. of the First Unitarian Universalist Church states:

I have never had anyone say this. I might say, "I don't blame you." But I'd probably add that there is no God who could cause or prevent this. It wasn't about God, either; it was about a disturbed woman/man who made (probably) a very bad choice, one that hurt many other people, robbed him or her of the rest of life's gift, and left permanent holes in those who loved them. I do remember, after the service of an eighteen-year-old who killed himself in which I had said it is all right to be angry with him or angry with God over this, several young (sixteen to twenty-two or so) people came up to me afterwards, very eager to thank me for giving permission to be angry, both at him and at God.

Father David Hoster of St. George's Episcopal Church explains his reply:

There is a whole world of how bad things could happen to good people; how can there be evil in a world that has been created by an all-loving, an all-good God? We have struggled with that for centuries and there is no good answer for it. Certainly I understand when somebody's in the immediate throes of trying to survive suicide, your heart may be one of the places you are trying to stay away from because it is very painful. I would also say that I understand perfectly that when the person has this painful and this alienating a thing happen to them, that they would feel completely alienated from all the goodness in the world, from the goodness in the universe, from the goodness of other people and from God Himself. I certainly appreciate it and I really do think that very well is something that the folks are going to experience, going to go to that place. I pray that is not where they will stay because it is painful and destructive, but I know they have to go there. I also believe with all my heart that the way out of that is God, that there are some things that are so overwhelming in life that we can't fix them ourselves, emotionally or psychologically. We can maybe get some handles on things; we can maybe get better some, but my belief is that it is ultimately God who wants us back with all His heart. He is the One who is going to be the solution. I just have to say that I understand where people are when they are in pain and feel completely cut off from anything good, but I also want to say that the way back has got to be with God in the end and let us keep talking until we get there.

Father Larry Mattingly of Cristo Rey Catholic Church discusses

how he would react and why:

One of the issues that all of us have to face is that God allows us to be who we are. That fact that God created us and that perhaps God knows what is going to happen, doesn't take away our ability to do what we choose to do. To say that God allowed the suicide to happen is to place on God something that is not His. I want people to understand how they relate to God and who God is for them. Often people think that God is out to get them or waiting to punish them. They have heard that God is all-powerful. But when something bad happens, we cannot attribute it to God. We need to look into ourselves.

When we are hurting, we say a lot of things, irrational things sometimes. For a person to get angry and yell at God is a good thing. The Psalms have lots of verses that express the anger of the people. God is okay with anger when it is an expression of something that went wrong in life. Anger is a normal part of life. Learning to cope with it is critical.

Rabbi Alan Freedman of Temple Beth Shalom first would sympathize, then talk:

Who's to blame them? I have a consistent response for someone who says they don't believe in God. My response is, "What don't you believe in? Then let us talk about whether it is a total non-belief or is it what you don't believe in is a God that would do this to you." I don't really mind people blaming God for things. That is a natural reaction. You can't say on one hand that there is no God and then say any real God should have controlled the situation so that it didn't happen. Okay, then which one is it? Are you prepared as a human being to say the world is totally random and is under no control by a higher being? Are you more comfortable with that or do you want to seriously look at this and say, "Well, is there a type of God that I can believe in and feel comfortable with and see as a source of comfort but who doesn't control everything?" So the exploration begins.

I would counsel against their leaving the Temple but sometimes people need a rest. I would say that's fine. Let us talk about it and see if that is really what you need. Is now the time in your life that you want to withdraw from any community? Is that what you should be doing now or should you be looking to be part of the community and share what you are going through and have others share this horrible time of your life with you? If you don't want to come to services because you feel you are false for praying, that is fine, but it doesn't mean you can't come to the Men's Club meetings. There may be different avenues of Judaism that are there for you now. I would definitely try to counsel them from withdrawing from the religious community entirely.

Seeking Religious Counseling

We asked the clergy with whom we spoke, "How common is it for families who survive suicide to seek religious counseling?" The importance of being sensitive to recognizing when people bring up such painful topics in an indirect manner or informal setting cannot be stressed enough. This may be a real clue for clergy, that is, to recognize that survivors may be very uncomfortable and uncertain as to how to test how receptive the clergy might be to their situation. The survivor may be indirect by approaching the clergy for some unrelated matter. It is possible that he or she has been hurt by clergy in the past. They might frequently test the clergy or individual and try to determine what attitude they might receive before bringing up their painful issues.

Rabbi Alan Freedman, Temple Beth Shalom:

In Judaism, we are non-judgmental in terms of the parent and son or daughter. It really becomes a matter of counseling along the lines of, "Well, how is this affecting you as a survivor of suicide? What, in fact, does this say to you about the relationship between people, between God and individuals?" Then you can start talking about those issues with that person. "Does this tell you that somehow there is something defective about God that would create a mind that would allow someone to take their own life? How could God have let my parent reach such levels of despair that suicide appeared to be the only answer?" That you can deal with a little more easily because their issues of why there are bad things in the world when the readings each week talk about how good life is and how good God is and how blessed we are. Then the counseling comes along the lines of, "Well, there is stuff that is unaccounted for in this world. It's part of the way of the world." At least at this stage, that is really the approach that focuses on the issues that this person brings. Talking about the nature and reasons for the suicide isn't productive. The suicide happened. The issue is, "How does it affect this individual sitting in the chair across from me?"

Rabbi Richard Zionts gives his opinion:

Many people will seek religious counseling, not in a formal sense, but they will seek it in an informal sense. For example, at a dinner at someone's home or some kind of a social gathering, a member of the congregation will be talking to the rabbi and will strike up a conversation about it. Sometimes, people will call and ask a question about something unrelated and lead into this, so it can come at any time really. Sometimes people do call and make an appointment to come in to talk. But very often, it happens in more informal settings, and of course clergy can be trained and we were trained to be prepared for that.

Father David Hoster of St. George's Episcopal Church states:

If one is active in a church, my sense is that s/he probably would go to his or her minister. However, someone who is not active in a church and has a member of his or her family commit suicide would be much less likely to seek religious counseling. For an individual who is not involved in church to say, "Gee, I think I'll go to a priest," I have difficulty imagining that I've never had anyone in almost thirty years of ministry commit suicide in any of my churches or have a relative who did. I don't know if that means we are doing a better job or having good luck or what but I have not had that happen. My sense would be that for a person to come to a clergy person, probably they would know the clergy person or probably they would have a relationship established because they are active in a parish or had been in the past and knew the person. I do think folks tend to be intimidated if they have had no contact with clergy. They would probably think more of going to a secular counselor than to clergy.

Father Larry Mattingly of Cristo Rey Catholic Church declares:

I am sixty-three years old and I was ordained in 1964. At that time, we received the usual course of philosophy and theology but little was said about how to deal with the difficulties and sufferings of the people. I had to learn on my own.

Younger clergy are given more preparation in the area of human needs. Through experiences and classes, they learn about the sufferings connected with issues such as suicide and have a better understanding of relating to the suffering of the people.

People tend to see us as distant or disconnected from their lives. If we can welcome them and reach out to them, they are likely to feel more open and able to talk about their sufferings.

Rabbi Alan Freedman of Temple Beth Shalom states:

If you happen to be the rabbi at the time that an event like that happens, I think it is very common. I think that what happens in the course of the years is that other issues rise and in speaking with a congregant about something else that is going on in their life, this gets mentioned. This becomes a backdrop to everything else that goes on. More often than not, it comes up in terms of the congregant's background as opposed to a traumatic event at a particular time. It doesn't just go away. It becomes part and parcel of almost every other event in that person's life.

Minister Davidson Loehr, Ph.D. of First Unitarian Universalist Church tells us his approach:

I've worked with people who lost a spouse, sibling, child or (more rarely) parent to suicide in three or four different churches. Sometimes, I'm not trying to do any more than establish a presence of being nonjudgmental and caring, someone to whom they can talk. I think each case has been different. A teenager thought she was responsible; that her mother committed suicide because the daughter was a pain in the butt. My general response is that no one is responsible for a suicide except the person who killed themselves, who chose that response. I've also found a lot of anger present, always. "Didn't she care that it would tear the rest of us apart? Did she think only of herself? What kind of love is that?" I tell people they have a right to be angry and to say so and that there often is a measure of aggression/revenge in a suicide. This has always seemed to offer some comfort, since the anger has always been part of it.

Chaplain Dora Robinson, Former Hospice Chaplain, Founder Place Ministries, gives her thoughts on a useful effective approach:

More than likely, suicide is not talked about that much. It's kind of hidden; it's kind of a scarlet letter. The issue that always comes out is: "I should have seen it coming." One of the things I will say to the person is "Was the day any different than any other day? Tell me what your friend did." Then I would explain to them that there is a phenomenon called looking back and saying what if I had done that. Then I would just let them talk about it and then tell them, "You know, if the person's going to do it, they're going to do it." It's also asking them about unfinished business; it's also giving them permission, the right to be angry, and to be able to say, it's okay to be angry. They will say, "Why did she do this?" The translation is, "Why did she do this to me?" Another question is, "Why didn't someone help her?" How many stories have you heard where there was no indication? Women tend to give more indication of trouble. With men, very often you don't know of their struggles.

I'll ask, "What do you need right now?" Sometimes they don't know what they need. As for helping them to let their anger out, I usually share my experience about my good friend who killed herself. I was really angry and went out into the field and ranted and raved because, "Why couldn't you hang on for just one more day?" Generally my experience has been that this gives them permission to open up. If they are of Christian tradition, particularly the females, and this is around any issue, I will refer them to Christ hanging on the cross and crying out the passage from the twenty-second psalm, saying, "My God, my God, why have you left me?" I will say, "If the Savior can get angry, why can't you?" That is amazing, particularly with women. I would also ask them to tell me about their relationship. I will use another phrase which is, "I never met your loved one. Can you describe him or her through your eyes so I could see your loved one?" There's something about the expression, "I never met him, I would like to see him through your eyes and can you paint the picture?" That just opens it up.

Suicide in the Name of Religion

Because of the advent of religious cults and figures who advocate mass suicide or suicidal acts, a number of which have been committed in recent history, we asked some of the clergy with whom we spoke to give us their opinions on such practices.

Rev. Tracey Davenport, Pastor of Stockbridge Presbyterian Church:

I was asked (after September eleventh) if suicide in the name of religion is valid. Does it guarantee a place in heaven, as some religions claim? The Presbyterian answer is that God is the giver and taker of life, and suicide/homicide does not guarantee a place in heaven. In fact, it goes against everything we believe God is about, as revealed in the life of Jesus: love, joy, peace, reconciliation and salvation by God's grace alone. Heaven for us is not earned; it is a gift.

Rabbi Alan Freedman of Temple Beth Shalom:

The Jewish response to that is that there is a passage in Leviticus that talks about the fact that the commandments are to be lived. In other words, the commandment is that always you adjust the laws of the particular religion so that they promote life. Consequently, you are not to interpret the laws of religion to promote death. Even in Judaism where you must accept death rather than commit idolatry, sexual offenses or murder, your death in such cases is not your doing it. It is someone else trying to force you to commit a crime and then killing you if you refuse. There is no call that you have to kill yourself. I can't think of any circumstances where suicide is permissible.

When Suicide is a Thought-out Act

Rabbi Alan Freedman of Temple Beth Shalom tells us his theory on this difficult subject, often causing survivors' pain:

There is ambivalence in Judaism and in most western religions. The one constant in western religions is that God is supreme and has control over life and death. Suicide is seen as an affront to God's exclusivity in this area. Consequently, religious doctrine is that someone who commits suicide has done something really heinous against God. There can be varying degrees then of excluding them from the community. For example, some highly traditional rabbis might exclude a person who committed suicide from being buried within a Jewish cemetery. This person is entitled to a funeral, but I would imagine certain prayers would be excluded from that burial service. That's really a very small minority, however. For the most part, it is viewed that the taking of one's life is not a rational act, and consequently we don't hold people guilty for acts that are insane. Everyone wants to live, so by definition you are insane if you kill yourself. I think that line of thinking is accurate and it reflects religious sensibilities.

We don't want to exclude somebody from the community who has committed suicide. On the other hand, it is reality that on some people's part, suicide is a rational act. The reasoning becomes a little artificial and if it becomes legal in more and more places to end one's own life, I think we are going to have to revisit the reasoning and make it clearer. We are going to have to work through the philosophical issues of whether or not God has exclusive control or whether God has spoken already by virtue of putting someone in a position where they are going to die, but as humans they have the ability to choose when and under what circumstances. We have this rational way of viewing suicide that gets us where we want to go, but at some point we are going to have to take a serious look at it.

There are people who are in the midst of serious diseases who are terminal, who choose to die because they want to die at a certain stage as opposed to waiting until total deterioration. Religions are not comfortable with that concept. We also need to face a certain reality. It's not something that I am prepared to address because I haven't wrestled with it enough. But it is something we are going to have to address as an organized religion. If nothing else, we are beginning to have to advise people who want essentially their minister to give (in a Catholic sense) absolution. For Jewish people, they want a rabbi to say that it's okay. They want to hear a religious person say, "I am not endangering my soul by doing this" and that is a tough spot. We really have to work that through quite carefully because the basic tenor of religion is that you aren't entitled to control that. First of all, you obviate the possibility of a miracle and you don't know what God has planned for the next few months of your life, whose life you are going to touch, who you are going to affect and what is your role in dying. It's an easy question if someone kills one's self because they are mentally ill. Now we are facing a more difficult question.

Overview

Talking about suicide, especially with a person who has just lost a loved one to suicide, can be a difficult task for anyone, including clergy. Taking one's own life is a difficult topic for most people to deal with. We found, in our research, that general education on this topic in seminary is limited, if any instruction at all is given. Therefore, as a general rule, many clergy have to take responsibility for their own on-the-job training. After talking to many participants and from our own experience, we believe there are some good guidelines: clergy first and foremost need to consider who they are talking with. The age of the person is primary to consider; a child should be handled differently than an adult. For any age, being a good listener is of utmost importance, and this may be, and probably will be, what the individual needs most at first as well as dealing with immediate concerns such as preparing for funeral arrangements or in the case of a child, preparing the child for what he or she can expect. The second aspect to consider is at what stage the individual is in recovery. Has the suicide just happened or is it three years or more after the suicide? The third consideration is to take into account how much, if any, help the survivor has received up to this point. There are those who have not even told anyone about the suicide prior to talking with the clergy, and whether it has been one year or fifty years, the wound in the survivor remains as open as it was immediately after the suicide.

In this chapter, parent suicide survivors discussed their positive and negative experiences with clergy. Also, it is important to note that some survivors do not give their clergy a chance, no matter how willing and able the clergy may be to counsel with them.

The importance of the funeral and eulogy for the grieving process should not be minimized. The service for a suicide can be handled with an approach that will accelerate the process of the son or daughter's recovery by sensitivity and thoughtfulness or slow down the process of healing by thoughtless or cruel comments by the clergy about the deceased and the suicide. Throughout this chapter we heard from Christian, Jewish and Unitarian clergy on how to handle, discuss and comfort survivors so that those who are grieving can mend, recover and heal.

CHAPTER 9

Unexplained Happenings

Early on, as we spoke to other survivors of parent suicide, we began hearing of experiences in which a dead parent appeared to a survivor. These were frequently spoken of as dreams by sons and daughters after the suicides of their parents and also believed by many to be quite authentic. Recurrently the survivors articulated an uncanny feeling of realness to them. This had occurred at such frequency that we began asking the participants as part of their interviews whether or not these types of happenings, ranging anywhere from dreams to visions, were part of their experiences.

We found that it was common for our participants who were children (either adolescent age and younger) at the times of the events to believe their deceased parents were watching over them and actually protecting them.

Judy explores in her poem, which was edited by Irene Parker, how and when she has felt her mother's presence in her life:

A pregnant young mother,
depressed, filled with strife,
delivered a girl child,
then took her own life.

God said, "You've done wrong.
You make me so sad.
What you did is taboo.
It's terribly bad.

You abandoned your children.
You've left them and died.
Go back and protect them
and stay by their side."

She responds, "It's too late.
I can't be their mother.
They won't know that I'm there.
Give that job to another."

God said, "You'll be unseen,
but they still need your love,
nor may you get credit,
you must help from above.

Their lives will be harsh
and at times filled with dangers.
Without you, they're vulnerable
to cruel family and strangers."

And so it was true,
we were hurt by another.
Then out of the blue came help;
it could be my mother.

And so years ago
having babies of my very own,
I thought she didn't love me.
She left me so alone.

Then something strange happened
lying awake in my bed.
That morning was a presence
of someone kissing my head.

While tensing with fear
wondering who could this be?
It wasn't my children
nor husband next to me.

Like on a baby's bald head,
loving lips were so cold.
I dared not turn to look
for what I'd behold.

What flashed through my mind,
as warmth flowed, replaced strife,
were memories of kisses
before Mom took her own life.

Or did my mother return
to my bed to convey
assurance of her love
on that miraculous day?

Kate, sixteen at the time of her father's suicide, tells her experience:

I know my dad watches over me; I know he protects me. There have been times where I've felt him around me. It was his presence, such a strong feeling, I could only cry. And there have been dreams that felt so real, like it was him trying to let me know he is there. Although he has yet to talk to me, I just know one day he will. In life that's how our relationship was, we didn't really have to say much to each other because we had such a strong bond that just a simple hug had enough words and emotions in the embrace to last a lifetime. I remember our last hug; it was in the room he killed himself in, my old bedroom. We didn't say anything but I knew and he knew how much we loved each other.

Our participants report that their unexplained incidences may come in different outward appearances. For most, these have been very real, comforting, reassuring and healing experiences.

Shanna, twenty-seven years at the time of her father's suicide, reveals:

Since he's been gone, actually about a week after my father's funeral, I was in the parking lot waiting for my husband when I looked up in the sky and there was one soaring bird. I don't know why this bird caught my attention. It wasn't a habit for me to look in the sky and to look at birds but there was this one soaring bird and none other around and he kept soaring above me. It was just so beautiful. I almost felt like that was my father for some reason, I don't know. It's really strange because now when sometimes I hear a bird, I will look in the sky and there will be only one. So I have this connection with Daddy and the soaring bird. Normally there is not just one bird in the sky but a flock.

Later as we spoke of other subjects, such as rituals and some things that families do (sometimes serious and other times fun) when remembering their deceased parents, Shanna offered:

Now that I think about it, there is a ritual that we do. My father's favorite sign was "flipping the bird" so when things weren't good, that is what he would do. One of my father's favorite sayings was, "The whole world is full of it, so flip the bird."

We found this an interesting play on words.

Vonny, thirty-three years at the time of her mother's suicide, calls herself a pragmatic individual but reports a series of dreams:

I am a "see it to believe it" type. That is why these experiences are really profound to me. My mother took her life on October twenty-second of 1995, and I remember driving more than a three hour drive over a mountain range to where my father was still living at the time. I drove over there and spent the first week with my father and my brother, who was the one to find my mother. I remember the first night I spent there after my mother's suicide. I went outside after dark all by myself and looked up to the sky and thought, "What in the world is going on; how could you let this happen?" I was basically talking to God.

Let me backtrack. After my mother did this, my father was in the house where she died and it was a fifty-five hundred square foot Victorian mansion that was just full of stuff. We wanted to get him out of there and sell the house so that he didn't have to keep living there. I was working full-time, of course, and had to drive up there every weekend to try to help pack up everything. It took me seven solid months of driving over there every single Friday night, coming back Sunday nights. The first weekend that I went back, I was in the house and went to sleep and had this dream.

My father and my cousin were standing in the dining room and I heard them talking to someone who sounded very familiar. I got up out of bed and walked into the dining room and there they were standing and talking to Mom. I looked at Mom and I said, "You're not supposed to be here; you're dead." Everybody just looked at me like, "Well that's okay; she just came back to talk to us."

It wasn't necessarily that I dreamt that but the feeling that I had when I woke up after I dreamt it was almost like she was trying to talk to me and communicate to me in some way. I didn't have another dream until the following week. It was always when I went back to the house.

In the second dream, it was just the two of us, my mother and me. We were doing what we did when she was alive; we were spending an afternoon together; we went shopping; we went to a little sidewalk café and had lunch and we were laughing and joking and talking and having a good time.

When I woke from that dream, it was almost like Mom had come back and said, "Remember all these good things we did together; I am going to always cherish those, too." I can't explain why I had that specific feeling after I had the dream. It was like somebody was trying to send me a message. These may have been the conjurings of my own overactive imagination and my attempt to pacify myself or rationalize what was going on. Some believe my mother had gone to a better place and I was trying to convince myself of that. I think your unconscious psyche can help you do things like that. It is not necessarily a bad thing when we do that to ourselves. Bear in mind that these are my thought processes because I am a pragmatic individual.

The following weekend when I went back, I had a dream that really got to me. First of all, the house had seven bedrooms and four bathrooms. It is huge. My father had tried to spend the night in their bedroom where they slept together and couldn't do it. I said, "Dad, there is a trundle underneath the daybed in the guest room; just sleep there. You don't have to sleep in your bedroom if it is too much for you to handle." So when I went there every weekend, I slept on the daybed and he slept on the trundle. It was a comfort to be just a few feet away when we went to sleep at night. So the third weekend, I went to sleep and the "dream" I had that night was so vivid; it was unbelievable!

I woke up and sat on the edge of the bed and I saw Dad in the trundle asleep. My mother was sitting right next to me on the bed. It was so real, I could reach out and touch her the same as I am touching this chair right now. I could feel her. I looked at her and I could see her face, I could see her pores as clear as day. She looked very pretty; she looked rested. I tried to wake my father up. I said, "Dad, Dad look who's here; it's Mom; she's here to talk to us." I tried for a couple of minutes to wake him up and he just mumbled and rolled over and he absolutely did not wake up. My mother put her arm on me and looked at me and didn't say it out loud but it was a look that said, "I'm not here to talk to him, I'm here to see you." He just didn't wake up. She looked at me and said, "Vonny, I wouldn't recommend going the way that I did, because God was very firm with me. But I want you to know that I am all right." That is exactly what she said. That was pretty much the extent of the conversation. Then she left. But while she was saying that in just the few split seconds that it was happening, I studied what she was wearing because I thought to myself, *I'm going to go to her closet after I wake up and I am going to find the dress that she was wearing.* I was planning to pack up all her clothes that weekend.

For a person to have such rational thoughts during a dream, according to psychologists and dream experts, is not supposed to happen in most cases. (In other words, it is not usual in a dream to just sit there thinking, "I realize this is a dream but it is really a visitation and when I wake up, I'm going to the closet to find this dress.") It's unusual to have such coherent thoughts during a dream. When I woke up the next morning, I started packing her clothing and looked and looked and looked for that dress because I recognized the dress from when she was alive. I had seen her wear it several times. I could not find it anywhere so I just let it go.

About three months later in December or January, we finally got the report back from the autopsy. It was difficult to read. Being the kind of person that I was and because of everything that was happening physically with my mother, I tried to get some clues, some answers to exactly why she did what she did. It was confirmed in the autopsy that she had a couple of strokes that she didn't tell anyone about. An autopsy report is really a tough thing to read, especially when it describes someone you love. The coroner describes every single detail of her in their examination of her body right down to how much her brain weighs, how much her liver weighs, what color pubic hair she had and what color fingernail polish she had on. It is that much detail. It wasn't morbid curiosity as much as the search for answers. Not only did they describe all the physical details but they also described exactly what she was wearing. The description of her dress that she was wearing matched the dress in my dreams exactly. That's the part that blew my mind. So three months later, I received confirmation as to why that dress was missing. It was strange because emotionally, intellectually and spiritually all at the same time, I decided for myself that that really was Mom coming through to reassure me that she was all right. Never have I so willingly accepted something like that, being the pragmatic person that I was and still am and then three months later, I get this confirmation in no uncertain terms that this was real. I had never experienced anything like that before; nothing has ever happened like that since, but it did happen. It was profound. To borrow an expression from the nineteen-seventies, "It was a trip." In my heart-of-hearts, I know that Mom came back to tell me that she was okay.

Katherine was seven years at the time of her father's suicide. Five months later, she witnessed her mother's murder:

I have a brother who died years ago. I went to be with him. It was very, very difficult when he was dying. I don't know another way to put it but if you have done a lot of grief work, you reach a point when you are thinking, "Would you either die or get well." It was one of those things where he was hanging on and hanging on and he had wasting syndrome. I went to him one day. I went in and sat down and I talked with him; he was pretty much comatose at that point. I told him I would be here for this specific length of time. "If you want me to be here when you die, I am going to be here for the next two hours; otherwise I won't be able to come back until late tonight." So I started talking to him about our childhood, the things that I knew that he enjoyed. All of a sudden I could hear my mother calling to him and I climbed into bed with my brother. I told him what she was saying and his eyes lit up and started moving back and forth. He clearly was watching something as I told him, "Go because she is calling you," and within minutes he died.

I've had numerous dreams, more of my mom than my dad since they died. My very last dream of my mom was about one and one-half years ago when she came to me and told me that she knew that all of this was very, very difficult and that she was okay.

Shelby, twenty-three at the time of her mother's suicide and twenty-nine at the time of her father's suicide, tells of this dream:

I was in my apartment. When I was a child on up until I was a teenager, one of the things my dad used to do was he would come into my room and tuck my feet under the covers. It was a playful thing he did. One night about a month after his death, I was in bed and I felt him sit on my bed; I couldn't see him but

I felt it once again that he gently tucked my feet under the covers. He was showing me affection. I was asleep and partially waking up. My feet weren't actually tucked in, but I felt it.

Steven, fifteen years of age at the time of his mother's suicide, speaks of an incident that has affected him through his life:

One defining incident after her death affected me to this very day. When I was in college living in a boarding house, I was experimenting in ESP and self-hypnosis, spiritual things. I was looking for something. I got turned on to self-hypnosis. I do it to this very day. It's something I learned very young and I learned fast. And if I don't feel good in the morning, I hypnotize myself in the shower and tell myself I'm going to have a good day. And it all comes from visualization. But while I was learning this, I was gazing into the mirror at the boarding house. It was quiet and dark. I had incense burning; my hair was long—hippie long. I was standing in front of the mirror, not looking at myself but through myself and gazing into a long, deep tunnel. I couldn't believe who was standing in the mirror looking at me. It wasn't me. It was my mom. And that was the first time I ever saw that resemblance. Growing up, people told me I look like my mom. And there I was, standing in front of the mirror, gazing into the mirror. And there stood my mother looking back at me. That shocked me. I grew my beard in 1978 and have never shaved it off simply because of what I saw in the mirror.

Sometimes these dreams or happenings are less than comforting but can still be useful in providing insight.

Ambur, fourteen years at the time of her mother's suicide, reveals:

For a long time, I had this recurrent dream. The dream was always that my mother was alive and my dad was around and she was slipping away. I knew what was going to happen, like she was still alive; yet I still couldn't do anything to stop it. It was this helpless feeling of knowing what was coming next and feeling so powerless to do anything about it. I also had a lot of dreams where she wouldn't hug me. I saw her and she wouldn't show any emotion to me or any affection. She was almost like a statue except she wasn't. I had those dreams for many years, mostly from a year after the suicide until two or three years ago. The dreams felt completely real, like it was happening.

I guess I wrestle with the feelings that if she had loved me, she wouldn't have done this. She wouldn't leave her fourteen-year-old daughter alone to deal with all these problems by herself. So it came out in the dream, so cold and unloving.

Janelle, ten at the time of her father's suicide, speaks of her strange experience:

About a year after my dad's death, we were having a sleepover with friends and playing this dumb game. We called it "samurai" and it consisted of one person hiding in the basement with all the lights off and everyone else coming downstairs and trying to find that person in the dark and then making them "give up." (Yes, it was stupid, yes, we occasionally had injuries and no, Mom didn't know about this stupid game.) Anyway, I was the samurai and was in the dark basement and I swore I saw my dad walking towards me from across the room. He was wearing his white sleeveless undershirt and cut-off jean shorts that he always wore in the summertime. I got freaked out and started screaming for them to turn the lights on. When they did, he was gone.

Visions, Dreams, Psychic Experiences of a Pending Tragedy

Rachel, fifteen at the time of her father's suicide, tells:

The most special, extraordinary event happened the night he killed himself, like when he took his life. We don't know exactly when he did it but my mom was on the phone with him in the early evening and tried to call back later but he didn't pick up; he was already dead. I don't know what time it was but I know exactly when he killed himself. I was studying for my chemistry test, and I took a break. I think his soul entered mine, because I went straight to the piano, which I hadn't done in years but my dad was one of the most musical people I had ever known. I just started playing the piano and played and played and then I went back to studying. I know that that was when he died.

Sharon, forty-two at the time of her mother's suicide, recalls:

Recently my mother's older sister died. The night that she died, I was lying in bed and feeling like my mother was very close to me; I felt her spirit. I did not know yet that my aunt had died. She was ill but not expected to die this soon. It was the next morning that we got the call that my Aunt Rosie had died, and I went over to see my cousin that next day and had a talk with her. I asked my cousin what time she had died and I learned she had died the very same time that I had gone to sleep. I also learned that Aunt Rosie had told her that before she went into the coma the day before that she had been visiting with my mother whose name was Selma. She told my cousin that she saw and spoke with Selma and her deceased husband (my uncle). I was just overcome; I knew my mother had been right there with me that night.

Eddie, the father of Bob who had an unsuccessful suicide attempt and then murdered his wife and baby during a psychotic episode, sadly remembers:

Prior to our horrendous ordeal, I talked to a fortune teller one week before it all happened. I was out and saw a gypsy who was charging five dollars for a fortune and there was a parking space right there for me to park. So I went to talk to this lady and she said my life was going to be a shambles, none of it would be my fault and that lots of people were going to be talking about me. She made me feel horrible. I walked out of there and said this is ridiculous. Then it all happened as she said. I was spooked and frightened around our own house after the tragedy. We kept lights on all night for a time.

Shanna, twenty-seven years at the time of her father's suicide, says:

My mother and I were in California visiting one of my brothers who just reconciled back into the family. My parents were separated and getting ready to go through a divorce. My father called and was in a really bad stage of alcoholism. He did not realize I was there.

The night before his phone call, she had this dream:

My father had committed suicide. I was dancing with my brothers at my wedding to Mariah Carey's "Same Day." I saw myself dancing with each of my brothers to that song.

I had not said anything to my mom as yet about my dream. When I hung the phone up with my father, I said to my mother, "Do you think Daddy would ever commit suicide?" She said, "That's an interesting question, why do you ask me this?" I told her I had this dream last night. He killed himself on July the tenth and that discussion was July the eighth.

Many of the survivors with whom we spoke told us of strange

experiences happening at a time of great turmoil in their lives and after several attempts at forgiveness.

Jill M., twenty-seven years at the time of the event, reveals:

I got to the point where I thought I was going to explode because there was so much to understand and my anger was so great. There was nobody to help me with all that. I don't remember whether it was four, five or six months or even a year after the suicide, I just finally said, "Okay, here it is; I can't deal with it and I can't find anyone to help me deal with it. You are going to have to help me deal with it." I just had that kind of conversation with myself and I literally handed it over, you know, to Him.

I asked for help and I got it. It's the weirdest thing because I had a dream of my dad and he was, like, talking to me in the dream. Everything was great and not to worry about him anymore. It was like he was right there. We were walking down the road and I remember him running through the house, which for years he was unable to do, and then we walked outside, walked down the road. I think it is reality; it was just too vivid.

Angela, nine years at the time of her dad's suicide, recalls:

My dad's abuse was so bad. I have had times when I'm sitting in a room and I feel someone is there. I sensed my dad's presence and it had scared me to death. I had a dream when I was twenty-four after I got into therapy and had been depressed for years, waking up at 1:00 every morning. This dream lifted me out of my depression.

I woke up one night and had this dream that I was standing on the porch of a plantation house; my dad came to me in white and said, "I'm so sorry."

Lori, twenty-three years old at the time of her father's suicide, tells us:

I had been looking for my dad always because I didn't live with him. My mother left him on Christmas Day when I was eleven, and so I had always been looking for him. I continued to look for him after he died; I still kind of look for him.

One day, I saw my dad; I just knew I saw my dad. The air just came out of me and I went to follow this guy to get a better look at him to make me see why I thought this was my dad, and I couldn't find him. At home that day, I was just sitting in my room; the kids were out playing or something. I heard my dad's voice say, "Lori" clear as a bell. I hadn't heard his voice since I was pregnant with my daughter (when he killed himself) and my daughter was, at this time, in eighth grade. When I heard his voice, I was wide awake; I was sitting on that bed thinking about what I was going to fix for dinner and I heard his voice clear as a bell. He didn't say anything to me, just my name. It was weird and it never happened since. A couple of nights later, I dreamed he came and sat on my bed. He just sat there and I didn't feel afraid. Normally when he sat on my bed, I would feel afraid. I hadn't realized before that his sitting on my bed was a dangerous thing when I was a child. This time he sat on my bed and didn't hurt me.

Lori goes on to comment:

I have tried over and over again to forgive both my dad and my stepfather, not for the suicide of my father but for the many years of rape from both my father and then my stepfather. I would dream of getting even with them, and I knew I was the only one being tormented while I focused on my anger. I tried as hard as I could for five years to muster everything up to forgive and I could not do it. One day I was in a Quaker meeting (you know Quakers are peaceful people) and I was sitting there. I am not a superstitious, supernatural person; I stay away from that as much as possible. I only told this story to one other person because I am kind of embarrassed to tell it because it sounds so hippie-dippie. It really happened to me.

There was an empty bench behind me and all of a sudden I felt a slap on my head. At first I questioned why a Quaker would hit me in the head so I turned around and nobody was there. I was confused and sat there in bewilderment because I am not a ghost person. I felt something just washing over me like water.

It's still a complete mystery to me, a mystery as to what that thing was, what hit me on the head and what made me feel like something was flowing over me. It was also a mystery to me why I was suddenly able to forgive when I had tried so hard and couldn't. Something did happen that I forgave at that time. I had to rationally explain it to myself as quickly as I could. I couldn't explain the mystical part of it, but I have explained it to myself that I tried so hard for so long, I had laid the groundwork and I was ready and whatever that was that happened, I was really ready for it. At the time I was pretty religious and I explained it to myself as having received grace. It was an incredible experience.

Judy reflects in this short poem on how these occurrences can heal grieving hearts:

> Our unexplained happenings
> can have momentous power.
> Remember them, use them
> for joyfulness to flower.

Overview

We have highlighted in this chapter the incredible stories of a few survivors who had unexplained interactions with their parents in the form of dreams or occurrences. We offer them here as a forum for discussion by other survivors so they will feel freer to reveal and review experiences they may have had that hold so much meaning. We have purposely chosen not to discuss possible rational explanations. Perhaps there are none. Therefore we also share them to offer the possibility that indeed our parents have contacted us in our subconscious, and we have found that often this provides enormous therapeutic value.

CHAPTER 10

Journey of Forgiveness

"Forgiveness is the accomplishment of mastery over a wound. It is the process through which an injured person first fights off, then embraces, then conquers a situation that has nearly destroyed him."

From *Forgiving the Unforgivable: Overcoming the Bitter Legacy of Intimate Wounds* by Beverly Flanigan, MSSW

Mia reflects on the difficult issues of forgiveness that affected her again when her first child was born:

As I write this, my baby boy is sleeping in the next room. He is my first child, and it amazes me every day how much I love him. One of my best friends (a woman who has "adopted" me as her third daughter) told me that I wouldn't love my baby right away. It would take a little while. But when this love blossoms, you feel as though you could go through concrete walls for your child. She was right. I had no idea and could not have prepared for what it would be like to be a mother. I read so many books and magazines; I talked to several mothers; I went to a ten hour Lamaze class and I asked my OB-GYN and his staff many questions. But when my baby finally came home, I had no idea

221

what I was doing. Now I'm more into the groove of this mother thing, but I wonder how my mother could have left me.

This thought hit me hard about a month ago on Mother's Day. People sent cards, my husband gave me gifts, made my favorite breakfast and my tiny son wore an adorable mommy outfit. I felt like being a mother was natural for me. The responsibility, the seriousness, how he depends on everything from my husband and me is amazing. But there I was, wondering as I had done so many times in the past twenty years, how could my mother have left me? On this day the feeling was different than any time before. I wondered about so many other things. Did she breast-feed me? Did I sleep in her bed when I was a newborn? Did she look at me with amazement and love and think how lucky she was to have a daughter, like I do with my son? I could ask my dad, but chances are he wouldn't remember and wouldn't want to. She left me when I was twelve. Maybe it was easier for her then, as opposed to my being a baby. I don't know. I guess I'll find out more about how I feel when my son is twelve. But in my heart I already know that answer.

When I think about forgiving my mother for her suicide, I have a hard time separating that from every other rotten thing she did leading up to that event. There were so many other abuses—emotional, mental and physical as well as abandonment. Her suicide was the culmination of twelve years of stress, sadness and constant anxiety on my part. My first reaction, as with several of our participants, was relief that she was actually gone and all that suffering would end. Now I'm left asking myself if I can forgive her for all that pain during my childhood or if I can forgive her for the suicide, or both.

Judy thinks about her feelings on forgiveness:

February 12, 1942...It's Thursday night at 11:30 p.m. As the doctors and nurses are scrambling about, the long labor of a twenty-nine-year-old mother advances to the last stage of delivery, the birth of her baby girl. The medical staff awaits as a newborn bellows out her first cry and breathes her first breath. The reddish, wailing, kicking infant protests strongly as she makes her first contact with the outside world. Thus far the journey into life has been a difficult one for this baby, as her mother has already made more than one attempt at suicide during pregnancy. First she strived to die by overdosing with sleeping pills, no doubt causing her unborn child much undue stress having to struggle for oxygen, having to fight for life. Then the mother made her final unsuccessful effort while in labor to die with child when the hospital nurses pulled her back from the window as she dared to leap.

When I turned seven weeks of age, my mother made her final attempt to die. She grappled between life and death for two days and on April 3, 1942, the third day of Passover and also Good Friday, my mother surrendered to her departure from life.

Although I have grown with a certain emptiness inside me because of this loss of my mother at such a young age, it is very difficult to comprehend what part forgiveness plays for me in regards to my mother. I look at my only photo of her and me together and I see despair and I feel compassion. I also speak silently to my mother, "You left me at a time when I was totally helpless."

Forgiveness is an emotional issue. We have found in our research and interviews varying opinions on forgiveness from our participants. You may find that different sections may pertain to you at various stages of your journey. If so, you may want to read all of it at one time or only what is pertinent to you at your present phase of your journey, saving other parts for later.

Now we will look at some important issues in the healing process through the views of the authors, our participants and other sources.

1. Forgiveness is a journey
2. The word "forgiveness" has varying degrees of differences
3. Clergy define forgiveness
4. Some survivors reject forgiveness
5. Suicide is frequently connected with conflicting emotions
6. Those who forgive may still feel unwanted feelings
7. To forgive does not mean to forget
8. Our clergy views forgiving and forgetting
9. Guilt, fear and resentment
10. Religious views of heaven, hell and suicide
11. Clergy responses to survivor blame
12. Long forgiveness lists
13. Forgiving does not mean condoning poor or sick behavior

1. Forgiveness is a journey

For most survivors of suicidal parents, the question of how and whether to forgive their parents is recurrent. As we spoke and reflected on the responses of our participants, we came to the conclusion that forgiveness is an expedition. Each and every survivor must choose whether or not to embark on this journey. Only the traveler on this passage can determine the time needed to progress as well as when and how to travel through their journey of forgiveness. It frequently is an excursion that takes an entire lifetime. Perhaps the process may be as important as the final outcome. The process of forgiveness and recovery may continue to creep back into the survivor's life and that can occur because of the many life cycle events in our lives—those we consider as major and some that appear on the surface as inconsequential. No matter how significant or insignificant these events might appear to the survivor or onlooker, they remind sons and daughters of suicidal parents of their losses.

Mia, who at age twelve lost her mother to suicide, as we've discussed, says:

I think it takes a while because there are so many life events—big and small— that constantly remind me that my mother isn't here. Then, it's like my old wound resurfaces and I feel everything all over again. I would think that I had "moved on" with my anger, my grief, my forgiving her but it really is just an ongoing process for me. However, for me with forgiveness, it just comes down to acceptance. I had to accept the circumstances that existed way before my birth that made my mother who she was and ultimately influenced her to choose what she did. I also had to accept that I would never be able to hear from her the answers to my questions, "How could she leave me? How could she leave my brothers and sister?" For me it has had to be enough just to understand that she was in too much pain having had an undiagnosed bipolar condition and being unable to help herself out of her despair.

2. The word "forgiveness" has varying degrees of differences

We asked our participants, "What does forgiveness mean to you?" What we discovered is that forgiveness for the survivors of suicidal parents is a loaded word that frequently has diverse meanings to different individuals. Commonly the word is a dreaded one for those who have lost a family member to suicide, particularly when there is outside pressure for the survivor to forgive. We heard several emotions and confusion in most participants as they grappled for the meaning of the word in the context of their tragic experiences. Many had been told it was something they ought to do. On the other hand, sons and daughters frequently heard from an acquaintance or said themselves that their parents' suicides are unforgivable and their parents do not deserve forgiveness. We learned that the words "to forgive" are used and interpreted in subtle and sometimes not so subtle ways. Consequently, much misunderstanding can result. Frequently advice is given by others who may be well-meaning, but still can be reckless and clichéd with opinions of what needs to be done by the survivor. Being told what the son or daughter "should" or "should not" do by well-meaning (and occasionally not so well-meaning) individuals actually may slow the healing process of the survivor of suicide.

In addition to our research on forgiveness, we read books and publications on this topic written from different perspectives. We spoke with various clergy of different houses of worship to hear their personal and religious interpretations of this complicated and loaded word. Like our participants, there were similarities and diversity among authors and clergy. We also learned that we ourselves had a rudimentary understanding of the word and that we, too, had work to do in processing forgiveness before we could process our thoughts. In this chapter we will share with you what forgiveness means to our participants, what it means to us, how some authors define it and how it's interpreted by various clergy from different Christian, Jewish and Unitarian denominations.

First we look at a sampling of the varied and interesting definitions that our participants shared with us as to what forgiveness means to them. We find them all meaningful and true from their own individual perspectives. Each comment may depict only part of the process of forgiveness, as everyone is in different stages of forgiveness with different lengths of time since the loss of each one's parents through suicide. Some were babies or children at the time of suicide; some were adolescents and others were adults. Most lost one parent to suicide and four of our participants lost both parents to suicide. Some had therapy and others did not. There were differences in family stability during the childhood years of each participant. All of these are significant factors. As we've mentioned, there was diversity in the responses of our participants as to the degree that suicide was or was not a defining event in their lives. These range from some saying it was not to others calling it the most defining event in their lives. Because the subject of forgiveness brings to light such emotional responses, as you read through this chapter, we ask each and every reader to please exercise gentleness with yourself and others around you.

In our interviews, we asked our participants these questions:

1. What does forgiveness mean to you?
2. Was forgiveness an issue that you had to come to terms with concerning your parent's suicide?
3. Is there anyone you felt you needed to forgive in your recovery? (This includes everyone, including you.) If so, would you care to share what that process was like?

Katherine, seven at the time of her father's suicide, witnessed her mother being murdered several months later by her stepfather. These were her feelings about forgiveness:

I found forgiveness when I grew up and I began to understand my stressors, and I realized that my parents' deaths weren't about me. It wasn't about me not being a good enough daughter, and it wasn't about me not taking care of my father. I think from a child's perspective, you're appropriately narcissistic and you think everything is about you, and then I grew up and I saw the world and the stressors that come with the world and I began to realize a little bit more how hard life was. It wasn't necessarily a simple choice. To me that's how I operate. I do real well when I begin to understand things. I recognize things that leave me frustrated, and once I am able to make a little bit more sense of it all, then it may be easier for me to stop being so angry with them and to bring upon some forgiveness.

To me, forgiveness was when I stopped making them responsible for why my life was such a mess. And I have a really good life. I have my legs, my arms, you know. To me, forgiveness was I quit being so angry and I quit blaming them for everything. I quit blaming them for being the reason that I did or I didn't do things. I still have sadness; I still hurt at times but not day-in and day-out. I can look at my parents in my memory and laugh at times. So forgiveness was for me, in a sense, it was a way to let go of being mad all the time, which I used to be. The pissed off part came from holding myself responsible for their deaths and I was fuming at them for their bad judgments because I had to carry their legacy. You know, forgiveness was giving it back saying, you know, you were in charge of your life; you made this decision. This decision did impact my life but as an adult, I make the decisions about what happens now. It didn't make the sadness go away; it didn't make the pain go away but it did give me an opportunity to sort of restructure my journey and my life instead of letting my anger guide where my journey was going.

Tammie's mother took her own life when she was only two years of age. Her father was out of her life and did not come forward to gain a relationship with her even after the suicide. Her maternal grandmother became her guardian, but Tammie was not allowed to talk about her pain or to ask questions:

I honestly had no clue what forgiveness meant at the beginning…At first I thought that forgiveness meant that you just let it go as if it never happened. I also believed what I was told by so many, that what happened is in the past and I needed to put it in the past. Forgiveness has played a huge part in my healing. The longer I was in therapy, I came to realize that forgiveness is not an event, not something that you just do and then it is gone and over with. I discovered that forgiveness is a process. As I began to feel the anger, the resentment, the acceptance and then the letting go, I saw forgiveness with new awareness. I define it now as letting go and not holding on to the events, getting the other person off the hook, allowing myself to feel the pain and anger. I see forgiveness as a gift for me.

Many of us have been told that our parents' suicides happened in the past and to put them there. But to those of us like Allison, such clichés do more harm than good.

Allison was an adult in her forties when her father killed himself. He was suffering from alcoholism and emphysema. Allison viewed her father's suicide "as him being sick and he had no way out." She was around when he was preparing to kill himself and called his psychiatrist who phoned the police. Out of necessity, she removed her mother and herself to safety away from the house.

It was the only way that he knew how. I don't view it as being selfish.

She also shared with us her view that it was the most traumatic event of her life. Forgiveness is a term we should not use without first being aware what it means to the individual to whom you are speaking. For Allison:

Forgiving is loving someone enough to understand and to believe that they did the right thing for themselves. I had to forgive myself for not doing things differently, forgive myself for leaving instead of staying and forgive my mom for being so angry and giving up on him.

Cynthia was in her late thirties when interviewed and was twenty-five when the tragic event in her life occurred. At first she blamed herself for her mother's suicide, saying she didn't visit her mother enough as Cynthia lived seventy-five miles away. Later Cynthia came to realize there were many other reasons not connected to her as to why her mother might have taken her own life. Cynthia says:

For me, it's different for different situations. I think that it's accepting that suicide was her choice, that it's not my fault and that I couldn't have stopped it. I had thought, "If I was only there." Forgiveness to me is realizing that she's now at peace and that she would want me to be happy, to go on with my life and that she didn't do this to hurt me. Forgiveness is feeling thankful for the time I had with her, realizing how lucky I was to have her all of the years that I did. Basically, it also means replacing the bad memories with the good ones. Now there are more good days than bad days. My thoughts are of the happy times instead of any of the fights or arguments, not really fights, but any of the bad times.

David, who has memories of a poor relationship with his parents as an adolescent, was thirty-three when his father committed suicide and thirty-four when his mother took her life. David discusses forgiveness:

Do I forgive my parents? Yes, I forgive my parents. I get mad at them sometimes. At a service I went to, the pastor was saying during a sermon how many times do we forgive? What does the Bible say? The Bible says seven times seven times seven. That was something that stuck with me. That would be my definition of forgiveness. You just have to keep forgiving. The hard part is doing that. I think that is the one thing I've learned with my parents. I had to forgive them. I don't want to forget them because I don't want to do what they did. They made their own choices and I have to forgive them. That's one thing that I struggle with at times, is God says to forgive seven times infinity. You are supposed to forgive everybody. The world would be a better place if everybody did.

3. Clergy define forgiveness
Like our participants, the clergy to whom we spoke have different concepts of forgiveness, which add to our understanding of the concept in relation to survivors.

Chaplain Dora Robinson, Former Hospice Chaplain, Founder Place Ministries, states:
To me it is where you come to a place that you can acknowledge this is what

happened to me, and you have worked through the horror and the anger as best you can and you're able to say, I forgive you. Forgiveness is that point where you can say, "I have let it go because if I keep it, it destroys me and I don't want to be destroyed so God will forgive you." So I'm going on and to go on, I don't want to consume myself with bitterness and pain. It's working with people to try to let it go. There are reasons why people choose to keep the bitterness and pain and to keep the fire and flames going. Sometimes it is because they feel guilty about something they did, so it's actually an act of self-punishment. It is as much being angry at the parent who committed suicide as of getting at the root cause of the survivor's belief that "I brought this on myself." Forgiveness is not just a process to go through; forgiveness is a life-long process. It will always be with you. I think that is part of the myth, that you might think that by forgiving, the feelings are over and done with, as opposed to being able to say, "I am having these anger feelings again."

I have my own term for this called the S.M.F., which is the spiral mind factor. You will start a thought and you will think another thought and it will spiral all the way down until you are just nuts again. And to me, the life-long process of forgiveness is to say, "Hmm, I am really feeling angry again. Okay, I know what this is about. I need to take a moment and sit so I don't go down that path again of beating myself up and raging." It is coming to acknowledge the feeling and also know what to do with it and to say, "This is part of my life; this is not part of who I am." I've had people who write letters; I have had people write letters when they lost a leg and then have the leg write them back. It's acknowledging that you have lost someone or something and this triggers the memories. Hopefully, it comes to a point when one is able to say, "I can see a gift." No matter what it is, one can see a gift. Holocaust survivors and those who get to that point will tell you the gifts. This would be an indication that there has been a significant amount of healing. It's a very long process.

Father Larry Mattingly of Cristo Rey Catholic Church discusses this topic from his perspective:

One of the things I remember when I deal with this is the experience of Jesus with the woman caught in adultery. The law said she should be stoned. Jesus was more interested in the woman and healing than in the law. So he forgave her and told her to go and try to change her life. For me, that is how forgiveness is. It's about God's love and His beginning to mend me from the hurt, the pain and the resentments that separate me from Him. God forgives so that I can forgive myself and feel more at home with others.

Jack R. Harris-Bonham, intern Minister at First Unitarian Universalist Church, brings up another interpretation of forgiveness:
If you think forgiveness is difficult, you're right, but probably not for the right reasons! Inability to forgive is a symptom. The real problem is anger, because we can't forgive someone without first being angry with them. And not many people want to own their anger! The reason we have trouble forgiving is that we have not allowed ourselves the luxury of our anger. Acting out our anger can kill others, stuffing our anger can kill us. We seem to be caught between a rock and a hard place. If the source of anger is threat or fear, then we must understand what threatens us, what we are truly afraid of. It is rather human-like to defend ourselves when we are being threatened. We all tell ourselves stories—that's how we make our lives meaningful; everyone does it from childhood to old age. These stories are sometimes known as core narratives. They are no more or less true than the narrative of Jesus itself. The stories we tell ourselves are there to keep us in a comfort zone—whatever makes us happy or strokes us is in. Whatever we don't like, we either keep it out or expand the story to contain the discomfort.

To forgive, one must first realize what has scared us into being angry—what has pushed us out of our comfort zone. Reality has a way of not cooperating with our comfort zones. If you're angry a lot or feel powerless to forgive those that have dumped upon your dreams, then the stories you are telling yourself might sound like this, "This isn't fair, I'm a good person. Things like this don't happen to good people. Where is the justice in what has happened to me?" You see the problem doesn't lie in the events themselves—in reality. The problem lies in your interpretation of the events—how well you have or have not included these threatening events in your core narratives. For in the end the only thing that actually counts is your interpretation of reality: can't forgive someone for what they've done to you, how they abused you, discarded you, betrayed you? Rewrite your story. Put their actions in perspective, deal with them, their actions, your reactions, de-triangulate yourself, redefine yourself so that your understanding of grace and justice is not so narrowly construed. Try to remember, if you've allowed someone to stomp on your dream, when there was a time that you thought this person worthy of your dream. It helps to again give that person as much credit as you can for being a good and worthy human being. So…let go of the story that hurts you. Write a story that heals and blesses you.

Sensitivity is extremely important in dealing with a survivor about the issue of forgiveness after the suicide of a parent. We feel the best route to take is for friends, family, acquaintances and counselors including clergy to be respectful and supportive when a survivor speaks of his or her own readiness to let go of bitterness and blame and begin the process of forgiveness. It is important as well to be supportive when he or she lapses into anger, sadness and other emotions, as the ability to forgive generally ebbs and flows throughout one's lifetime. This is normal and to be expected. None of us should judge the rightness or wrongness of another's emotions. If the timing is right and only if the survivor is open and interested in such conversation, it may help to discuss with the son or daughter one's own personal journey of forgiveness or to share suggestions of books pertaining to this topic that might be helpful. Never tell the survivor that they must let go or forgive anyone. Insensitivity from individuals and clergy giving indiscreet advice to the recently bereaved to forgive in the early aftermath of the suicide or during or after funerals has caused piercing and lasting pain to the survivor as well as more work for the survivor in order to move forward in the process of healing.

Several of our clergy reflected on their views of forgiveness and suicide survivors:

Rabbi Steven Folberg of Temple Beth Israel says:
In the person choosing suicide, there is frequently some degree of rage, anger or desire, however buried, to hurt the survivors. Wrestling with that reality in so many cases combined with the issue of forgiveness would certainly be huge.

I think there are a couple of pieces to that. One piece is understanding that forgiveness can come only from the victim of whatever the act was. Nobody else can do that for the person; nobody can tell somebody that they should forgive that person because it has got to come from the person who was harmed. Every Yom Kippur we fast and say prayers of atonement for sins that don't involve other people. The prayers are just between God and me. Yom Kippur doesn't do anything to atone for sins between one person and another until those people have made peace with each other. Here you have a case where one of those people is gone and that's the rut; there is nobody to make peace with.

Forgiveness must be done in one's own way and in one's own time. I believe it takes a great deal of time, and I think it is also one of those things that you return to again and again and again. I don't think you figure this out once and then that is it. I suppose someone may get to the point that they begin to get a sense of the emotional toll of not letting go of anger or hatred, a sense of the toll that the anger is taking on the person who is holding on and nursing it. I don't think you can tell anyone when that is. There may come a point where you say, "You know what, I had this very human, kind of control fantasy that if I stay angry enough, somehow it is going to control or stop what already has happened. What it is doing is eating my insides out." Forgiveness is largely a choice to let go of anger, rage and hurt and begin to allow one's self to accept the reality of whatever that reality is, not the way things should be. Forgiveness isn't something you give to the perpetrator; it's something you give to yourself. We're saying this was wrong; it shouldn't have been that way but it was. Eventually, we hopefully will get to the point that we say, "But it happened so where does that leave me?" I don't think anyone else can say that to somebody. I think someone can be supportive of that person as s/he works through the process.

The things that I am saying to you now are not something I would say to a person who is freshly dealing with something like this because it takes on the tone of "What is wrong with you?" I think one of the reasons why forgiveness or letting go is really hard is because people fear if they let go of the anger, then the other person either clean got away with what they did or the person who might forgive feels that they are giving sanction to what was done. "If I am not angry about it anymore, then it must have made it okay to do." Understand that is not the case. The fact that I have forgiven somebody doesn't make it okay; it means I have moved to a place where I am not in the center of it the same way that I was.

Again, I would not say this to someone who is fresh in grief. However, the second Jewish piece of it is that on Yom Kippur, when we do the confessional, we stand up as a congregation together and we all say that we have done this and we have done that. People often say, "Well, maybe I haven't done all those things. Why do I have to say these in front of all those other people?" My response is, "The message is that nobody is perfect; everyone screws up and we admit that communally... One of the things that blocks forgiveness and reconciliation is maintaining the fantasy that I am okay in the sense of being perfect. When I get in touch with my own foibles, weaknesses and blindness to things, I can look at somebody else's stuff and wonder how much anger can I nurse towards that person when I realize that I have a lot of these same qualities anyway. Some of the most unforgiving people are really perfectionist people who sort of walk around with a rulebook on their shoulders dictating how other people "should" act. Again it doesn't make wrong okay. Unless I am willing to apply the same sort of perfectionist rulebook to myself, then I can't hold the other person to those impossible standards either. It's kind of like people being in therapy, which I highly recommend to people in trying to work through their issues with their parents, even let's say without a suicide. It's getting to the point that I understand that my parents were people. Now, if someone is lucky, they're in a situation where they can say that their parents did their best. It is a different situation if someone has parents who are genuinely disturbed enough to be really hostile or violent. Maybe for a person in that situation, it's a matter of saying what kind of home did my parents grow up in? What was done to them? To be able to say well, within the limitations of whatever hand they were dealt with in life, they did their best. When I get in touch with my own imperfections, to the extent that there is a sort of self righteousness in my anger, it deflates some of that because I can say, "You know what, I can be sort of a jerk too."

4. Some survivors reject forgiveness

Forgiveness is for the person who is doing the forgiving, not for the forgiven. It does allow a person to move on, but generally only after experiencing the stages and symptoms of grief: shock, sadness and loss, loneliness, panic, guilt, anger and resentment, hope and finally acceptance. We do not necessarily experience all the symptoms equally (and may even skip some) and do not go through the stages necessarily in this order. People approach grief and forgiveness in their own manner. Who is anyone to say whether each and every person must do it in a specific order or at all?

Karen, age twenty-four at the time of her mother's suicide, began to cry as she spoke:

I've never forgiven my mother and I think that is okay. I just think it's an unforgivable act. My siblings don't feel that way. I hope I retain some of my feelings so that when I see my mother again, I can talk with her about it.

A few of our participants stated that forgiveness was not something they had even thought about or given much thought to until we asked them. Others said forgiveness was never an issue for them. This surprised us until we understood their viewpoints better. Judy states there was a time in her life when she questioned that forgiveness might not be an issue for her in regard to her mother's suicide. While in the midst of our research, it became evident that for her this was not the case; work on forgiveness was clearly of utmost importance to her in regard to her journey of healing from her mother's suicide.

For survivors who clearly don't want to forgive but really want to remember their own feelings in regard to this subject, we feel one consideration might be to keep a notebook for the purpose of writing down all these feelings that they wish to retain. This way one can be sure that these feelings will not be buried or repressed. This was a useful technique that the authors used effectively for their own healing.

After studying this subject and listening to our participants' views, we believe there are reasons why survivors might not feel any need to forgive or may not have even thought about forgiveness:

- Some parents were so physically ill, suffering for so long, that the survivor understood why the parent made this decision. It might not be a decision that the survivors or others agreed with, but it was understandable to our participant.

- The parent may have suffered severely from mental illness and a son or daughter may not believe the parent was actually responsible for his or her own actions.

- The survivor may not have reached the point in their recovery to be able to recognize that there might be an issue with forgiveness.

- The survivor may be feeling relief after his or her parent's suicide and then consumed with feelings of guilt for feeling relief. Relief is actually one of many normal feelings.

- The survivor might not feel the need to forgive because of not ever knowing or remembering the parent. The survivor might have been too young. (In Judy's case, her young age at the time of her loss and subsequent early indoctrination in her family that she needed to leave the past in the past made the forgiveness part of her journey more complicated.)

Jill W., who is now in her mid-thirties, witnessed her mother's multiple attempts at suicide during Jill's formative years. Her mother took her life when Jill was sixteen. Jill states:

No, I had no need to forgive my mother. I knew that my mother suffered tremendously and tried everything she could to get professional help for many years. For as much as I loved her and still miss her, I know that she no longer suffers. I concentrate on the good things and am thankful for what she taught me. She was the most compassionate, caring person I have ever known.

Diane, age twenty-one when her mother took her own life, feels similarly:

Forgiveness is not an issue. No, because she is in a better place. She wasn't really happy here so I think wherever she is, she is happier.

In his late twenties, James refers to his father's suicide as one of the most defining events in his life. His father committed suicide when James was twenty-five:

Regarding forgiveness—I did not struggle with forgiving my father for killing himself simply because he spent all his life making sure I had everything. He was a loving, caring and giving father until the day he killed himself. It was a selfish, impulsive act, but it was the only thing I can remember that he did without thought for me and the people he loved. I had some small struggles at first forgiving my stepmom and aunt and grandmother for hiding his depression from me (something he adamantly requested of them). Those feelings have subsided.

Billi Sue was in her mid fifties when her mother, who was suffering from degenerative arthritis, died from suicide. She reports being very close to her mother and, like many of our participants, says the suicide is the most defining event in her life:

Forgiving isn't anything I thought much about. At the office, my therapist did get a little peeved at me from time to time because I refused to acknowledge anger. I didn't let anger sap my energy. "You have to go through the angry stage," she would say.

I never did get angry with my mom. My mom was my rock, the one who kept me whole and sane during a major crisis in my life. The suicide was so out of character because I thought she had the strength that I didn't have. How can I possibly be angry with her? Anger saps energy; it makes people sweat and sick inside; it raises blood pressure. I refuse to go there. Through this whole process I have never had a time when I've gone into the bedroom and shut the door and covered my head up.

Lori, a woman in her mid-forties, lost her father to suicide when she was twenty-three years old. She was four months pregnant when she learned of her father's suicide. She explains:

It's difficult to disentangle the effects of my father's suicide from his extreme alcoholism and abuse of me.

I had never thought about having to define forgiveness and have had to think about this a lot. I'm glad I had to think about it. What I came up with is that forgiveness is a final way to understand something enough that you quit hurting the person and yourself about it. That is what it meant to me because I had to forgive a lot of people. At the bottom of it, when I finally got to the point of forgiveness that I was able to do it, the realization came that I wasn't hurting them; it was just eating me up inside. It was destroying me to carry around this hatred, all this pain. I needed to quit hurting myself. When I finally got there, I realized that I even understood a little bit. I would never have made the same choices as he did. I still do not think these choices should have been made, but I can understand that my father was in pain.

5. Suicide is frequently connected with conflicting emotions

The emotions one experiences from a suicide are generally more complicated than from a death caused by illness or old age for the survivor. Intense love and anger may be felt concurrently and can be unsettling for the survivor. However, keep in mind that conflicting emotions are frequently experienced in different circumstances during one's lifetime. Mia tells about her own conflicting emotions:

Immediately after I learned of my mother's suicide, I felt so many emotions. I was relieved because she had been such a tyrant in my life and had scared me for so many years. Then, I felt guilty for feeling relieved. I was scared that she was not really dead. What did she look like and would she come back to haunt me? I had to sleep with the light on for several months after that. I was sad because there were some good times and positive memories; she was my mother. I also knew that she loved me (although this area has come into question for me repeatedly over the years). I was confused as to who she really was. What kind of person takes his or her life? If I listened to my step-mother, my mother was crazy and completely unfit as a mother. So, what did that mean about who I was and what part of my mother was genetically passed down to me?

Donna lost her father at fourteen to suicide and was in her late twenties at the time of the interview. She explained to us the fact that there were many unknowns regarding her father's suicide. His body was never found: his jumping off a bridge was witnessed after a failed attempt to die from a vehicle accident. The suicide was not discussed in her family. Talking about this trauma was not acceptable in her family, and Donna became disconnected from the whole event and her father's death. Donna says that for a long time she talked about him as if she were talking about someone she hardly knew.

In some ways I've forgiven my father, and in some ways I haven't. I have a hard time defining it because I could give a definition for both ways. I'm on the fence with that. I think that I am always mad because how could he commit suicide when he had kids? How could he be so selfish and weak? But on the other hand, I think it's a disease and maybe he couldn't help it. I believe both ways. I don't know if that'll ever change.

6. Those who forgive may still feel unwanted feelings

Forgiving does not mean that the individual who has forgiven his or her parent is now pain-free regarding the parent's suicide. The survivor may feel sadness, anger or grief. It doesn't mean that the son or daughter hasn't felt judgmental or honest hate toward the parent for causing him or her heartache and turmoil. Many of our participants and we the authors feel that forgiveness is much more about acceptance and understanding and frequently about going through the process of forgiving again periodically.

Kris lost her mother to suicide immediately after Kris gave birth to a baby at the age of thirty-one. She was in her early forties at the time of her interview:

I'd have to say that, if I could have anything, I would have her back, living a life where she didn't have to suffer from depression. So, even though I was angry with my mom for doing what she did when she did it, I know that it had more to do with her whole chemical makeup, her whole chemistry, her whole being and nobody would wish to live that way or choose that kind of life. And so, more than forgiving her, I'd have to say that I'm just sorry that my mother had to live through that horrible depression. I do realize why she didn't want to live. I'm just sad that she chose suicide as opposed to fighting the battle. It was a tremendous battle for her.

7. To forgive does not mean to forget

"To forgive and forget" is a confusing phrase that has been used and an old adage that has caused bewilderment for many to whom we spoke who are trying to achieve forgiveness. Mia discusses this adage as it applies to her mother's suicide when she was twelve:

A lot of people live their lives by the motto, "Forgive and forget." Personally, I think that only applies to superficial occurrences, such as poor service at a restaurant or bumping into someone without saying excuse me. The message of forgetting was drilled into me after my mother died by people who didn't know me very well and who couldn't handle the seriousness of the situation. They thought if I could just forget, I could move on with my life. Wrong! These people would have been quite satisfied if I had forgotten it all and never spoke of my mother and her suicide again. Being twelve and looking for guidance, I did somewhat forget because I was never allowed to talk about her, ask questions, mourn or even put up pictures of her. However, forgetting my mother and who she really was, both good and bad, really slowed my healing. I had to take a long, hard look at the person my mother really was. She was brilliant, gifted, angry, depressed and a plethora of other attributes, both positive and negative. I had to find out for myself and not just blindly accept the recollections and memories of those who knew her.

About eight years ago, I was on a mission to find out all I could about my mother. I read through her diaries and her letters home from college. I talked to my dad, her sister, her cousin, her sorority sisters, some of her professional colleagues and some of her close friends. I read a letter she wrote me when I was four days old that I had never read before. I looked at several pictures of her throughout her life. I watched home movies that spanned twelve years. The more I did my personal research, the more eager I became to know everything. But finally, I realized this would never happen. I had to take all that I knew and then learn to be satisfied that that was as far as I could go. What I learned for sure was that my mother was highly intellectual and driven academically and that yes, she did love her children. But her lack of appropriate role models of loving parents and her traumatic childhood left her clueless and hopeless at ever truly succeeding in maternal relationships.

Carla's father died from suicide when she was eleven years old. She was in her late twenties at the time of our interview. She commented that when her mother first told her that her dad took his own life, all she could think was:

And whose life did he save in the process? I did not immediately realize that he had committed suicide. Unfortunately, this ignorance lasted only moments and when the realization of what actually happened struck me, I experienced a wide range of emotions.....anger was never one of them.

Forgiving someone is possible when you understand that they are sorry for what they have done and are able to let it go—"forgive and forget." My problem is forgetting. There is a great quote in John Irving's book *A Prayer for Owen Meaney* that accurately describes my dilemma in terms of "forgetting"—it basically says something to the effect of "you think you have a memory, but it has you"—meaning, no matter how much you want to forget something, sometimes your memory won't allow it. Luckily, time does.

David lost both his parents to suicide one year apart from each other when he was thirty-three and thirty-four:

I just have to keep forgiving and that is the hard part. In my opinion, when people do me wrong, I want to hold a grudge. That is the one thing I have had to learn from both the suicides. My parents made their own choices and I had to forgive them. I don't want to forget because I don't want to do what they did.

8. Our clergy views forgiving and forgetting

Interviewing different clergy from diverse faiths, we learned they have various interpretations of the phrase "forgive and forget." All had something valuable to contribute while each gave a different slant. Three clergy speak here of their various viewpoints.

Father Larry Mattingly of Cristo Rey Catholic Church states:

It seems logical that if I say I forgive and still hold grudges, I really haven't forgiven. I said I forgive but the experience of forgiving has not touched me. Jesus forgave and didn't seem to ask a lot of questions. He always counseled them in to trying to get them to change their lives after they have been forgiven. But forgiveness without letting go of the hurt is not going to affect a person very profoundly. Forget can mean a lot of things. We really never forget experiences that impact our life. To this day I remember where I was standing when I heard that John Kennedy was assassinated. When I heard my mother had died or my father had died, I remember where I was. So obviously you are going to remember those things. When we say forgive and forget we're talking about the resentments and hurts and those issues that affect no one but me. I could hold resentments and grudges and that person could care less if I hold the resentment. I am the one who suffers because I keep that within me. I think the forget part of forgiving is that healing of those inner hurts and resentments and feelings that keep me from being at peace.

Father David Hoster of St. George's Episcopal Church gives his view:

Forgiveness is about restoring the health of the relationship before whatever it was that came along and broke it, to get back to that state of grace and union. Forgiveness is not just saying, "Oh, forget it." It is not like playing that something bad never happened, because I think we know that from psychology that when you play like something never happened, then you don't deal with it and in fact there is something that stays cold, stays disunited in the relationship with the other person. You don't do what needs to be done to overcome that and get back into the relationship. You just pretend that something never happened. When you are pretending, you are not back into the relationship. Just saying, "Forget it, let's move on" is not a form of forgiveness. The old phrase is "forgive and forget."

There are degrees of forgiveness in ordinary human experience. For example, with suicide, it must be awfully important for the survivors to talk about forgiving the person who committed suicide. It seems to me that the person who committed suicide has done something that is incredibly selfish, an assault on the relationship. It's saying, "I don't care enough about you to continue to live in the relationship with you." Therefore, there is some real searching work that has to be done, spiritually and psychologically, for a suicide survivor in order to get back to that union with the person. Of course the person isn't there so you're not talking about a union in which you are actually face to face, but a union in which you can be at peace with who the person was. Gee whiz, that means coming to some state of peace and forgiveness and acceptance of whatever it was that you hold yourself responsible for in that relationship that led to the failure, if in fact you do. I guess the way I would define forgiveness is being able to move ultimately, in time—it takes a lot of time—but ultimately be able to move, in time, with all your heart into the reality of the brokenness of that relationship in order to come to a place where, by the grace of God, you can take a deep breath and be at peace with that and say, "Yes, we are talking about this person, a human being and not God and s/he was flawed. I am a human being and not God and I am flawed, but I can live with this." The act of forgiveness is saying I accept you and I accept myself and I accept our relationship with all of this sinfulness and all of this brokenness. That's a very grace-filled and marvelous and wonderful kind of healing moment when you can do that. To me, that is what forgiveness is about.

The forget era is part of that same era that I was talking about a few moments ago when basically you set a standard for how things are supposed to be good and right. If they are not good and right that way, then what you want to do is cut off and get rid of this stuff that doesn't feel good and right, which is as I said before: a denial of who we are, and a denial of who the other person is or was as a human being. We all have our dark sides. God knows that and God can live with our dark sides. We have this immediate response of feeling that, "I have to forget this if I am ever going to get past it. I have to pretend that this didn't happen, that this doesn't exist, that this person isn't this way and this person hasn't done that." Pretending is not life. Forgetting is pretending. I think once you've gone through the forgiveness, there may be sort of a forgetting of the horrible pain, the immediate pain of something being done in that you've come to peace with it so you don't reenact that pain every time you think about the person. Even when you have forgiven, you do have moments when you go back. The anniversary of a death, for a lot of folks, is always a moment when feelings come back with force; they come back from outside your conscious control and they really can bite you pretty hard. That's not even with suicide but that's with any sort of death or difficult event. Forgetting is not a virtue. I really wonder, and I don't presume to know or understand the minds of folks who commit suicide, but my sense is that the compulsion to forget or to deny can lead you to that kind of desperation to start with. If you feel that life ought to be good in this way and that your life is awful because it is not like that and you can't live with that, you have to deny it and will want to forget it. But you can't. I think doing that could make you desperate in just the sort of way that I think may lead some folks to suicide. I think this business about forgetting is really pretty dangerous, pretty awful. Denial is a terrible thing and it costs people their lives sometimes.

Rabbi Folberg of Temple Beth Israel discusses:

There is a Jewish folk expression, and I don't know where it comes from and I am going to mangle it, too; it says something like a mean-spirited person forgets but does not forgive. This is like holding a grudge. "I don't even know what I am still angry about but I am still angry." A different kind of person neither forgives nor forgets. The wise person forgives but does not forget, forgiving in the terms of saying that I don't need those emotions anymore, I have found a way to a different place, but forgetting, in a lot of circumstances, means that one is in the position to be hurt by that person again if they are still alive. Memory is part of what we get, for better and for worse. There is a book on mourning and grief that I like where the author gives an analogy in terms of mourning and he says the difference between fresh mourning and mourning which has years behind it is that when grief is fresh, it is like a book which is just sitting on the table all the time and every time you sit down to the table, the book is open to that page. But after a while, mourning is more like a book that you put on a shelf and you can take the book down and open it up and look at it when you choose to, knowing that it is always there. The book is still on the shelf in the library but it isn't on the table, open all the time.

9. Guilt, fear and resentment

Hanging on to feelings of guilt, fear and resentment may cut us off from ourselves and others around us and may cause us to be incapable of love. Mia shares her thoughts on her mother:

I think of how this describes my mother perfectly. She carried so much guilt and resentment that she could never work through. It ran several layers deep for her and spanned through most of her life. When she would make a small attempt to address it—just acknowledge that it existed—the need to hurt herself was too great and she would fall back into her self-destructive patterns and try to take those closest to her along with her.

Friends, family, therapists and clergy can all tell you that you're not to blame for the suicide, that you never could have changed what happened. But if you do not come to this realization on your own and believe it in your own heart, it will never bring you peace. Judy, seven weeks when her mother died from suicide, tells about her aunt:

My aunt was twenty-six years of age when my mother took her own life and was eighty-three when she died. I called her at least every weekend, as I lived 1500 miles from her. She never talked much before about my mother (her sister). When she was very ill, I told her about my research and that I planned to write a book to help other survivors. I asked her if she might speak with me about her sister. This was really the first time we had a heart-to-heart conversation about my mother. This talk took place only one month before my aunt died, and I never had any idea what she had been thinking for the past fifty-seven years. I believe she tortured herself all these years. In that call, she sobbed as she spoke. She said she never wanted to remember how my mother died. What was so obvious to me was that she never forgot it for the rest of her life. At the end of our talk, she said she felt much better, and she asked, "Are you going to put this in your book?" I told her yes, and she said she was pleased. Here are the words my aunt spoke to me:

"It was terrible. Ah anyway, before she did that, I called and told her I'm getting married and she says, 'Oh, are you going to invite me?' and I said, 'Of course, I'm going to invite you, you are my sister; what do you think?' That was the last I heard. I'll never forget those words: 'Are you going to invite me?' I felt so bad because of course I was going to invite her. She could be still living, you know and we could be together with her and everything. Ay, it's tough. I miss her a lot because I was, well she and I were close. Maybe she was mad at me, I don't know. I never even thought she would actually kill herself. It has always bothered me. I don't always do the right thing. Look at me now. I'm lying here in bed. That's what I have to realize. I keep thinking maybe that's why she did it, because I was going to get married. She was begging me to take her home when she was in the hospital the last time. Then she died that night. Where could I take her to? I was living in somebody's room that I rented. I couldn't take her home. And she had a husband. It was awful. I never want to remember that anymore."

My aunt had always felt responsible, but she talked about it and we spoke again the next day. She laughed and sounded so much better. She sounded free of guilt.

10. Religious views of heaven, hell and suicide

We asked the clergy with whom we spoke two questions relating to this topic.

1. Does your religion believe there is a heaven and a hell?
2. Will a parent who committed suicide go to hell?

Here are some very different responses which we hope are indicative of the many interpretations those who are grieving may turn to for comfort.

Rabbi Alan Freedman of Temple Beth Shalom told us:

In Judaism, there is a heaven but it really is undefined. There is no hell. "It may take certain people longer to get to heaven." I use that in quotes. But everybody gets there. I don't have a lot of trouble saying to people who have had relatives who committed suicide that death brings a certain peace and rest to everybody. It's kind of equal. The anguish that their loved one was in during life. It's funny because we are very dismissive of physical pain and anguish during life. We say, well at least they are out of pain. We're seemingly less so about mental anguish. I sort of view mental anguish and physical pain as the same. If someone is that troubled that they would take their own life, well they are as much at peace as someone whose last days were racked with physical pain. I think in a way we can be just as grateful for the fact that they are out of that mental anguish. There is nothing in Judaism that it deters or penalizes one's relationship with God and where you go. Afterlife is undefined in Judaism and purposely so. Judaism isn't about what happens after you die. Judaism is about what you do while you are here. The source of an afterlife is "what you did here that reminds people that you were once here." It's really of that nature as opposed to "if you conduct yourself in a certain way, you are assured of some sort of paradise." That is not part of the religion.

Father Larry Mattingly of Cristo Rey Catholic Church states:

I would say the same I say about people who die, we have to believe in God's mercy; we presume that a person who harms himself was not acting rationally at the time and I believe God will save them. No one knows what happens to a person but we do know how God loves people. God's mercy and kindness towards us is obvious, and I think my job is to communicate that sort of message to people.

Dr. Gary D. Kinnaman, Senior Minister of Word of Grace Church, says:

Now, I know some people believe that if you commit suicide you're going to hell because you don't have a chance to ask God for forgiveness. Yes, we need to confess our sins daily to keep our lives clean, but not to make sure God doesn't turn against us. Certainly suicide has terrible social consequences. It's way up there on the bad sin scale. But to God, sin is sin, large or small. I'm here to tell you that there are a lot of things I do that I don't even know I'm doing, and I don't always ask specifically for forgiveness for everything I do. Sometimes I just forget. So what if I die suddenly right after committing some sin, any sin, without a chance to confess? For me, I have to trust that Christ forgives not only my sins, but my forgetfulness and frequent failure to confess those sins, too.

Father Benedetto Ravano, Monk of the Santuario Madonna de Sasso order, opines:

The Catholic faith will not argue whether suicide is condemnable or not, it will stress that life is a gift from He who is Good, the only Good One. He is also the only Judge and He has knowledge of all that agitates and troubles the human heart. We trust in His wisdom and mercy, knowing that He became a man like us and experienced death for us who were doomed to despair. Probably in the past, when society was more deeply Christian, suicide was contemplated as a lack of faith in God and thus considered more sternly. There were times in which someone who had committed suicide would not be buried in a Christian cemetery, since such an act was considered as serious as an apostasy. Today this is no longer the case, and people who commit suicide receive a Christian funeral and burial, trusting that God, in His infinite mercy, has touched their heart before actual death occurred. However, I believe that a strong faith, well-nourished throughout a man's life, is the great antidote against this temptation which affects almost everyone at one time or another.

As far as I am concerned, I remember meeting only one person who committed suicide and who was coming to our religious house at the very beginning of my religious life. She was convinced that she had to commit suicide for the good of her family, to give them a moral shock and "bring them back to their senses." She was very depressed and not even the word of our founder convinced her. I also talked to her many times, but in the end she jumped into a river. So even this single case made me understand how difficult it is to understand and share what takes place in a human heart and mind. There is probably a point in life in which we have to overcome a crucial temptation which wants to overturn our mind, and maybe a single word, or smile or kindness, even from a stranger, but so much more from someone you know, may change your destiny. Such is the attention which clarity requires, but the mystery remains. As to forgiveness, we all know that suicide is sometimes meant to hurt those who are left behind, and hurt them badly. Here too we should forgive, but we are able to do so, in a deep true way, only with God's help, with God's all-powerful mercy and compassion, with a real experience of faith in His love for us.

Chaplain Dora Robinson, Former Hospice Chaplain of Founder Place Ministries, gives this view:

Generally when people ask me that question, my answer is always, "There's a beautiful line from the philosopher William James who said, 'I know there's a God because I can feel God's breath on my heart.'" So I'll say to the person, "I can't prove it but I just do believe it." I also believe that there is a place of profound love that we all go to and so I anticipate I will see everyone there. Now what happens is if someone says to me, "Will Hitler even go?" My response is I believe in an all-powerful, loving God and when you stand before God, you may see all the wrongs that you have done and you may grieve and weep over them but love transcends over the evil and you go in. So that's my theology. This is hard sometimes for people to hear.

Pastor Dan Davis of Hope Chapel tells us:

I would start by inviting them to validate and express their anger at the parent for what they did. In my theology, the parent who committed suicide sinned against their child. It is a terrible offense against their children. I believe this is the appropriate starting point, because the survivors almost always are tempted to take the guilt upon themselves. Our family relationships are almost always incomplete and we can always find ways to blame ourselves for something that we should have done, or something we shouldn't have done.

Then I would ask them to empathize with the severe emotional pain that their parent was in to do such a terrible thing. I would then move on to walk them through a process of forgiveness for their absent parent's act. Suicide is not the unforgivable sin. I understand depression well enough to know that the emotional pain is so severe that people can do very irrational things. God's love and grace is far bigger than ours. Obviously, my commitment to Christ's love and forgiveness would be central to everything that I asked them to do. As a Christian, I believe in heaven and hell. If they had confidence in their parent's relationship to Christ, I would actively encourage them to know that they would see their departed parent in heaven. If they were not certain, I would press them hard to know that God will always do things right and that they can trust His judgment in the matter. Even in the last fleeting moments of a person's life, Christ can meet them. I would never tell them that their parent went to hell. The Bible is clear that neither I nor anyone else is qualified or permitted to make that judgment.

Father David Hoster of St. George's Episcopal Church has different thoughts and feelings:

I have all sorts of complicated thoughts and feelings about the notions about heaven and hell. I feel what matters is intimacy with God and whether a person can find union with God; that's heaven obviously. I'm primarily concerned about that in my business. I feel it is very destructive in the church for us to threaten people with hell and emphasize that kind of horrible and negative side-effects. Certainly I think clergy are very punishing of suicide survivors if they are told their parent is going to hell. Equally bad is, "I don't know if your dad is going to hell or not" and then sort of weaseling out of it that way without clearly stating and being willing to go on-line that God could mend this. Of course, ultimately to me, who the heck are we to say this anyway? God has the power to do that; if there is any message in scripture at all, it's that God has the power to redeem us; God has the power to come back into a relationship with us. I do think we have some choice about that and something to say about that. "I don't want to be with God. Maybe I want to be in horrible isolation forever." I certainly don't think that is God's choice for us. I guess when we start talking about heaven and hell, where things go from here; I would simply want to say that is God's world and God's business. I can't speak for God except to say that I know that every iota of God's being is directed toward redeeming us; that is why our God sent Jesus Christ to die on the cross, to go to the very worst place that we could ever possibly be, just to wake us up. If God is really serious about this, then you just can't escape Him by killing yourself. Sorry, you can't get out of it so easily.

11. Clergy responses to survivor blame

We asked our participating clergy how they would respond if a survivor of suicide came to them and said: "I can't forgive my dead parent; I can't forgive my surviving parent; I can't forgive myself; I can't forgive God; I just can't forgive."

Chaplain Dora Robinson, Former Hospice Chaplain of Founder Place Ministries, says:

Sometimes I say to a person, "Who can you forgive?" I also am very visual and if the person is open, I'll say something like, "It strikes me like this is your wound: (_____). You have this incredible wound, and can you tell me what is inside here?" Sometimes that visualization of what is inside here is helpful. I say to the person, "You may never come to the place of forgiving your parents but my prayer for you is that your wound, by working it through, will look something like this (_). My prayer is that you will come to a place where you are not consuming yourself, where you can get your anger out and have it be okay that you are angry." One of the wonderful opportunities is that hospice gives people who are caring for your dying loved ones opportunities to do reconciliation. The other thing I will ask people at some appropriate point in this arduous, exhausting journey, "Can you see the gifts?" It is pretty amazing the conversations that I will have with people. They will look at me and say, "Gifts?" I'll say, "Yes, what are the gifts? Can you see any gifts?" They will begin to talk. They say things like, "I did get to sit next to Dad; I did get to hold his hand; I did get him to look at me and say something. My brother and I finally talked after all these years. My baby sister who I thought was an absolute dingbat was the one who took over and handled the whole thing. I always thought my mom was a strong woman and now I see her as this person who's real fragile." There is lots of stuff that comes out.

Father David Hoster of St. George's Episcopal Church gives this response:

That is just such a struggle; you can't forgive God; you can't forgive the person who left; you can't forgive family members who let them down. Ultimately I wonder if there is some sense that the person can't forgive themselves. That may be part of it. I certainly would not pass judgment on anybody like that. I just wonder if there is not some way in which the way back to health is to kind of let down and stop being harsh on the world and harsh on others and on him or herself. We certainly know people who are just harsh as all get-out, not necessarily because they had someone commit suicide but for any reason. It could be that someone was elected president that the person didn't want. Lord knows what, but they just get angry and bitter, you know, a recession and got laid off, life stinks and their wife left them. They are mad, angry, unyielding and unforgiving about life. I think that is a real hard place to be. Forgiveness is about stepping back, taking a deep breath and saying things are this way, but this isn't the whole world. You forgive God for the world being the way it is. You forgive yourself for hardness of heart.

12. Long forgiveness lists

Many participants spoke of having to do a lot of forgiving after the suicide of their parents. One participant speaks of this issue in detail.

Candice was in her mid-fifties at the time we spoke to her. Thirty years had passed since her father's death. He had been a clergyman and her mother was adamant that his death be attributed to a heart attack.

So many changes had occurred in my life that year. My soon-to-be father-in-law died of cancer in April, I graduated from college in May, my father died by suicide in June, I was married in August and my grandmother died in September. Later that year I was diagnosed with Muscular Dystrophy. My life felt completely out of control. I put myself back in "control" in the form of anorexia. Little did I know at the time that I was anything but in control. My body deteriorated, my heart went numb and my spirit left my being. The anorexia was my friend and way of coping (or not coping) for over twenty years.

Candice said she had a difficult time struggling with guilt over her father's suicide:

I felt guilty and could not forgive myself for not being a "good enough" daughter. I felt guilty and could not forgive myself for not preventing Daddy's suicide. I felt guilty and could not forgive myself for what I thought was my part in his suicide. The guilt made me physically and psychologically ill. Eventually I realized that I had to forgive myself. I even needed to forgive my dad for his act, my mother for not letting me talk about it and God for allowing my dad to be sick in the first place.

The hardest forgiveness was to forgive myself. I believed that it was my fault because Daddy had difficulty accepting that his "baby" daughter was marrying a Roman Catholic. He had been counseling a family in our church whose daughter was also marrying a Catholic. He told them, "Ecumenism is coming. There are more similarities than differences, and we will need to learn to accept other faiths." Yet, he was upset about his own daughter's impending marriage to a Catholic. He could not tolerate his own hypocrisy. To me, the situation meant that if I had not been engaged to a Catholic, Daddy would not have felt like a hypocrite, which led to his suicide.

My parents, fiancé and I all had to go to be interviewed individually by a priest in order to be married in my church. My dad was to officiate at our wedding along with a priest friend of ours. The purpose of the interview was to determine that we would not use birth control and that our children would be raised Catholic. My parents had to sign papers declaring this, as did my fiancé and I. My dad came home from that interrogation and he just shook his head and said, "I feel like I signed my daughter's life away." My mother told him he was being melodramatic. Daddy's depression developed into a vegetative state. I found him in an overdosed stupor and he died two days later. I had been angry with the Catholic Church for many years. It was just too hard to forgive.

I also realized that I needed to forgive my mom for telling us to keep the secret. Daddy was a wonderful pastor, a compassionate counselor and a dynamic person. People loved him. I loved him. I now think that my mother was wrong. Daddy's final act did not "undo all the good he had ever done." I also needed to forgive her for calling me "stupid." Stupid referred to my revealing the truth about his death and because I was in so much emotional pain over an event which happened so long ago. Fortunately, I have been able to forgive my mom. She had always been a great mom but she made a big mistake.

And then there was forgiving God. I think I was angry with God for allowing my dad to be bipolar in the first place. I also had difficulty differentiating my dad from God. I know that seems silly, but as a small child I had thought of my dad as God, standing in the pulpit dressed in his white robe and saying "God-like" things. By extension, because I felt responsible for my father's death,

I felt that God was dead to me, too. All those years I attended church religiously, taught Sunday school, lead the youth fellowship, served as an elder, sang in the choir and all that stuff. I had a lot of religion but I had no spiritual base and no real relationship with God. With lots of help, I was on my way to healing physically, emotionally, mentally and spiritually.

I do not believe in "forgive and forget." How could I ever forget finding my dad like that? I think forgiveness is remembering without resentment, retribution and recrimination toward self or others. I learned to forgive and remember.

Candice ended her interview with us by speaking of the issue of acceptance:

Acceptance does not mean liking it. I will never like the fact that my father ended his own life. I will never like that he felt desperate and lonely in the preceding years and especially in those moments prior to taking the overdose. I will never like any of it, but I can now accept that it occurred and use this tragedy to deepen my love for God, for others and for myself.

I have now found peace in my soul. Healing from the guilt and pain has allowed me to love others in ways I could never have dreamed. I loved my dad and my dad loved me. Lastly, I can now take solace when I visualize finding my dad laying in his bed with the Bible opened to the twenty-third psalm.

Margaret, twenty-nine at the time of her father's suicide, made a list of people she needed to forgive:

1. family members who failed to obtain appropriate mental health intervention,
2. my father for "abandoning" me in such a way,
3. my stepmother for not recognizing his serious problem with depression,
4. his psychiatrist for failing to provide appropriate treatment and
5. the psychiatric hospital that released him on a pass (on which he completed suicide).

13. Forgiving does not mean condoning poor or sick behavior

Josephine, nineteen at the time of her father's suicide, says:

Forgiveness is to allow people to have made mistakes and continue to value/acknowledge their presence in your life and development.

Mia reflects on how Josephine's theory affected her:

I had to read Josephine's sentence over and over to really get the message. It released me in a way from what people would tell me about my mother—that she was sick, a bad person who did a terrible, unforgivable thing and she wasn't a good and loving person or mother. For twelve and a half years, I had a good and loving mother who took care of me the best she could, considering her handicap, her impairment that went untreated. I can separate who she was in her soul from what her condition would make her do. I can separate the abandonment from the act of suicide. Knowing this and understanding this has lifted a burden from me and has allowed me to have some compassion for my mother. I can also look at myself and recognize the positive traits from her that we share, and I feel good about that.

As does Judy:

As my research continued I became aware I was horribly blocked on the issue of forgiveness. It was a difficult and painful subject for me. Then I realized that I needed to go through old photos. I did this and found four photos of my mother, which I looked at and studied for hours. The one photo that I had of Mother and me, the only photo that exists of me with her, was full of shadows and in poor condition. I took this photo and had it refurbished. Then I knew that these photos needed framing. They now add the right sentiment to my office. In the process of all this, something strange happened within me. I felt as if I was acquainting myself with my mother and much to my revelation, I felt intense love towards her.

Overview

Forgiveness means different things to different people, so it is important to understand how the son or daughter who has survived a parent's suicide defines forgiveness. Through our research and our own tragic experiences with suicide, we have come to believe that there are many things that forgiveness does not mean. It does not mean that once the process of forgiving has been worked on that the person who has forgiven does not feel pain or sadness connected to the suicide. It does not mean that we who are survivors condone suicide. It does not mean that the tragic experience that has impacted our lives is forgotten. It does not mean that once the person has forgiven that the process is complete forever. Generally, we have found survivors work on forgiveness for a lifetime as individuals might tend to fall back into old patterns and might need to redo some of the work to regain peace once again. However, once forgiveness has been achieved, these periods of relapsing into old behaviors, as a general rule, become less severe and less frequent as our process of forgiveness becomes stronger.

Forgiveness does mean, however, that we have let go of the anger, resentments and hurt. We understand that hanging on to these feelings for an indefinite period of time is punishing to ourselves. These feelings cause emotional disorders and may precipitate physical illness as well. Certainly, we cannot lead fulfilling lives when we are paralyzed with grudges and other such emotions. Also, we will alienate others by grasping so desperately to these negative emotions for years. However, all these emotions are normal for survivors of suicide and usually need to be felt at first. Forgiveness also means we can allow ourselves to feel compassion towards all involved, including ourselves.

Forgiveness does not happen overnight and may take time to work through, perhaps years. Sensitive and skillful therapists, medical professionals and clergy can be instrumental and therapeutic in guiding survivors through the process, but first a sufficient amount of time needs to be allowed for the survivor to let him or herself feel the pain and sadness precipitated by the event. Others may also be supportive in assisting the survivor through this process, such as a good friend who understands forgiveness or a facilitator of a support group.

surgery or buying your first house. It can be the simple everyday
ons or a random comment or question from a friend. In the end,
authors felt a sense of comfort in the stories of our newfound
r friends who told us they shared the same phenomena. We shared
d been a secret and not to be spoken. We broke the silence.

different experiences we heard depended mainly on the age of
ticipant at the time of his or her parent's suicide. We note that
oung children who lost a parent to suicide have a sense of shame,
d lack a sense of belonging. They often tend to be more
le to family abuse and psychological trauma. They can have a
rame of reference for their own place in the world, i.e. their own
history. They may have difficulties connecting with others, and
y have anxieties about becoming a parent.

ing adolescence, acting out and self-destructive behaviors may
er a parent's suicide. This age group struggles with self and
entification issues as it is, which is only further complicated by
suicide. They want to feel "normal" but that can be near
e to define. It's a difficult line to walk with this group to give
support and help they need while not overwhelming them and
tly causing them to withdraw into isolation.

adult, having a parent who chose to take his or her own life is
more difficult and painful to deal with than a death as part of
l lifecycle. More often than not, the son or daughter has
n playing the role of a parent to help with financial, physical
chological problems. This group has likely already fought a
to keep their parents alive despite all the circumstances. Many
ith felt primarily abandoned by their parents' acts.

we as authors walked away with from these interviews were
ficant themes. First, no matter what age the survivor was at the
arent's suicide, finding the right kind of help that is provided on
basis is undeniably so essential. Friends, family members, co-
acquaintances are all well-meaning, but that support eventually
le the pain and grief of a parent's suicide goes on—almost begins
day for some. Second, we learned that in talking about one's
ne can begin to feel some healing, some hope for themselves.
feelings associated with the suicide, discussing with a therapist
n in the quest for reasons for this event (even when there won't
finitive answer), shouting, crying and writing a letter to the
this releases the myriad of emotions and brings healing.

CHAPTER 11

Destinations

This book is one of our ways of creating something positive from our tragic events. Before we wrote it, we as authors knew about our own individual experiences of parent suicide and somewhat about our siblings', although the topic wasn't really discussed between us in a healthy or therapeutic way. We had explored our grief as it pertained to us—how old we were at the time, how old our mothers were when they died, the manner in which they passed, how our friends, family and acquaintances treated us and eventually how we entered or re-entered the world with this legacy. We had lived with our own stories for so long—the majority of our lives. We knew them so well from many hours spent with therapists, spent journaling and spent thinking, crying and reliving our pasts.

Voices of Strength: Sons and Daughters of Suicide Speak Out has taken on a life of its own since our journey began. Initially our goal was to offer constructive information and suggestions to the sons and daughters of suicide. Very soon thereafter, it became evident that to thoroughly accomplish this, the larger issue of society and its responses to suicide survivors needed to be addressed. Should the readers be students studying for vocations or professions that would bring them into contact with a survivor of any age of parent suicide, we hope our book will increase their knowledge and help them to guide survivors with respect and empathy on how to purposely respond.

253

For those who have lost a parent to suicide, we hope that they will find comfort in the knowledge that they are not alone and that their experiences and feelings are similar to others who have been through a parent suicide. We have tried to explore the issues that are faced by the offspring who experience parent suicide and to elucidate the steps towards healing. We are hopeful that *Voices of Strength* will be an inspiration to survivors to begin or to continue to work towards rebuilding their lives.

Lastly, for those parents who are contemplating suicide or who have already attempted it in the past, this book shows the damaging ripple effect that occurs with such an event. It shows how that effect really never ceases for the survivors. It is our hope that all our readers will conclude that suicide is never an option.

We have spent ten years in researching and then deciding to write this book together, but the content spans more than 2,629 years of accumulative individual lives. When we started, we only knew that we wanted to know the personal stories and the experiences of other survivors of parent suicide. The journey, in fact, began when we actually started contacting people and hearing their stories. In one situation, we interviewed grandparents who spoke on behalf of their grandchild who did not survive her father's attempted parent suicide. It has never ceased to amaze us that so many people, mostly strangers, were so willing to tell two women they didn't know of such traumatic events that shaped their lives. We remember our first tape-recorded phone interview. Fueled by excitement and overly-prepared with numerous questions, we conversed for over an hour. All our participants shared momentous emotions and memories and were easy to talk with. When we finished our research and interviews, it was time to write this book. In some ways it felt like the journey began all over again.

Voices of Strength is a major way of creating something positive from our tragic events. Definitely *Voices of Strength* has been part of our journey and a very significant part of our healing process. It is our way of giving back to our community of survivors and to help others to eventually build fulfilling lives after a parent's suicide. It is our hope that you, the son or daughter of a suicidal parent, will decide to work towards thriving and reaching the goal of finding your own constructive ways to turn your tragic event into a fulfilling and rewarding life.

Survivors of All Ages

The majority of the work we did on our book invol we met and interviewed. This process was more tim actual writing of the book. It began with a search for lost a parent or stepparent to suicide and were eigh older. (Their age at the time of the suicide could be people who had resources available to them: ther groups, close friends or family members. We f questionnaire and follow-up interview could bring events that our participants might need to deal with sure that in such cases they would have someone a experiences with. On the internet we searched for and contacted the facilitators at that time, who newsletters, made announcements at support gro flyers at a Suicide Survivors national convention were Tri Valley Survivors of Suicide in Livermore Suicide Loss in Sacramento, California; The One Texas; Heartbeat in Colorado; and Survivors (SOLOS) in San Antonio, Texas. We advertise Suicide (SOS). We posted ads in the Texas Psy Network. We had a couple of referrals from a th from a religious congregation. We knew s personally. Mia had co-workers who, unkno parent suicide. It was amazing that often anyon book with, that person would know of anoth parent suicide or someone close to them, themselves.

Our questionnaire and follow-up inter Some people wrote additional answers to offered to read their parents' suicide notes; to contact us with other memories to sh participants we spoke with. Not only had suicide but also we had felt many of the relief, fear, guilt, sadness, anxiety, depressic that continues to ebb and flow at any tin us into any one of these states; it doe moments: getting married, having a c

having
occasi
we the
surviv
what h

Th
the par
many y
guilt ar
vulnera
skewed
personal
they ma

Dur
occur af
group id
a parent
impossibl
them the
inadverte

As ar
frequently
the norm
already be
and/or psy
long battle
we spoke

What
several sign
time of the
a consistent
workers and
subsides wh
anew each
experience
Exploring th
one's obsessi
ever be a de
parent—all o

Immediate and Later Consequences

One December morning in 2007, I received a call from Janelle, one of our participants who was calling from South Korea. Janelle, who was age ten at the time of her father's suicide, wished to make one more contribution to *Voices of Strength* by letting our readers know that life goes on and one can still have a fulfilling life after suicide. She gave us an update of her life:

I graduated from my Internal Medicine residency and am currently serving Active Duty for the U.S. Air Force. I am the Internal Medicine physician here at Osan Air Base in South Korea. I am on a one year "unaccompanied" (my husband is still living in our home in the U.S.) tour and I am scheduled to return to the U.S. in July 2008. At any rate, I don't know where my next assignment is, so life is one big adventure.

However, this part of the journey does not occur until one is on the road to recovery. At different times for different individuals and in different ways, survivors can, and most will, find positive ways to facilitate their own recoveries. First, however, we must recognize and work through various steps in order to reach this goal, beginning with coping with bereavement.

Bereavement is normal after a loss. Even though at times, going through a myriad of emotions, one may question his or her own sanity, grief is not a mental illness. Initially we very well may be in shock and denial, a disbelief in what has happened. In some cases, others may view us as handling the situation well, because a sense of calmness and not crying is frequently the initial reaction to loss, known as being in shock. After that there are four other stages of grief that occur definitely not in an orderly manner but frequently as a cycle, or as one phase moving to another.

Anger frequently is the second stage of grief. "Why me?" is a question often asked or, "Why have you (the parent/s) done this to me?" Eventually we need to accept that suicide is about the person committing this act and not about the survivors. This realization does not generally happen right away.

The third stage of grief may be trying to bargain with God to change this outcome, trying to make deals to reverse this irreversible event. We may find ourselves wishing to bring the deceased back, to try to make things right for the parent or loved one. We cannot do this but we may try anyway.

The fourth stage of grief is manifested by feelings of helplessness, depression, being out of control or even suicidal ourselves. You may feel as if you will never be happy, well or stable again. We strongly urge you to seek help at this point and can assure you, from our own experience and research, (though you may find it hard to believe if you are mired down in this stage) that this stage is a temporary one.

The final stage of grief is that of acceptance of the fact that the suicide has happened and cannot be reversed. This phase is followed by a final step of feeling peace and comfort. One must remember that after reaching this point, it does not mean that we stay there indefinitely, but we may relapse for a temporary period of time and replay the other four stages. However, once reached, this stage indicates that recovery is well on its way.

Sometimes, one may get stuck in a phase and not move on. Seek help from a professional, clergy, counselor or another individual qualified to assist you through the mourning process when you feel hopeless or stuck. After a suicide, this is particularly important, because survivors must cope with grief and bereavement of so many kinds and dimension. Feelings of pain and loneliness, though natural, are often mixed with guilt and blame, which complicate the healing process because of the trauma of the parent's death. Reaching out for professional help in this problematic time is not a sign of weakness but of reason and strength. The stories of many of our participants and our own experiences reinforce this. We do not and should not have to heal alone.

After an accident, one becomes physically injured and then allows the lesion to heal; scar tissue forms. The skin is tougher now because scar tissue is stronger, that is if we allow the healing to happen. The same is true with emotional wounds. Eventually, if we allow ourselves to heal from trauma, the scars can make us stronger. Within time, we can choose for strength to prevail. We as authors have yet to meet a person who has gone through childhood and not been wounded. Some of us may be more wounded than others, but nonetheless, it seems to happen to us all eventually. As parents, we do what we can to prevent our children from getting hurt, but there are too many outside influences that are beyond our control. Also, as less than perfect people, we make mistakes and may unknowingly hurt the ones we love the most. Even a protected and shielded child may be wounded because s/he has not learned to face reality, make his or her own mistakes and is unable to learn about this world we live in. There is no getting around we all bear wounds at one time or another in our lives. The question becomes, can or will we recover? As we've seen through the stories of the participants in this book, time and effort can indeed heal. Being there for others who have survived suicide and helping them to heal will strengthen the healing powers within ourselves.

For those of you who have suffered the tragedy of a suicidal parent, there are many signs that the healing process is happening. Laughter and having fun is one such change that is indicative of recovery. The survivor may start choosing more color in his or her wardrobe. Planning the future is another positive sign. These are only three of the many ways that reflect that one's healing is taking place. Think of all the ways that you, the survivor, are showing renewal of life, which means your journey of healing is progressing. Be comforted.

The healing process is on-going; it continues throughout life and gets stronger and more resilient the more it is worked on. This progression can look different for different people and for various stages of recovery. Certainly we as authors believe in therapy and have greatly benefited from it. We have also participated in support groups. However, reading self-help books and reading, in general, the plethora of information available online is immensely helpful, too. The most important thing to do is to get help, wherever that comes from. If you decide to speak with a therapist or a clergy member, make sure it's the right person for you. The bottom line is, if it doesn't feel right, pay attention to what you are feeling. This may not be the right person for you. Do not give up on finding help. It is out there, and sometimes it's in the least likely place or person.

Hope Persists and Recovery Emerges

Of all the chapters of our book, "Journey of Forgiveness" was perhaps the most complex and complicated one to write. As authors, we spent the most time with this idea, both personally in our own situations with our mothers as well as how to discuss it with our participants. It is a topic that can be as controversial and problematic as suicide itself. We discovered that there are numerous schools of thought and theories on just how to go about forgiving someone. However, the more we tried to define it for the purpose of our book, the more we realized how intricate the process could become.

When thinking about forgiveness as it pertained to our mothers and their suicides and knowing that they were both mentally unstable individuals who did not receive proper medical care as we know it today changed our perspective. They both had histories of depression and many cries for help that went unanswered. With Judy's mother, psychiatric care was ineffective and unavailable in the 1940s. Medications did not really exist for psychiatric disorders and, to a lesser extent, this was true for Mia's mother as well. In addition, Mia's mother was abusing alcohol and prescription medication for years. So our questions were, are they responsible for their suicides? Or was it inevitable given their psychological states and the realities of their lives at the time? And does forgiving them come easier if they weren't responsible for their actions? The answers are not that simple, as logic says one thing, but blame and a need for forgiveness do not necessarily follow a pattern of logic. Judy has known for a very long time that her mother was probably not responsible, given the severity of her mental illness and the era in which she lived. Yet during the course of writing this book, Judy found that she needed to go through a process of forgiveness before beginning to write the chapter on forgiveness.

We had several conversations about these questions within the backdrop of mothers in the news who were clinically depressed individuals on trial for murdering their children. These questions became part of the follow-up interviews we conducted with our participants. Their responses were very interesting and frequently indicative of their stage of recovery and/or the amount of time that had elapsed since their parents' suicides. For Mia, it was fascinating how different the responses were among her three siblings. She also noticed that the way in which her siblings responded on forgiving their mother over twenty-five years ago has also defined how they have forgiven anyone in their own lives since then.

Another reality shared by many of our participants was the fact that the suicides were compounded by other abuses suffered at the hands of their parents before they died. We heard many stories of emotional, physical and sexual abuse that complicated the forgiveness process considerably. They spoke of their difficulty in thinking about forgiveness when there had been no closure to these other tragic events.

Our discussion of forgiveness also centered on other individuals. First, many participants felt they needed to forgive themselves. In their minds, they had played a role in the circumstances that led up to their parents' suicides. Some felt they could have done something to prevent the outcome. Second, other participants felt blame should be shared by the other parent (whether a spouse or an ex-spouse) and thus needed to forgive the surviving parent. Some of our participants included God in the list of those to forgive. The thinking went that if a higher power controls everything, then blame could be placed there since He let it happen.

In the end, the journey to recovery has forgiveness as one of its final stages. No matter how long the process takes or how many times it needs repeating, coming to terms with the suicide is essential to allowing it to be a part of your life instead of controlling your life. However, we cannot say what that will look like for everyone. It is a subjective term that seems to evolve for some with the passage of time. Still for others we hear them say that it is an impossibility or that they choose not to forgive.

What we as authors and survivors can say about the journey is to trust yourself and listen to your inner voice while you go through the various stages. Pay attention to your needs and seek support from trusted family members, friends and health professionals. This is something that many of us have trouble accepting and need to learn how to do. It's okay to sometimes feel stuck or frustrated with an aspect of recovery. It might be necessary to spend some time there to work on and gain insight into an issue. Above all, bear in mind that even though our lives will never be the same as they were before our loved ones' suicides, if we choose, life can still be quite rewarding and joyful. Life is well worth living. In fact, it is or can become possible one day to soar, to thrive and to live a fulfilling life as a son or daughter of parent suicide.

The loss of a parent and the suicide of a mother, father or both leaves internal scars, but we have revealed that these can heal with sensitive help, time and support. *Voices of Strength: Sons and Daughters of Suicide Speak Out* shows how to begin curing the physical, mental and emotional trauma of parental suicide. The recovery process is a long road and may often leave an individual feeling silent and solitary—but we the authors hope this book will help other survivors of parent suicide to find their own voices and move forward.

CHAPTER 12

Making Lemonade:
An Epilogue

On April 3, 2007, our agent, Dr. Sydney Harriet, called to inform Mia and me that he had just received word from New Horizon Press that they were making us an offer to publish *Voices of Strength: Sons and Daughters of Suicide Speak Out*. April 3rd was not just an ordinary day for Judy, not only because we rejoiced that our book, which we had worked on for so long, would reach the public, but it was also her mother's yahrzeit according to the Gregorian calendar. In Judaism, a yahrzeit is the anniversary date of the death of a Jewish person. This memorable day was also the first day of Passover. Passover is the Jewish holiday commemorating the liberation of the Israelite slaves of Pharaoh from Egypt. This allowed the Israelites to become servants of God instead, and as described in the Book of Exodus, Passover marks the "birth" of the Jewish nation, thus the birth of Judaism. On the Hebrew calendar, Passover always begins on the fifteenth day of the Jewish month of Nissan. Judy checked the Hebrew calendar for the dates in 1942. Her mother died on the seventeenth of Nissan but she actually carried out the act on the fifteenth day of Nissan (the first day of Passover). Two days later, she was declared dead on the third day of Passover. Was the occurrence of our good news on the exact day Judy's mother died coincidental? We do not believe this was the case. We felt it was a message of hope.

Judy's cousin, Ellen Steinberg Karch, and she were discussing not long ago their lifelong relationship together that began when Ellen was born, the day after Judy's fifth birthday:

I recall that special time when I boasted proudly to all that Ellen was my birthday present. We remain close to this very day. Our histories have been lived and shared together. In recent days while talking about our complicated childhoods, I commented to Ellen, "We were served a lot of lemons during our lifetime and we made lemonade out of them, Ellen." My cousin responded back, "Yes, and we are still drinking the lemonade."

As our book draws to an end, we want to say it's possible to have had this tragedy in one's life but to come through it as a whole person who strives to have a happy and fulfilling life. This is what we have done. We hope our readers feel the stories in this book inspire them. We believe one needs to put forth much effort towards the recovery process. Our own journeys and the journeys of most of our participants illustrate both the challenges to be faced and the future fulfillment we wish for them and you.

Today, Mia speaks of where the journey has taken her:

By 1998, my mom had been gone for seventeen years. In that time, I had been to five therapists and two support groups. At one point I felt like I had identified and explored all my feelings surrounding my mom's suicide. What more could there be? But new and familiar feelings surfaced as we wrote this book. Now I understand they will accompany me for the rest of my life.

During the years that have passed, I have revisited my anger with my mom for leaving me. While writing this book, I became a mother and that shed a whole new light on her. I thought I had cleared her of any responsibility for what she did, because I knew (and still know) that she was an untreated and undiagnosed manic-depressive. She had never been happy in her life except for brief time periods when she was first married, became a mother and attained some professional recognition in her career as a political psychologist. Initially after my son was born, my anger intensified. I couldn't foresee anything in life that would make me turn my back on him. But then I've never been clinically depressed. I still haven't resolved the issue of abandonment by my mother and maybe I never will. Her sadness and disappointment with life has inspired me, however, to always show my son unconditional love and support.

Six years ago, I embarked on my new career as an elementary special education teacher. My mom was a high school social studies teacher at one point in her life on the way to obtaining her two Ph.Ds. She continuously worked as long as I can remember. In each home we lived, she had her own personal study/office/library. Her constant dedication and personal drive to succeed made her an influential female role model. One of the positive legacies she left me was the pursuit of higher education and love of one's profession.

As a child, I spent most of those evenings lying down with my mom on my bed while she read chapters to me from novels such as *Charlotte's Web* or *Stuart Little*. I laid my head on her chest and was rhythmically rocked into sleep by the steady beat of her heart. It was the safest place I had as a child and my fondest and most loving memory of her. I can't recall specific dialogue between us, but the unspoken bond this ritual provided has left me with her true maternal sentiments.

As a result of coming to accept and coping with her suicide, I see her, as well as others in my family, as human. Growing up and into my early twenties, I put high and possibly unreal expectations on my mother, my father and my siblings to be the type of family I wanted: strong, resilient, consistent and available. I believe this came from being the youngest child and growing up in an emotionally unstable household. I have always felt a sense that I didn't get what I deserved as a child while I watched it happen for my friends around me. The stable foundation of my youth crumbled when I said good-bye to my mother and father living in the same house and my childhood home of ten years. All I felt was anger and resentment. I thought, "Why me?"

At the time of her suicide, nothing made me angrier than people telling me that time would heal all wounds. This phrase did not mean a great deal to a girl of twelve who had already lived through six years of her parents' violent fights, a bitter separation and divorce and a depressed and alcoholic mom who frightened her almost daily with unpredictable behavior. But it was the passing of time, the ability to let years go by that gave me the feeling that I had some healthy control on my life. This eventually put the perspective on my family that I needed. My parents were people trying to let time heal their wounds of sad and emotionally empty childhoods with over-bearing mothers. My siblings were also going through adolescence while trying to establish their own identity amid the confusion and chaos of our parents. They could not have done anything different.

Although I still search for answers, I have also not come to terms with my own spirituality. Not all of this relates to my mom's suicide. Some of it belongs to the role the church I attended played in my childhood. Our minister was more like a grandfather to me, with his short, white hair, soft, wrinkled skin and kind eyes. He hugged us sincerely after each service and then reached into his robe pocket to give us a piece of candy. Outside of these services, we never discussed God in our house, and the notion of faith was not a shining beacon that helped us through the hard times. Thus, by the time my mom died, the church had not been a strong spiritual foundation in my life, and I felt so angry with God. I had no faith that my life would get any better. Perhaps the right minister could have guided me through this time and helped me to find my way back to God. Hopefully, I will find that person one day.

The events of this will be a part of me for the rest of my life, and that's okay. I have incorporated it into the character and history of who I am. As so many participants have noted, a parent's suicide is much like a stone thrown in a lake—there is a ripple effect that reaches all boundaries of the world around us. But I've learned to go with the flow of that current, holding on tightly to survive at first when it was the strongest, then learning to accept the help around me as I endeavored to stabilize myself. The reeds that grow in my world that I cling to for support are my husband, my son, my sister, my brothers, my friends and my work. At times I still cry when I miss my mother and at other times I still rage when I feel her absence. I still smile when I remember our holidays; I still laugh when I think of her mannerisms. I will always honor her as my mother.

Judy speaks of where the journey has taken her today:

My earliest experience in life was learning of my mother's last part of her life, with hallucinations and suicide attempts during her pregnancy and even during labor. Babies are not born with a blank slate and unaware of their surroundings. I did experience her suicide at age seven weeks. I was right there during all the commotion and the police and ambulance activity and the outpouring of family emotions and horror. While I did not understand nor do I have conscious recall of what was happening, I certainly had to feel the extreme emotions and troublesome atmosphere. All I could do was cry; I could not discuss my feelings and what happened. This does not mean that I did not experience the painful confusion of it all. Do I consider her a bad person? No, I do not. I see her as having been mentally ill and in total despair. But coming to this realization did not happen overnight. It took time and maturity. As to whether she attempted to harm me physically after my birth, I believe that she did not. Before my birth was entirely a different story.

Because of my mother's repeated suicide attempts, my life was out of control and unmanageable even before my birth. As a young child, I worried about death and feared dying. I frequently felt like I could not breathe and could not get enough oxygen in my lungs, probably a body memory from being in utero and oxygen-deprived during times of her overdosing. I began my life under chaotic circumstances, and my lifelong task has been to bring order into my life.

I have had people in my life who have had strong and positive impacts on me. I've had many people in my life who have made a significant difference, but two are prominent as being vital to my survival during my early years. Marguerite Ertel was one such important person. She was my grandmother's nurse and took over mothering and loving me when I was seven weeks old. From Marguerite, who I called Mommy, I learned to love. From her I also learned an extremely tough lesson about loss when she was gone from my life just two months before I turned three years. Yearning painfully for the loss of Mommy became part of who I was until I was almost fifty years of age. At that time, my psychotherapist knew how to help me recover from chronic longing. But by age three, I had already learned how to love, and that I did not lose.

Florence Capedas came into my life as my speech therapist at the University of Pittsburgh when I was in the second grade. As a very quiet child who was believed to be mute by some adults, I mostly talked only with children. To me it made sense, being that there were too many topics that I was firmly told to avoid talking about, mainly my entire life. Meanwhile Florence, a student speech therapist taking on her very first client (me), had been instructed by her professors not to expect success with me. However, when we first met, I did not hesitate. I spoke with Florence immediately, as she and I were the same height; I was tall for my age but still the size of a child and was more comfortable with someone who did not tower over me. She had childhood rheumatoid arthritis and had spent her pre-school and childhood years in a school for crippled children. Both of us shared the commonality of knowing pain from the earliest moments of our lives. It turned out that my only speech impediment was pronouncing L's and S's. But Florence taught me much more than speech. She taught me that I was just as important as the next person. After her coaching for six months, I believed in myself. I reminded myself constantly that I was just as good as anyone else and although my shyness slowed me down, I refused to allow it to keep me from accomplishing what I wanted. I learned much about life during that period of time; I incorporated her teachings into my own thinking and they became part of me. I went on from there building on the wisdom that she shared with me about survival and the early foundation that she began to structure for me.

During my forties, when I met her once again, Florence told me that any good parent could have done for me what she did to help me with my speech. I took her a book collection of Norman Rockwell's pictures; I knew she would like them but knew not why. When I presented my gift to her, she burst into tears as she replied, "You remember!" I questioned, "Remember what?" She said, "Those were the pictures that I used to get you to talk about during your sessions." As for her success with me, I was talking again with adults and she informed them that I was not slow but actually intelligent. She was reprimanded for her arrogance in challenging the findings of the guidance clinic, where I had previously been. She was told not to think that she knew more than they did. Florence assured me that she never forgot me. "You were my first client," she said.

However, in my youth I still had bouts of sadness and I told myself just to survive until I became an adult. I decided that as an adult I could get the help I needed and start living the life I was meant to have. This was definitely true but not nearly as simple as I believed it to be as a child. Nevertheless, that is exactly what I did.

I graduated as a professional nurse at the age of twenty-two and began the next phase of my journey as a Registered Nurse and an independent adult. On January 2, 1965, I left Pittsburgh on a bus to Houston, Texas, as my parents warned me that I could not survive on my own. I responded, "Watch me!"

I loved my job as a medical nurse at Methodist Hospital in Houston, Texas. In Houston I met my husband-to-be. We now have four daughters. I loved (and still do love) motherhood and knew for sure that suicide could never be an option even though depression was my unwanted companion. Therapy, with the help of antidepressants, helped to keep that companion mostly under control. I later received my bachelor's degree as a Social Worker and enjoyed some interesting jobs as an RN/Social Worker.

In May of 2006, one more major event occurred in my life; I had open-heart surgery. My leaking heart valves had become life-threatening, along with other complications that followed my surgery. I have traveled a long way from the beginning of my life (when I heard as a child that it was a shame that I was ever born) to the present time. Not only were my family and close friends joyful with my recovery but also there were many others whom I never realized would care so deeply. My rabbi, Rabbi Alan Freedman, was genuinely and spiritually supportive of me during my successful recovery. What a great opportunity this was for me to put a new frame on my earlier experiences!

Our four daughters are adults now, and we have eight grandchildren and three great-grandchildren. I am doing what I want to do, enjoying my family, my many wonderful friends, my synagogue and, of course, writing this book. Learning to thrive has been an ongoing process. I have learned not only to enjoy the momentous happy occasions in my life but also the seemingly small, everyday contacts that bring joy and sweetness to life.

As this book draws to a close, so does the part of the journey our participants, Mia and Judy have shared with you. However, our hopes that you will continue to heal and move forward to find future fulfillment and happiness are ongoing. Our thoughts and prayers go out to you. May you heal and prosper, finding love and contentment.